M000105017

HEARING God Speak

52-Week

INTERACTIVE ENNEAGRAM DEVOTIONAL

EVE ANNUNZIATO & JACKIE BREWSTER

Ink & Willow

All Scripture quotations, unless otherwise indicated, are taken from the Holy Bible, New International Version®, NIV®. Copyright © 1973, 1978, 1984 by Biblica Inc.™ Used by permission of Zondervan. All rights reserved worldwide. www. zondervan.com. Scripture quotations marked (ESV) are taken from The Holy Bible, English Standard Version, copyright © 2001 by Crossway Bibles, a division of Good News Publishers. Used by permission. All rights reserved. Scripture quotations marked (TLB) are taken from The Living Bible, copyright © 1971. Used by permission of Tyndale House Publishers Inc., Carol Stream, Illinois 60188. All rights reserved. Scripture quotations marked (MSG) are taken from The Message by Eugene H. Peterson. Copyright © 1993, 1994, 1995, 1996, 2000, 2001, 2002. Used by permission of NavPress Publishing Group. All rights reserved. Scripture quotations marked (NASB) are taken from the New American Standard Bible®. Copyright © The Lockman Foundation 1960, 1962, 1963, 1968, 1971, 1972, 1973, 1975, 1977, 1995. Used by permission. www.Lockman.org. Scriptures quotations marked (NIV) are taken from the Holy Bible, New International Version®, NIV®. Copyright © 1973, 1978, 1984 by Biblica Inc.™ Used by permission of Zondervan. All rights reserved worldwide. www.zondervan.com. Scripture quotations marked (NKJV) are taken from the New King James Version®. Copyright © 1982 by Thomas Nelson Inc. Used by permission. All rights reserved. Scripture quotations marked (NLV) are taken from the Holy Bible, New Life Version. Copyright © 1969, 1976, 1978, 1983, 1986, 1992, 1997, 2003, Christian Literature International, P. O. Box 777, Canby, OR 97013. Used by permission. Scripture quotations marked (NLT) are taken from the Holy Bible, New Living Translation, copyright © 1996, 2004, 2007. Used by permission of Tyndale House Publishers Inc., Carol Stream, Illinois 60188. All rights reserved. Scripture quotations marked (TPT) are from The Passion Translation®. Copyright © 2017, 2018 by Passion & Fire Ministries, Inc. Used by permission. All rights reserved. ThePassionTranslation.com.

Copyright © 2021 by Eve Annunziato and Jackie Brewster
Illustrations copyright © 2021 by WaterBrook

All rights reserved.

Published in the United States by WaterBrook, an imprint of Random House, a division of Penguin Random House LLC. inkandwillow.com

Ink & Willow with its tree colophon is a trademark of Penguin Random House LLC.

Library of Congress Cataloging-in-Publication Data Classification:
LCC BV4597.57 .A56 2021 | DDC 242/.2—dc23.
LC record available at lccn.loc.gov/2020025421.
ISBN 978-0-593-23269-9
Ebook ISBN 978-0-593-23270-5

Printed in China

10 9 8 7 6 5 4 3 2

First Edition

Design by Sarah Sung

SPECIAL SALES Most WaterBrook and Ink & Willow books are available at special quantity discounts when purchased in bulk by corporations, organizations, and special-interest groups. Custom imprinting or excerpting can also be done to fit special needs. For information, please email specialmarketscms@penguinrandomhouse.com.

DEDICATIONS

EVE

To my mom: Thank you for reading the Scriptures daily and teaching it to all of us. In your last moments on earth, you defined your legacy as such: "For my children, my grandchildren, their children, and a thousand generations to know and love Christ." And so it begins . . .

JACKIE

To my amazing husband, Stephen: Thank you for seeing the depth of who God has created me to be and championing me along this beautiful journey. And to our four children, Isaiah, Ashlyn, Grace, and Hope: Thank you for encouraging me through your kind words, caring prayers, and big hugs as I have passionately pursued this new adventure.

CONTENTS

Your Peace

QUARTER ONE
YOUR PEACE

QUARTER TWO
YOUR PROTECTOR

Your
Protector

Your
Purpose

Your
Personal
Growth

DISCOVERING HOW GOD IS SPEAKING TO YOU IN YOUR ENNEAGRAM LANGUAGE

During this 52-week devotional, you will begin exploring how your heavenly Father is speaking to you by listening to God in your own Enneagram language. Using the Enneagram system helps you navigate the process of growing and developing into a healthier and more well-rounded human being. Through biblical truth and Enneagram awareness, you will uncover your deepest thoughts, unconscious motivations, and personality traits while you learn to identify patterns of behavior that drive your decisions. Simply put, once you understand how you are wired, you can engage with God and His Word in a fresh new way, bringing you profound knowledge of His truth. As you read Scripture through your own personality lens, you will clearly hear His message of who you are and whose you are—a message that drowns out the lies of the Enemy. As you begin to hear God's message with new awareness, you will recognize cycles and triggers in your life that have kept you bound. This acknowledgment will help you find freedom, allowing you to embrace your uniqueness and others' differences. After all, the more you understand God, the better you understand yourself; and the better you understand yourself, the more you can engage with God.

DISCOVERING THE HISTORY OF THE ENNEAGRAM

The Enneagram is an ancient personality typing system that was first brought to the United States in the 1970s by the American psychiatrist Claudio Naranjo. This highly effective process provides a roadmap to your patterns of behavior and helps you identify your distinct habits, thought processes, and response triggers that dominate your everyday life. The word *Enneagram* comes from the Greek words *Enna,* meaning "nine," and *grammos,* meaning "figure." This refers to the nine-pointed geometric figure, one point for each personality type, upon which the system was originally based. Since its introduction in the US, a host of teachers, psychologists, and psychiatrists have refined and expanded it to create today's Enneagram system.

DISCOVERING THE MEANING OF THE ENNEAGRAM

In the Enneagram system, you have a primary number that speaks to your dominant personality traits. In addition to this number, four other numbers are also important. The two **wing numbers**, those to the right and left of your primary number, help further identify patterns of behavior. Oftentimes, you will identify with one of your wings more than the other. However, you can learn to access the positive qualities of both your wings in order to become a healthier version of yourself. Also, you have a **stress number**, the one you go to in times of stress, and a **growth number**, the one you go to in periods of personal growth. You are encouraged to explore all of these numbers, since they will bring a new level of awareness to your life. On the opposite page is a chart listing each Enneagram number, its wings, and the numbers you tend to use during periods of stress and growth.

THE ENNEAGRAM NUMBERS
PRIMARY, WINGS, STRESS, AND HEALTH

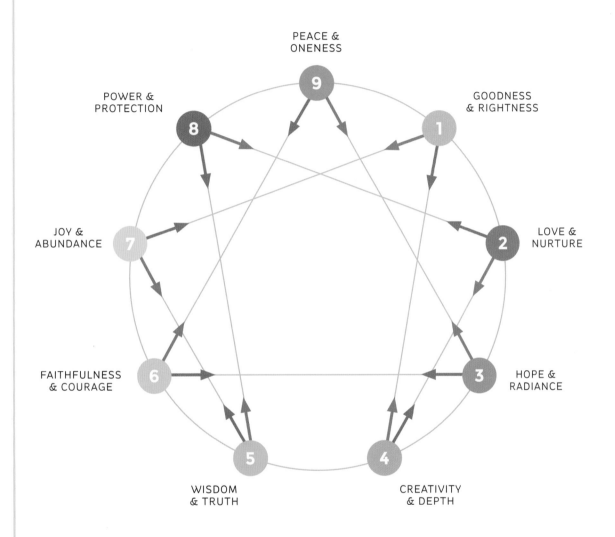

PEACE & ONENESS

GOODNESS & RIGHTNESS

POWER & PROTECTION

LOVE & NURTURE

JOY & ABUNDANCE

FAITHFULNESS & COURAGE

HOPE & RADIANCE

WISDOM & TRUTH

CREATIVITY & DEPTH

1	**Wings: 9 & 2** Stress: 4 Health: 7	4	**Wings: 3 & 5** Stress: 2 Health: 1	7	**Wings: 6 & 8** Stress: 1 Health: 5
2	**Wings: 1 & 3** Stress: 8 Health: 4	5	**Wings: 4 & 6** Stress: 7 Health: 8	8	**Wings: 7 & 9** Stress: 5 Health: 2
3	**Wings: 2 & 4** Stress: 9 Health: 6	6	**Wings: 5 & 7** Stress: 3 Health: 9	9	**Wings: 8 & 1** Stress: 6 Health: 3

DISCOVERING YOUR PRIMARY ENNEAGRAM PERSONALITY

If you do not already know your Enneagram number, don't worry! You can discover it through this devotional. As you explore the content each week with full honesty and vulnerability, you will begin to identify with one number more than the others. This number will feel most "comfortable"—as if the descriptions were written just for you. That's one of the beauties of this "narrative approach" to the Enneagram system: you discover your own number. It's not assigned to you.

Although no test is necessary, you can take a credible online assessment as a starting point, if you like. However, we encourage you to stay curious after receiving your test results, because you might find your motivations more accurately line up with another Enneagram number.

After identifying your main number, you can then explore your wings and the numbers you go to in stress and health. All of this will help you better understand your patterns of behavior.

DISCOVERING THIS 52-WEEK JOURNEY

PURPOSE: Our prayer for you as you work through this 52-week devotional is that you will achieve a better understanding of yourself and those closest to you with the help of the Enneagram system and biblical truths. Keep in mind, different personalities are not a problem to be solved, but a beauty to embrace. There is no such thing as a bad, better, or best Enneagram type. We are all magnificently complex individuals who are "fearfully and wonderfully made" by God.

PROCESS: While on this journey of self-discovery, you will engage with God by reading His Word, praying, meditating, and applying what you've learned. In exploring all the Enneagram numbers, you will also gain insight into others, thereby giving you empathy and compassion in all of your relationships.

This study will cover four main themes, with one per quarter: Your Peace, Your Protector, Your Purpose, and Your Personal Growth. Each week, you will delve into scriptures and topics relevant to your daily life and spiritual development under these themes. While reading at your own pace, you will have an opportunity to journal your thoughts to help clarify what you are learning and how you are hearing God speak to you in your Enneagram language.

PLAN: This devotional includes the following aspects:

Bible Verse: The Word of God is the anchor for each devotional, as written in varying translations. Don't hesitate to look up the week's verse in any of your other favorite translations.

Scripture Reflection: This section invites you to explore how the Word of God brings insight, awareness, and relevance to your daily walk. This is the on-ramp between the Bible verse and the nine Enneagram reflections.

Nine Enneagram Reflections: This section guides you through a search for the meaning of God's Word through all the Enneagram numbers. As you identify your primary number, you have an opportunity to investigate your four other important numbers that impact your personality type. These include your wings and the numbers you go to in stress and growth. Together, all five will shape your understanding of yourself through the lens of the Enneagram.

PRACTICE: Following each week's Enneagram devotional is an invitation to try one of four different meditation exercises, which are at the back of the book:

Box Breathing: Also known as "resetting your breath" or "four-square breathing," this relaxing technique helps you to clear your mind, relax your body, and improve your focus.

Concentration Meditation: As you focus on a single word or passage from the weekly scripture, this practice helps you to actually see the Word, breathe it in, and ask yourself, "What is God revealing to me in this moment?"

Reflection Meditation: This practice offers a time to reflect on the weekly scripture and to answer throughout the week one or two of the provided questions, such as, "What is lovely and praiseworthy about this passage?"

Contemplation Meditation: By journaling your answer to "What is God revealing to me in this scripture?" you will spend a few moments rewriting the scripture in your own words and unpacking what you are gaining from the weekly Word of God through your specific Enneagram type.

PRACTICAL APPLICATION: Journaling space is provided to answer questions about how you are hearing God speak to you through the weekly scriptures, based on your Enneagram type. This section also includes space for writing out a personal prayer and any other thoughts and notes.

MEET YOUR GUIDES

EVE ANNUNZIATO

Hi, my name is Eve and I'm an Enneagram Eight—the protective challenger. Honestly, I didn't want to be an Eight. However, after retaking the test half a dozen times and exploring the narrative approach while reading several Enneagram books, I realized I was challenging my number and thus behaving exactly like a formidable Eight. Subsequently, I educated myself by studying the numbers, warmly welcomed my personality and vulnerability, and am now loud and proud of my Eight-ness and all its splendor.

Learning about the Enneagram has been a defining moment in my life. It has helped me understand, unpack, and improve all of my relationships. I appreciate the fun-loving spirit of my Enneagram Six son, Gentry, whose reaction to my writing this devotion was, "Mom, we are all cheering you on." I admire the wisdom of my caring Five husband, Charlie. And I am thankful for the sweet, loving heart of my Two daughter, Oharah, who sits at lunchtime with any student who feels lonely. I now understand why my mom, also a Two, took me to nursing homes to hand out bananas and flowers and encouraged me to join her on the occasional visits to 69th Street in Philly to give sandwiches to the homeless. I'm beyond proud of my overachieving and philosophical Three dad and my focused creative-genius Four sister, Lori, who wished me into existence when she was five by tossing a coin in the well. (My parents heard and nine months later, I was born!) I have acquired mad respect for the ways they each approach life and process scenarios, even when vastly different from the ways I do.

I'm a writer and storyteller and have been for my entire life. Eventually, after trading in my hairbrush for an actual microphone, I became a professional storyteller, sharing others' stories in the 'nineties as a TV reporter. I transitioned from journalism into ministry and motherhood in 1997, and I've spent more than two decades telling the best story of all—the one about the God of the universe and His Son, Jesus Christ.

Over the years, I've enjoyed many small group studies, two decades of intense Bible study classes, and many beautiful, thought-provoking devotionals. Oftentimes, while reading my morning devotion, I find myself not quite relating to all the topics and will skim through the ones I think don't apply to me. Conversely, when I get to a part where God's Word instructs me not to overreact or stress about insignificant issues and instead to keep my mind peaceful, my heart humble, and my spirit less anxious, I lean in and listen! In those moments, I know God is speaking directly to me.

When I realized how I was selectively applying devotional material, I invited my dear friend and certified Enneagram expert, Jackie, into the conversation happening inside my heart—a conversation sparked by a desire to explore how God speaks uniquely to all nine of the personality types. This conversation grew into this book—so you can learn how He is speaking to *you*!

JACKIE BREWSTER

My name is Jackie, and I am an Enneagram Seven—the enthusiast! I look at life through the lens of glass half-full. I love to try new experiences and learn new things. I keep my days pretty busy, with the occasional need to slow down and really drive into my Enneagram Five (where Sevens go in health and growth). However, when I feel stressed and overwhelmed, I travel toward Enneagram One and become hypercritical of myself and others. I use both Enneagram numbers on either side of my Seven (Six and Eight). These wings give me strength in areas I might otherwise be weak in. I tend to lean a lot more toward my Eight wing in work environments. My Six wing shows up the older I get. I tend to look ahead toward the big picture so I am prepared for what may come.

I started studying the Enneagram more than eight years ago. I remember picking up an Enneagram book a friend gave me and then doing the test at the beginning, curious to see what I would learn about myself. In that season of my life, my children were very young. Isaiah, my oldest, was ten; Ashlyn was eight, and twins Grace and Hope were three. Our family had just endured a very difficult season. Hope had undergone major surgery, and there had been complications. Our family was in a continual state of survival as we tried to comfort and care for Hope while she worked to overcome many challenges, both physically and mentally. Through the months of Hope's recovery, the Enneagram proved to be a timely tool I believe God and my friend gifted me so I could understand myself better in that difficult season.

I have spent years reading books and exploring the Enneagram and many other facets of psychology. Along with being a certified Enneagram coach, I am also certified in experiential therapy. I have found using different methods to help people along their journey of self-discovery brings a deeper understanding to the patterns of behavior uncovered through the work we do.

After nineteen years of ministry, my husband, Stephen, and I decided in 2018 that it was time to start our own consulting company by taking our passions and skills into the world to help people overcome being overwhelmed. I love the work I do with my clients, helping them understand themselves and each other with the help of the Enneagram and the Word of God.

I'm confident that as you learn to read Scripture with a new awareness about yourself, you will find freedom from patterns in your life—and gain a greater understanding of why you do what you do and why you believe what you believe.

Are you ready to begin?

QUARTER ONE
YOUR PEACE

The God of the universe grants us a calm spirit that surpasses all of our understanding. Though we all approach tranquility, stillness, and surrender through our different Enneagram personality types, we all have access to peace promised by the Prince of Peace.

WEEK 1

YOU WILL KEEP IN PERFECT PEACE THOSE WHOSE MINDS ARE STEADFAST, BECAUSE THEY TRUST IN YOU.

ISAIAH 26:3

TRANQUILITY
STEADFAST MINDS

THERE'S ONLY ONE WAY FOR YOU
TO FIND AND FEEL A SINCERE
PEACE THAT FILLS YOUR HEART
AND SPIRIT.

Is peace a state of mind that comes naturally to you? Could you honestly say the words, "I feel completely at peace right now," and truly feel it? In many ways, finding peace is a lost art. Your world may be filled with distractions and meaningless babble that capture your attention and warp your sense of reality. If you watch too much cable news, your perception might be that the world is one step away from disaster. Binge too many fantasy features and you might get a warped sense of how your relationships should look. Or playing too much of the comparison game with your neighbors might make you feel inadequate. A sense of comfort can be difficult to come by if you are looking in all the wrong places. According to Scripture, there's only one way for you to find and feel a sincere peace that fills your heart and spirit. That is via a mind that is unswervingly toward Christ—meaning you are in harmony with Him and rooted in His Word. Put your trust in His promise; it's a much more beautiful melody than the noise of the world.

ONE

It is imperative for **ONES** to continually renew their minds with the Word of Christ. Spending time in Scripture and reading truth will ground them and help them feel more secure in their "yes" and "no" responses.

Awareness for Ones: When your trust is in the Lord and your mind is being renewed, peace will be with you. You won't get caught up in asking yourself, "Am I good?" You will know you are good because you are a child of God. This week as you meditate on Isaiah 26:3, ask the Lord to quiet your inner critic as you set your mind on things above. Write down the words you hear your inner critic whispering to you. Ask the Lord to take those words captive so you will have peace as you trust in the Lord.

TWO

Journaling is a great exercise for **TWOS**. Writing down on paper what they are really feeling helps them form their thoughts. This type of reflection brings them peace.

Awareness for Twos: Spending time reflecting on the Word of God that is truth will help you put things into perspective. When you can center your thoughts on God, you are able to put your trust in Him. This week as you meditate on Isaiah 26:3, allow yourself to feel God's perfect peace as you write down several ways you have put your trust in the Lord. As you journal, stay present in the moment and recognize the blessing of a renewed mind.

THREE

THREES find peace doing something for themselves that is not tied to achieving. They no longer chase people's approval, because they give themselves permission to be who Christ created them to be.

Awareness for Threes: When you are able to reflect on who God is, you find that your trust in Christ grows because you understand that He is Jehovah Jireh—our Provider. This week as you meditate on Isaiah 26:3, recognize the peace you have experienced from simply putting your trust in Christ. Write down the ways you have found peace in your life by renewing your mind in the Word of God.

FOUR

For **FOURS**, finding peace often means quieting their minds. They can get caught up guessing what will happen in situations and sometimes will replay events over and over until their anxiety level is overwhelming.

Awareness for Fours: Giving yourself permission to explore Scripture through a creative outlet can help you re-center yourself and remember your trust is found in Christ alone. This week as you meditate on Isaiah 26:3, allow yourself to see the benefit of seeking the Word of God first in all you do. Write down several ways in which you have experienced an overwhelming sense of peace because you have put your trust in Christ.

FIVE

FIVES often find peace when retreating into their "own space." They require and value a lot of alone time. They also gain peace of mind best by rooting their thoughts in the Word of God and quieting the constant need to investigate.

Awareness for Fives: Find how to trust in Christ by spending time learning His ways and recognizing that His ways are better than your own ways. This week as you meditate on Isaiah 26:3, allow yourself to see the benefit of seeking the Word of God first in all you do. Write down several ways in which you have experienced an overwhelming sense of peace because you have put your trust in Christ.

SIX

SIXES find inner peace through physical activity. By walking, doing yoga, hiking, gardening, or maybe even bike riding, they begin to awaken other parts of their bodies. This can help them process anxiety. Getting out of their own heads and not overthinking is key to finding peace in their day-to-day lives.

Awareness for Sixes: Connecting with God through physical activity allows you to process information while stimulating both sides of your brain. This week as you meditate on Isaiah 26:3, allow yourself to bring to mind scriptures that speak truth about who you are as you engage in a physical activity you enjoy. As you renew your mind through scriptures, ask God to quiet your anxiety. Rest in the peace that comes from spending time on yourself and being in the word of God.

Notes

SEVEN

The key to finding peace for **SEVENS** is to allow themselves to slow down and sit in the presence of God. They keep themselves moving to avoid painful feelings or memories that might come with slowing down. However, God desires to give them peace through a relationship with Him. But relationships take time to build, and trust has to be established. Understanding this allows them to be vulnerable.

Awareness for Sevens: As you spend time in the Word of God, your trust will grow and you will get a sense of peace. This week as you reflect on Isaiah 26:3, find a quiet place to spend some time meditating on this scripture. Allow yourself to sit in the presence of God and invite His peace into your mind. Write down the ways He has proven that He is trustworthy and that He cares for you.

EIGHT

For **EIGHTS**, finding peace in their lives will happen when they surrender to God. He is constantly pursuing them, knowing the peace they desire is found only in Him—not in their ability to take charge or control situations. Although they have the natural gift of leadership, their true peace and desire comes from seeking God in all they do and in all the ways they lead.

Awareness for Eights: Spend time in the Word of God to grow your trust in Him. This week as you meditate on Isaiah 26:3, allow yourself to trust that God is working behind the scenes on your behalf and that He is in full control. Write down the ways in which you have found peace in your mind as you have surrendered to His will and plan.

NINE

For **NINES**, finding peace will require them to speak up when they have something to say. As they lean into the Word of God and learn more about who they are in Christ, they will feel more confident to share more thoughts and share themselves with the world.

Awareness for Nines: This week as you meditate on Isaiah 26:3, recognize how renewing your mind with the word of God allows you to trust in God's timing. You are able to feel confident that He has your best interest at heart. Write down several biblical truths about who Christ says you are. Reflect on these thoughts often since they will bring you peace.

APPLICATION

As you reflect on your Enneagram number this week, do you feel more understood?

_____

_____

_____

How can you use this Enneagram reflection to help you move from understanding the *idea* of peace to actually *finding* peace in your life?

_____

_____

_____

When it comes to finding peace in your life, how can you relate to other Enneagram numbers this week?

_____

_____

_____

In what ways can you find peace during any current storms you might be facing? How are you hearing God speak to you about His peace?

_____

_____

_____

MEDITATION

Go to page 332 and try the Box Breathing exercise.

My prayer this week is:

_____

_____

_____

_____

_____

_____

_____

_____

WEEK 2

"

NOT ONLY THAT, BUT WE REJOICE
IN OUR SUFFERINGS, KNOWING THAT
SUFFERING PRODUCES ENDURANCE,
AND ENDURANCE PRODUCES CHARACTER,
AND CHARACTER PRODUCES HOPE,
AND HOPE DOES NOT PUT US TO SHAME,
BECAUSE GOD'S LOVE HAS BEEN POURED
INTO OUR HEARTS THROUGH THE HOLY
SPIRIT WHO HAS BEEN GIVEN TO US.

ROMANS 5:3-5 (ESV)

PATIENCE
LOVE POURED OUT

YOUR GOD AND HIS LOVE FOR YOU ARE *NEVER* CHANGING, EVEN DURING EVER-CHANGING SEASONS.

In a world full of "new normals" and unprecedented change, there is ONE constant: the God of all creation. Right now, you might be dealing with overwhelming suffering or shame from your past—something that needs a great deal of patience as you navigate in uncharted territory. The antidote to being undone by the unknown is holding on to the one true known: God's lavish love for you. Your God and His love for you are *never* changing, even during ever-changing seasons. God is the beginning and the end, "'I am the Alpha and the Omega,' says the Lord God, 'who is and who was and who is to come, the Almighty'" (Revelation 1:8, ESV). In his letter, Paul reminds the Romans that although troubles are inevitable, developing a habit of handing over control to our heavenly Father leads to patience. When you are facing trouble, rather than trying to fix it, ignore it, judge it, or control it, just simply let it go to Him. Shift your heart to praise and gain a spirit of expectancy, as your suffering yields endurance.

ONE

ONES can feel overwhelmed by life. A lack of consistency and discipline can frustrate them. When they look at this week's passage of scripture, they see that God is developing passionate patience in them through their frustrations. He is not asking them to clean themselves up or fix the problems that plague them. He is simply asking them to praise Him through and in their troubles. As God works on their behalf, they will be amazed at his goodness.

Awareness for Ones: As you process Romans 5:3–5 this week, ask God to show you where you are being rigid and ask Him to help you release your grip.

TWO

TWOS can get lost in overwhelming feelings and emotions, especially when they find themselves hemmed in by trouble. At times, they have a hard time waiting patiently on God to move on their behalf. They want to feel the Holy Spirit and praise God amid their troubles, but they often feel as though they are crumbling inside.

Awareness for Twos: As you meditate on Romans 5:3–5, lean into being alert and expectant, watching and waiting for God to show Himself to you.

THREE

THREES can get caught up in wanting to fix everything right away. They don't like waiting, and patience is not a word that typically describes them. However, they do desire to know God and see Him move, and they want to praise Him through their trials. They have a difficult time understanding the need for slowing down.

Awareness for Threes: This week as you meditate on Romans 5:3–5, ask God to slow you down to see His goodness. Ask Him to develop passionate patience and virtue inside you.

FOUR

FOURS can get caught up looking at the past by allowing their emotions to take over. Trouble can feel all encompassing, and praising in the midst of it is not always easy. Allowing themselves to feel the fear, pain, or hurt is their way of being fully alive. Learning to praise God in the midst of trouble is what will grow their passionate patience and virtue. This will result in their being more open to the present moment while being able to see God moving and making a way.

Awareness for Fours: This week as you meditate on Romans 5:3-5, allow yourself space to be present and open to seeing God in a new way.

FIVE

FIVES understand the importance of praising God in the midst of their troubles. They know that He will come through; however, they don't often allow themselves to feel the emotions attached to the trouble. Fives know that if they are willing to open themselves up to God in this way, He will meet them where they are in the moment. They will deeply grasp how much He has patiently waited for them and how much He loves them.

Awareness for Fives: This week as you meditate on Romans 5:3-5, allow yourself to express to God your feelings about what you are going through. Have hope knowing He loves and cares for you.

SIX

SIXES can get caught up in troubleshooting when problems come their way. They can forget to praise God through the situation because they are so caught up in the problem. But, obsessing never equates to peace. Though they understand their anxiety rises when they feel trouble around them and that God is by their side, learning to lean into God will help Sixes get out of their own heads and be more fully present to the world around them.

Awareness for Sixes: This week as you meditate on Romans 5:3-5, work on recognizing how God has already shown up on your behalf and how to praise Him in the midst of the trouble.

Notes

SEVEN

SEVENS have a hard time staying in the present moment. They often look to the future and want to forget about their troubles. Learning to stay present and to praise God in the midst of the trouble will allow Sevens to see God's goodness and faithfulness. As they lean into the trials and look toward God for their strength, they must allow themselves to be fully present and connected to Him.

Awareness for Sevens: This week as you meditate on Romans 5:3–5, allow yourself to feel the emotions within any troubling situations. Give yourself grace as you fumble your way toward the cross with great expectation to see God show up for you.

EIGHT

EIGHTS don't like trouble, nor do they tolerate messy situations well. Rather, they like to take charge and get things back to the way they should be. Romans 5:3–5 shows there is beauty in the waiting. Eights need to notice they grow in patience and virtue when they learn to praise God through all situations, and they do not have to always take control. This spiritual journey requires them to surrender who they are and invite God into their situations.

Awareness for Eights: As you meditate on Romans 5:3–5 this week, ask God to help you see where you are not allowing Him access. Ask for help in developing passionate patience so you can be alert to the goodness of God and all the gifts He is pouring out in front of you.

NINE

NINES tend to be patient and kind. Although they can praise God in the midst of trouble, they don't always allow themselves to have a voice in the pain. They are acutely aware of His goodness and mercy, as they love to watch Him fill others' containers with the help of the Holy Spirit. What Nines need to remember is that God is there for them as much as He is there for all those they care for and love. Just as they can feel God do things for others, they need assurance He will do likewise for them.

Awareness for Nines: This week as you meditate on Romans 5:3–5, be open and alert with great expectation, knowing God will never leave you feeling shortchanged.

APPLICATION

As you read each Enneagram number this week, which one do you find yourself resonating with most as it pertains to patience?

_____

_____

How are you becoming more aware of your Enneagram number and how you handle patience?

_____

_____

In what way can you relate to another person's Enneagram number and how he or she reacts in regard to patience?

_____

_____

How can you better develop the discipline of patience during times of trouble to continue to "shout His praises"? How are you hearing God speak to you when it comes to your patience?

_____

_____

MEDITATION

Go to page 334 and try the Concentration Meditation exercise.

My prayer this week:

_____

_____

_____

_____

_____

_____

_____

_____

WEEK 3

HE SAYS, "BE STILL, AND KNOW
THAT I AM GOD; I WILL BE EXALTED
AMONG THE NATIONS, I WILL BE
EXALTED IN THE EARTH."

PSALM 46:10

STILLNESS
CALMING SPIRIT

**TO BE STILL IS TO BE CALM
AND TO "LET IT BE."**

Take a moment and say aloud or jot down the top three thoughts currently racing through your mind. Next, think about three expectations others have of you. Then, name a few items on your "to-do" list that give you anxiety or worry. Lastly, picture several social media posts taking up space in your mind. Most likely, all this noise racing through your brain is overwhelming and exhausting. This week before you start your day, try to limit the mental noise swirling around your mind and be still, understanding that God is near. To be still is to be calm and to "let it be." In fact, the word translated as "be still" comes from the Hebrew term *raphah,* meaning "to let drop." Right now, ease your mind and let all of your thoughts land in the palm of God's hands. Remember you are loved beyond your wildest dreams. You are enough, and you have enough and exactly what it takes to conquer this day. Jesus paid the ultimate price just for you—you who are a priceless member of His royal family. Rest assured that you can hand over all your worries, burdens, and anxieties directly to Him. He will do your heavy lifting. Be still and let it all drop at the feet of Jesus.

ONE

To **ONES**, being still feels counterproductive. They wonder how everything will get done if they stop doing. However, it is in the stillness they will find peace. It is in slowing down and allowing themselves to "just be" that God will meet them right where they are.

Awareness for Ones: Allowing yourself to not feel guilty for this time is growth for you. Always striving for perfection is exhausting. Simply be still and know that God is who He says He is, and you are found in Him. This week as you meditate on Psalm 46:10, write down all of the overwhelming noise in your head you need to hand over to God. Allow yourself to be still in His presence, knowing He will help you accomplish what needs to be done.

TWO

TWOS desire time alone to process and feel their emotions. They are able to slow down and be still when they feel the need. Being still and turning their focus on God is when they get clarity. When they are able to be still in the presence of God, their thoughts and emotions become aligned with Him. They are able to see how He has been orchestrating all of their steps from the beginning.

Awareness for Twos: This week as you meditate on Psalm 46:10, allow yourself time to focus on your relationship with God. Write down the areas in your life where your thoughts and emotions are clouding your decision-making.

THREE

"Stillness" is not really part of the vocabulary of **THREES**. They have a strong drive toward success, which keeps them moving at record speed. Achieving makes them feel safe and as if they will gain the love and acceptance they need from others. However, when they get caught up in achieving, they lose sight of God being the source of their success and the anchor of their soul.

Awareness for Threes: This week as you meditate on Psalm 46:10, write down some ways you can put your trust in God. Allow yourself to be still and receive the love He has for you.

FOUR

FOURS long for calm and stillness. They appreciate it when others show who God is through kindness, and they enjoy noticing expressions of His goodness throughout the earth. However, they can often get lost in their emotions and feel God is not hearing their heart's cry. Their desire to be seen as unique can cause them to pull away from people and God. When their insecurities arise, they tend to get caught up in their emotions, and their feeling of shame overshadows God's love for them.

Awareness for Fours: This week as you meditate on Psalm 46:10, write down a few ways you can be more accepting of yourself. Your uniqueness is a gift to the world that God displays through you. Be still and know God is who He says He is and that you are found in Him.

FIVE

FIVES prefer stillness and quiet in their environment. They long for alone time, privacy, and personal space. In the stillness, they ponder the many mysteries of life. They lean in and investigate, searching for answers so they are never caught off guard. Yet oftentimes stillness doesn't develop into knowing God is present. On the contrary, it causes them to think about all the unknowns of this world.

Awareness for Fives: As you meditate on Psalm 46:10, invite God into your stillness. Ask Him to calm your anxieties. Write down areas of your life that you need to surrender to God. Allowing yourself this time to put your trust in Him and believing He desires to care for you is growth.

SIX

SIXES have a hard time sitting in stillness because it causes their anxiety to increase. Their minds have a way of racing ahead to scope out situations for safety purposes. They are always on guard, fearful of what could happen next. However, learning to be still and knowing God is who He says He is, is a freeing exercise for them to practice.

Awareness for Sixes: This week as you meditate on Psalm 46:10, write down your fears and bring them to God in prayer. Allowing yourself this time to be fully present with Him is growth.

Notes

SEVEN

SEVENS have racing thoughts and a need to keep busy. They avoid stillness because it causes memories and emotions to rise to the surface, which causes anxiety. Even when they slow down, typically they have some type of noise playing in the background.

Awareness for Sevens: This week as you meditate on Psalm 46:10, allow yourself time to focus on the goodness of God. Write down the distractions keeping you from being fully present with God.

EIGHT

EIGHTS have a strong desire to protect themselves and others. They have a lot of energy and prefer to keep projects moving forward. They do not like to seem weak in any situation, and the appearance of being still feels vulnerable. They do, however, desire to have God at the center of their decisions. Therefore, slowing down and being still is exactly what they need.

Awareness for Eights: This week as you meditate on Psalm 46:10, allow yourself to acknowledge God and His mighty power. Write down the areas you are trying to control and release them to Him.

NINE

NINES desire a harmonious environment. Even when they are at rest, their minds are still going. They hope their stillness doesn't look like laziness or apathy. Most of the time, they stay quiet so others are more comfortable. However, choosing to be quiet is not the same as choosing to be still. When they choose to be still, they are posturing themselves to receive what they need and desire from God.

Awareness for Nines: This week as you meditate on Psalm 46:10, allow yourself to be still in the presence of God. Write down the situations making you feel like you have to be quiet.

APPLICATION

As you reflect on your Enneagram number this week, can you identify with how you process the idea of stillness?

_____

_____

_____

What are some ways this week you can allow yourself fifteen minutes of space to simply "be" without reading, watching TV, listening to music, or scrolling through social media?

_____

_____

_____

After reading each of the Enneagram reflections, can you allow those close to you to take some time to explore what stillness looks like for them?

_____

_____

_____

In stillness, how do you know God is near? How are you hearing God speak to you when it comes to your stillness?

_____

_____

_____

MEDITATION

Go to page 336 and try the Reflection Meditation exercise.

My prayer this week:

_____

_____

_____

_____

_____

_____

_____

WEEK 4

"

ARE YOU TIRED? WORN OUT? BURNED OUT
ON RELIGION? COME TO ME. GET AWAY WITH
ME AND YOU'LL RECOVER YOUR LIFE. I'LL
SHOW YOU HOW TO TAKE A REAL REST.
WALK WITH ME AND WORK WITH ME—
WATCH HOW I DO IT. LEARN THE UNFORCED
RHYTHMS OF GRACE. I WON'T LAY ANYTHING
HEAVY OR ILL-FITTING ON YOU. KEEP
COMPANY WITH ME AND YOU'LL LEARN
TO LIVE FREELY AND LIGHTLY."

MATTHEW 11:28–30 (MSG)

REST
LIVING FREELY AND LIGHTLY

TRUE TRANQUILITY IN HIM IS THE PERMISSION TO CHANGE YOUR RHYTHM TO HIS GRACE, PEACE AND TIME SPENT HANGING OUT WITH JESUS.

Today, social media platforms expand the base of those who shape your view of the world, often creating unrealistic expectations, unhealthy goals, and an idealistic pace of life. "Do more," "get more," and "be more—right now" are often the messages bombarding you. Inputting these posts into your psyche every day becomes a burden and is incredibly exhausting. Subconsciously, you can begin believing the lie that you are failing in life because yours is not as perfect as everyone else's appears. However, you are often only seeing the very best moments in these quick video bites and momentary snapshots. You need rest, you need a break from this weary practice, and you need God's unending grace so you can reclaim your joy and contentment. True tranquility in Him is the permission to change your rhythm to His grace, peace, and time spent hanging out with Jesus. There is no better influencer than our Creator. After all, He is your Holy comfort and company as He encourages you to live freely and lightly in Him—a promise calming to your soul with permission to reclaim your life!

Notes

_____

_____

_____

_____

_____

_____

_____

_____

_____

_____

_____

_____

_____

_____

_____

_____

_____

_____

ONE

ONES are always doing what needs to be done. They don't allow themselves time to enjoy life unless all the chores are finished. However, when they cultivate a relationship with Christ and seek His approval above all others, they are able to find rest and freedom within themselves.

Awareness for Ones: This week as you process Matthew 11:28–30, ask yourself, "Am I feeling tired and worn out?" If you answered yes to this, then go to Christ— get away with Him. Ask Him to lift the heavy burden you have been carrying. Write down what is weighing on your heart and mind and surrender them in prayer trusting you will find rest in Christ.

TWO

TWOS are always hoping they are wanted and needed. They work hard to ensure others are happy. They are highly relational and nurturers by nature, therefore giving to those they care for is just who they are.

Awareness for Twos: This week as you process Matthew 11:28–30, allow yourself to recognize areas in your life where you have become tired and worn out. Has trying to do for others as a loving Christian caused you to neglect your own personal needs and desires? Journal several ways you can find a sense of renewal by spending some time alone and building your relationship with Christ. Make an appointment with yourself; even schedule this intentional time on your calendar, to follow through with creative ways you can enjoy self-care so you can live more freely.

THREE

THREES are always working on something. They don't allow themselves time to enjoy life. They fear that if they are not accomplishing something great, people will forget about them. However, when they are able to surrender their lives to God and allow His grace to fill them, they find they are loved for simply being themselves and not only for their accolades.

Awareness for Threes: This week as you process Matthew 11:28–30, ask yourself, "Am I burned out?" You may find yourself burned out on hustling, striving, and achieving, which leaves you little time to spend with God. Get away with God this week and ask Him to teach you how to walk with Him and work with Him. Write down areas you can surrender to Christ and learn to live more freely.

FOUR

FOURS get caught up with looking at what others have and lose sight of the blessings in their own lives. They struggle seeing their own unique qualities as gifts from the Lord. However, when they are grounded in the Lord and cultivating a relationship with Him, they can find rest from the comparison game. They know they are children of God, created exactly as they are for a purpose and a plan.

Awareness for Fours: This week as you process Matthew 11:28–30, see how you can find real rest in your life. Get away with Him, walk with Him, work with Him, and—as God says—"Watch how I do it." Write down or draw a picture of what you think the unforced rhythms of grace look like. Ask God to reveal ways in which you can live more freely and lightly.

FIVE

FIVES are always researching and learning. They enjoy alone time and often have a hobby in which they put a lot of time. But, allowing for rest is different from being busy with hobbies. True rest comes when you put your trust in God and can believe He will provide for you.

Awareness for Fives: This week as you process Matthew 11:28–30, recognize if you are feeling worn out trying to do what is right. Go to Christ and surrender, knowing He will never lay anything heavy or ill fitting on you that you will have to walk through alone. This week as you pray, write down a list of the areas in your life in which you desire freedom. Trust God is listening and eager to give you rest.

SIX

SIXES feel the constant need to be on guard and keep order, but that kind of constant attention is exhausting. The "what if's" can consume them and create an undercurrent of anxiety that plagues them. However, when they can surrender to Christ and trust He is going to protect them, they are able to let down their guard and live much more freely.

Awareness for Sixes: This week as you process Matthew 11:28–30, ask yourself, "Am I tired? Worn out? Burned out on religion?" If you answered yes to any of these, then go to Christ—get away with Him, walk with Him, work with Him, and learn God's unforced rhythms of His grace. Write down all the areas in your life in which you are seeking freedom and peace. Lift them up to God in prayer, knowing He desires to give you rest.

Notes

SEVEN

For **SEVENS**, rest is not something that comes easily, especially when there is repressed underlying anxiety. Sevens like to keep themselves busy with constant stimulation, as a way to avoid difficult conversations, situations, or relationships. However, when they are cultivating a relationship with Christ and are grounded in their faith, they seek silence and solitude to recharge.

Awareness for Sevens: This week as you process Matthew 11:28–30, ask yourself, "Am I keeping myself overly busy to avoid feelings of being worn out, burned out, or spiritually dry?" If you answered yes to any of these, then go to Christ and ask Him to renew your mind. Pick three objects in your home that symbolize spiritual and physical renewal. Use these objects to write a sentence or two about how you can find rest and freedom in this season of your life.

EIGHT

Rest is not something that **EIGHTS** desire. They are big-picture thinkers and have a lot of energy. They like to keep busy and love to work on projects. However, when they feel confident in their relationship with Christ and safe within the relationships in their lives, they can slow down and be fully present in the moment.

Awareness for Eights: This week as you process Matthew 11:28–30, ask yourself, "Am I functioning from a place of hyper-awareness trying to protect myself? If so, am I feeling tired, worn out, or even burned out?" If you answered yes to any of these, write down how this is making you feel. Lift these concerns to Christ, knowing He desires to carry your heavy burdens and give you freedom.

NINE

NINES love rest. They enjoy a comfy couch with cozy blankets. They like to numb themselves by enjoying their TV shows, books, and movies. However, when they seek a relationship with Christ, they find a peace within themselves. They can rest, knowing their voice and presence matter.

Awareness for Nines: This week as you process Matthew 11:28–30, recognize the areas in your life in which you have become worn out trying to keep the peace and do the right thing. Take some time to get away in nature with Christ. Ask Him to reveal the areas in your life that are keeping you from living in true freedom. Write down what you need to feel true freedom and rest in Christ. Pray He will help you to live lightly as you seek Him in all you do.

APPLICATION

As you reflect on your Enneagram number this week, how do you see yourself relating to rest?

_____

_____

_____

How are you able to allow yourself to rest this week without feeling guilt or shame?

_____

_____

_____

Can you write down a few things you discovered about the people in your life through these Enneagram reflections?

_____

_____

_____

When you are weary, how can you go to God to find true rest? How are you hearing Him speak to you about taking time to rest?

_____

_____

_____

MEDITATION

Go to page 342 and try the Contemplation Meditation exercise.

My prayer this week:

_____

_____

_____

_____

_____

_____

_____

_____

WEEK 5

"

TAKE A GOOD LOOK, FRIENDS, AT WHO YOU WERE WHEN YOU GOT CALLED INTO THIS LIFE. I DON'T SEE MANY OF "THE BRIGHTEST AND THE BEST" AMONG YOU, NOT MANY INFLUENTIAL, NOT MANY FROM HIGH-SOCIETY FAMILIES. ISN'T IT OBVIOUS THAT GOD DELIBERATELY CHOSE MEN AND WOMEN THAT THE CULTURE OVERLOOKS AND EXPLOITS AND ABUSES, CHOSE THESE "NOBODIES" TO EXPOSE THE HOLLOW PRETENSIONS OF THE "SOMEBODIES"? THAT MAKES IT QUITE CLEAR THAT NONE OF YOU CAN GET BY WITH BLOWING YOUR OWN HORN BEFORE GOD. EVERYTHING THAT WE HAVE— RIGHT THINKING AND RIGHT LIVING, A CLEAN SLATE AND A FRESH START— COMES FROM GOD BY WAY OF JESUS CHRIST. THAT'S WHY WE HAVE THE SAYING, "IF YOU'RE GOING TO BLOW A HORN, BLOW A TRUMPET FOR GOD."

1 CORINTHIANS 1:26–31 (MSG)

YOUR GIFTS
RIGHT THINKING AND RIGHT LIVING

YOU ARE NOT MAN-MADE;
YOU ARE HANDCRAFTED BY
THE KING OF CREATION.

You are exceptionally talented and exceedingly gifted. Regardless of your status or finances, you are enough. You are not a mistake; you were created on purpose for His purpose. When you receive accolades for your talent, remember who has given them. When you make a comeback and are given a second chance, remember who has offered it. When you are praised for accomplishments and feats, remember who has given them. The Holy Spirit did not make any mistakes when he granted your immeasurable gifts. In fact, the Greek translation for spiritual gifts is the word *pneumatikac*, which means "spirituals" or "things of the Spirit." This word is derived from the word *charis*, which means "grace." Your gifts are given by His spirit through His grace. You are not man-made; you are handcrafted by the King of creation. Therefore, keep in mind which horn to blow during your successes: "Blow a trumpet for God." It is a much more contagious, pleasant, and humbling sound!

ONE

ONES have the gift of wisdom and discernment. As they walk out their gifts here on earth, using them to advance the kingdom of God, Ones have a natural ability to establish order and bring clarity. They have high moral standards and care very deeply about what is right and wrong.

Awareness for Ones: This week as you meditate on 1 Corinthians 1:26–31, allow yourself to see your divine attribute as an extension of Christ in you. You are a child of God, so do all that you do in your life as unto Him. Spend some time reflecting on how you have used your gifts for Christ. Write down the impact you have had in this world through your gifts of wisdom and discernment. Thank God for trusting you with this gift.

TWO

TWOS have the gift of nurture. They have an ability to care for themselves and others with compassion. Understanding that God specifically gave them these gifts for His purpose here on earth is both comforting and humbling for them.

Awareness for Twos: This week as you meditate on 1 Corinthians 1:26–31, recognize how the gift of nurture has helped you love people well. Find comfort knowing you are exactly where you need to be for God to use the very gifts He has given you. As you process the many ways you have been able to be the hands and feet of Jesus to others, write down the feelings that arise. Take some time to praise God for allowing you to be a part of His magnificent plan.

THREE

THREES have the gift of encouragement. They have an ability to help people see their talents and gifts. They champion other people to pursue their passions. Their own desire to be seen as valuable positions them to see and acknowledge the value in others.

Awareness for Threes: This week as you meditate on 1 Corinthians 1:26–31, allow yourself to see your own value in the Kingdom of God through the gifts placed within you. Identify the ways God has been walking alongside you and positioning you to be a voice to others who need encouragement. Make a list of the people God has put in your life for you to encourage. Pray for influence and favor as you allow Christ to use you in this way.

FOUR

FOURS have the gift of forgiveness of others and themselves. They have an ability to help people realize how their different situations can be used for their own personal growth. They are compassionate people who desire for all people to be seen and accepted for who they authentically are.

Awareness for Fours: This week as you meditate on 1 Corinthians 1:26–31, allow yourself to see how your ability to forgive others is a picture of Christ in action. Sometimes your insecurities may cause you to think you have no voice or value to influence others for Christ, but you are mistaken. Write down the ways you have experienced true freedom by seeing the power of forgiveness in your own life.

FIVE

FIVES have the gift of seeing infinite possibilities. They are pioneers and able to innovate and discover new ideas. Knowing God is walking alongside them, guiding their steps, and working all things out for their good, allows them to take risks and be adventurous.

Awareness for Fives: This week as you meditate on 1 Corinthians 1:26–31, allow yourself to see your value in the Kingdom of God through the gifts placed within you. Make a list of these gifts and pray for favor as you display your talents with thanksgiving.

SIX

SIXES have the gift of courage. They can take on the challenges in their lives and conquer them head-on. They are problem solvers by nature and are naturally inclined to look toward spiritual guidance to help them throughout their lives.

Awareness for Sixes: This week as you meditate on 1 Corinthians 1:26–31, recognize the areas in your life in which you have leaned into Christ and conquered challenges that were set before you. Are you able to recognize that He has been the one walking alongside you, guiding and directing your steps and working out all things for your good the whole time? Write down a few ways you have witnessed Christ actively filling your mind with "right thinking" and continually giving you a clean slate.

Notes

SEVEN

SEVENS have the gift of joy. They have an ability to bring happiness into all situations. They enthusiastically encourage others to pursue their passion. The joy they feel from knowing that Christ is continually choosing them allows them to love others in that same way.

Awareness for Sevens: This week as you meditate on 1 Corinthians 1:26–31, allow yourself to see the many ways God has used you to bring joy and gladness into others' lives. As you walk out your gifts here on earth, using them to advance the kingdom of God, always remember to give Him all the glory. Write down what fills your heart, mind, and soul with true joy. Thank God for giving you the ability to see life the way you do.

EIGHT

EIGHTS have the gift of strength. They can effect positive change for this world. They champion others to believe in their dreams. When they are tethered to Christ and grounded in their faith, they are an unstoppable force.

Awareness for Eights: This week as you meditate on 1 Corinthians 1:26–31, humble yourself as you seek to understand the value that your strength and gifts bring to the kingdom of God through your many talents. Make a list of the gifts God has given you and the ways you have used them throughout your life. Pray God will continue to grant you favor as you pursue your passions.

NINE

NINES have the gift of healing. They have an ability to show the world kindness, acceptance, and peace. They are patient with others and allow them to share their experiences and situations without judgment.

Awareness for Nines: This week as you meditate on 1 Corinthians 1:26–31, allow yourself to see the tender heart God has placed within you as a reflection of who Christ is. Your ability to care for others regardless of their situation, social status, past mistakes, or current circumstances is truly a beautiful gift from heaven above. As you reflect on the ways God has used you in this way throughout your life, write down a few memories that bring you joy. Thank God for allowing you to love others with compassion and empathy.

APPLICATION

As you reflect on your Enneagram number this week, can you identify with your specific gift that you show the world?

_____

_____

_____

How do you use your gift on a daily basis?

_____

_____

_____

In what ways can you see those around you displaying their specific gift described in these Enneagram reflections?

_____

_____

_____

How are you using your God-given gifts to pursue your passion? How are you hearing God speak to you when it comes to your humility?

_____

_____

_____

MEDITATION

Go to page 332 and try the Box Breathing exercise.

My prayer this week:

_____

_____

_____

_____

_____

_____

_____

_____

WEEK 6

> HE HAS SAVED US AND CALLED US
> TO A HOLY LIFE—NOT BECAUSE
> OF ANYTHING WE HAVE DONE BUT
> BECAUSE OF HIS OWN PURPOSE AND GRACE.
> THIS GRACE WAS GIVEN US IN CHRIST
> JESUS BEFORE THE BEGINNING OF TIME.

2 TIMOTHY 1:9

GRACE
FREE OF CHARGE

GRACE AND PURPOSE
ARE AVAILABLE TO THE ENTIRE
HUMAN RACE...

Have you ever played the moral comparison game? It goes something like, "I might have done that, but at least I am not as bad as she is." Or, "Yes, I am making bad decisions, but at least I would never disown my family like he did." Maybe, you think, "I will never be loved by God, because He is disappointed in my bad decisions." This is a dangerous game, because it assumes you are being judged by a virtual sliding scale that rates you and others. Also, it implies you can either work your way up to God or that you already arrived at the top ahead of others. However, the truth is clear in this scripture: you are saved not because of anything you have done or did not do, but by grace given to you by the King of the universe. You, like all of us, process information differently. The Enneagram distinguishes the three different ways we each process information called Triads: the gut or instinctual triad, heart or emotions triad, the head or thinking triad. Whether you process from your gut, heart, or head, there are two significant truths: First, you are not above or beneath any certain rung on a virtual ladder of goodness. Next, your neighbor from across the street or across the globe is not on another rung higher or lower. Grace and purpose are available to the entire human race and are freely given to you because of what Jesus did on the cross.

ONE

It is hard for **ONES** to let down their guard and accept a life not walked out by "works." Ones are in the instinctual—or some call it the "gut"—triad. They process information from their gut first. Because of their keen intuition, they guard themselves by trying to protect and defend themselves.

Awareness for Ones: This week as you meditate on 2 Timothy 1:19, allow yourself to see the importance of trusting God. When you are walking your life out full of grace, you can lay down your life and take up the cross. You will be able to trust that you will not be overwhelmed by the world or be in danger of losing your freedom. Write down all areas in your life that you have been attempting to control. Release these areas in prayer to God and ask Him to help you put your trust fully in Him.

TWO

It is hard for **TWOS** to let down their guard and believe others will care for them and their needs. Twos are in the heart triad. They process information from their hearts or emotions first. Their ability to feel and sense emotions keeps them on guard because of their fear of losing their relationships. They are loving, caring, and compassionate people who desire to know they are wanted and needed.

Awareness for Twos: This week as you meditate on 2 Timothy 1:19, can you see how putting your trust in God can feel overwhelming if you are worried about being rejected by the world or afraid of emotional abandonment. As you process your emotions that are surfacing, write down all the thoughts coming to your mind. Ask God to fill you with peace, joy, and true freedom as you seek His grace in all you do.

THREE

It is hard for **THREES** to let down their guard and believe others will love them just as they are. Threes are in the heart triad. They process information from their heart or emotions, but their emotions are not easily accessible. They suppress their emotions out of fear that these emotions will hinder their ability to achieve. Because of this, they put up their guard and try to be what others need them to be, in hopes of being seen as valuable. However, when they are able to surrender their lives to Christ, knowing it is by grace they have been saved, they can access their feelings and trust that God's love for them is not fleeting.

Awareness for Threes: This week as you meditate on 2 Timothy 1:19, allow yourself to embrace the grace that has saved you. As you accept God's grace and allow it to be activated in your life, you will be able to accomplish your goals, even when you allow yourself to feel your emotions. Make a list of emotions you have kept at bay and pray for God to help you embrace all of them, knowing you are loved just as you are.

FOUR

It is hard for **FOURS** to let down their guard and believe others will accept them just as they are. Fours are in the heart triad. They process information from their hearts or emotions first. Their emotions can override their ability to stay present in the moment. They guard themselves by trying to prove their worth through gaining attention and being different or unique.

Awareness for Fours: This week as you meditate on 2 Timothy 1:19, embrace the grace extended to you by laying down your life and taking up the cross. Living with Christ at the center of all you do requires you to trust Him. As you place your trust in God, you will see the value you bring to the world by being your authentic self. Try a new creative outlet this week and write down the ways God reveals to you how His grace has given you new life.

FIVE

It is hard for **FIVES** to let down their guard and believe their needs are not too much. Fives are in the head triad. They process information by thinking and reasoning. They put up a guard whenever they are keeping themselves and their loved ones safe. They try to take care of themselves and those around them without being perceived as demanding.

Awareness for Fives: When you are intentionally connecting to God and reading the Bible, you can see God as your provider and protector. This week as you meditate on 2 Timothy 1:19, allow yourself to see the importance of embracing the grace of God in your life. As you learn to put your trust in Him, you will find comfort in knowing you will not be overtaken by the world. Take time to write down the areas in your life you are afraid to trust God. Bring your list to Him in prayer, asking for Him to help you experience true freedom only found in Christ.

SIX

It is hard for **SIXES** to let down their guard and believe they are safe in this world. Sixes are in the head triad. They process information by thinking and reasoning. They are always testing and questioning people to determine if they are who they say they are and will do what they say they will do. They protect themselves when they feel they need to keep themselves safe and secure.

Awareness for Sixes: When you are praying and reading the Word of God, you can relax and put your trust in Him. This week as you meditate on 2 Timothy 1:19, allow Him to reveal to you His infinite love for you. As you embrace the grace He has given to you by His death on the cross, you can begin to trust He will not leave you feeling vulnerable, overwhelmed, or taken advantage of by the world. Take a walk or run and breathe in the beauty God has created all around you. Pray for His peace that passes all understanding to rest on you.

Notes

SEVEN

It is hard for **SEVENS** to let down their guard and trust that others will take care of them. Sevens are in the head triad. They process information by thinking and reasoning. They keep themselves busy and are constantly looking toward the future. They fear being trapped in emotional pain or being without support. They protect themselves when they feel they are left to care for themselves.

Awareness for Sevens: This week as you meditate on 2 Timothy 1:19, allow yourself to see the importance of living with Christ at the center of all you do. This requires you to trust that God longs to care for you and loves you unconditionally. As you allow His grace and mercy to encompass all you do, write down the ways God has shown His love to you. Pray for overwhelming peace, joy, and freedom in your life.

EIGHT

EIGHTS struggle with letting down their guard and accepting they are loved even when they are not being productive. Eights are in the instinctual—or some call it the "gut"—triad. Because they are highly intuitive, they process information from their gut first. They are big-picture thinkers and like to involve others in accomplishing goals. They are protective when they feel the need to defend themselves and their loved ones.

Awareness for Eights: This week as you meditate on 2 Timothy 1:19, allow yourself to experience the true freedom that comes when you embrace the grace of God. As you put your trust in Him, you will not be afraid of betrayal by the world or of losing your freedom. Write down areas in your life in which you have experienced freedom because you have relinquished your control unto God. Ask God to fill your heart and mind with peace as you continue to draw near to Him.

NINE

NINES struggle with letting down their guard and allowing others to hear their opinions and ideas while having a hard time believing their presence or voices matter. Nines are in the instinctual—or some call it the "gut"—triad. They process information from their gut first. They can see all sides of a situation. They are protective when they feel their environment or relationships are becoming a source of stress and tension. When they can embrace the grace of God and trust He is in control, they can continue moving forward knowing they matter.

Awareness for Nines: This week as you meditate on 2 Timothy 1:19, allow God to reveal to you how much He loves you by simply embracing the grace He has given to you. As you put your trust in God, you will find that you will not be overwhelmed or overlooked in the world. Write down the ways you experience God's peace in your life. Ask Him to fill you with understanding, mercy, and grace.

APPLICATION

As you reflect on your Enneagram number this week, which part do you find most relatable?

_____

_____

_____

How are you able to embrace grace in your life as you reflect on your Enneagram number?

_____

_____

_____

In what ways can you relate to the struggle each Enneagram number has as it pertains to accepting grace?

_____

_____

_____

What are some ways God has shown you grace even when you did not think you deserved it? How are you hearing God speak to you when it comes to grace?

_____

_____

_____

MEDITATION

Go to page 334 and try the Concentration Meditation exercise.

My prayer this week:

_____

_____

_____

_____

_____

_____

_____

_____

_____

_____

_____

WEEK 7

"

YOU'RE ALL I WANT IN HEAVEN! YOU'RE ALL I WANT ON EARTH! WHEN MY SKIN SAGS AND MY BONES GET BRITTLE, GOD IS ROCK-FIRM AND FAITHFUL. LOOK! THOSE WHO LEFT YOU ARE FALLING APART! DESERTERS, THEY'LL NEVER BE HEARD FROM AGAIN. BUT I'M IN THE VERY PRESENCE OF GOD — OH, HOW REFRESHING IT IS! I'VE MADE LORD GOD MY HOME. GOD, I'M TELLING THE WORLD WHAT YOU DO!

PSALM 73:26–28 (MSG)

LIVING FREE
ROCK-FIRM AND FAITHFUL

THE LORD WILL NEVER LEAVE YOU FALLING APART.

If you are feeling weary or weepy or even bone tired, look to your God in heaven for strength and comfort. Be inspired and encouraged by the knowledge you are exactly enough. He created you for a divine purpose, right here and right now, regardless of your current situation. Because you are full of favor as a cherished member of His royal family, you can walk in confidence knowing God is all you need here on earth. Thankfully, you do not have to make a divine appointment nor wait to get His undivided attention, as you can be in God's presence anytime you ask! Ask Him to give you strength and confidence when you are feeling weak and to take your anxiety and angst when you are feeling overwhelmed. He can handle it all. Your relationship with the Father is built over a lifetime and on a strong foundation because your God is "rock-firm." The Lord will never leave you falling apart. Shout to the world what He does, as His invitation to His house is ALL-inclusive. Everyone is invited to sit at His table.

——— • ——— ONE ——— • ———

ONES no longer believe they must strive for perfection to be loved by God. They know they are loved right here, right now, just as they are. Allowing themselves to grasp the infinite love of Christ frees them from living in the bondage of criticism and judgment.

Awareness for Ones: As you grow in your relationship with Christ, you can see the world through other people's points of view without feeling the need to correct them. This week as you meditate on Psalm 73:26–28, thank God for His faithfulness. Thank Him for His unconditional love. Also, write down words of gratitude you have toward your heavenly Father.

——— • ——— TWO ——— • ———

TWOS no longer need to believe they must rescue others to be loved by God. They know they are loved just as they are. Allowing themselves to grasp the infinite love of Christ frees them from living in the bondage of people pleasing.

Awareness for Twos: As you spend time cultivating a relationship with Christ, you will be able to love people right where they are without feeling the need to save them. This week as you meditate on Psalm 73:26–28, thank God for being a solid rock in your life. Thank Him for His unconditional love. Also, write a declaration of love to God.

——— • ——— THREE ——— • ———

THREES no longer believe they must strive for success to be loved by others and God. They know they are loved for simply being themselves when they allow themselves to grasp the infinite love of Christ. They will find true freedom from living in the bondage of their achievements.

Awareness for Threes: As you surrender your life to Christ, you will be able to see you no longer need to prove your self-worth to those around you. This week as you meditate on Psalm 73:26–28, allow yourself to see how refreshing it is to be in the presence of God. Write down the thoughts that come to mind as you reflect on your decision to make Christ the center of your life.

FOUR

FOURS no longer believe they must be individualists in order to be loved by God. They know He loves them just as they are. They find the acceptance and freedom they have longed for all their life when they allow themselves to grasp the infinite love of Christ. This frees them from living in the bondage of their emotions.

Awareness for Fours: As you develop a deeper relationship with Christ, you will be able to use Scripture to help you balance overwhelming emotions. This week as you meditate on Psalm 73:26–28, thank God for His unconditional love. Also, write down how He has helped you see your true self with a new perspective. Share this revelation with someone this week.

FIVE

FIVES no longer believe they must store up treasures on earth for fear of scarcity. They know they are loved and taken care of by their heavenly Father who created them just as they are. Allowing themselves to grasp the infinite love of Christ frees them from living in the bondage of worry.

Awareness for Fives: As you grow in your relationship with the Lord, you are able to embrace His love for you, which will in turn build a sense of security within yourself. This week as you meditate on Psalm 73:26–28, allow Him to refresh your soul. Thank Him for His unconditional love. Also, write down all the ways, big and small, God has shown His love to you.

SIX

SIXES no longer believe they have to be on guard, waiting for the next crisis to happen. They are able to accept the infinite love of Christ. This allows them to live free from the bondage of fear and uncertainty.

Awareness for Sixes: As you seek the Lord in all areas of your life, you are able to let down your guard and trust that He will guide and protect you. This week as you meditate on Psalm 73:26–28, reflect on His goodness in your life. Can you see the ways He cares for you? Write down the ways you have seen God as rock-firm and faithful in your life since receiving salvation.

Notes

SEVEN

SEVENS no longer need to fear abandonment by those they love, because they are secure in God's love for them. They have a newfound confidence in knowing He loves them unconditionally. Allowing themselves to grasp the infinite love of Christ frees them from living in the bondage of trying to prove their self-worth.

Awareness for Sevens: As you continue to study God's Word and draw closer to Him through prayer, you will experience the comfort and peace you have longed for. This week as you meditate on Psalm 73:26–28, allow yourself to embrace God's presence. Thank Him for His unconditional love. Put on your favorite worship song and praise God for all He has done for you.

EIGHT

EIGHTS no longer believe they must stand their ground to be secure. Their protection is found in God. Allowing themselves to grasp the infinite love and security of Christ frees them from living in the bondage of control.

Awareness for Eights: As you seek God through His Word, you will find comfort in knowing He will fight for you and protect you. This week as you meditate on Psalm 73:26–28, allow His Word to refresh you. Thank Him for His faithfulness toward you. Write down the ways God has proven His love for you by being rock-firm and fighting on your behalf.

NINE

NINES no longer believe their voices are insignificant because they are confident in God's love for them. They can walk out their purpose, knowing their voice and their presence matter. When they allow themselves to grasp the infinite love of Christ, they can then live free from the bondage of self-doubt.

Awareness for Nines: As you continue to cultivate your relationship with the Lord, you will experience a peace that passes all understanding. This week as you meditate on Psalm 73:26–28, allow yourself to be refreshed and renewed. Thank Him for His unconditional love. Go out into nature and take note of its vast beauty, thanking God for giving you eternal salvation.

APPLICATION

As you reflect on your Enneagram number this week, what feelings stir as you read the words "You are loved right here, right now, just as you are"?

_____

_____

_____

How are you able to see the world through other people's points of view?

_____

_____

_____

After reading the Enneagram reflections, how can you encourage those around you to be their true selves?

_____

_____

_____

In what ways have you seen God act "rock-firm and faithful"? How are you hearing God speak to you when it comes to God's invitation?

_____

_____

_____

MEDITATION

Go to page 336 and try the Reflection Meditation exercise.

My prayer this week:

_____

_____

_____

_____

_____

_____

_____

_____

_____

_____

_____

_____

WEEK 8

"

SUMMING UP: BE AGREEABLE,
BE SYMPATHETIC, BE LOVING,
BE COMPASSIONATE, BE HUMBLE.
THAT GOES FOR ALL OF YOU,
NO EXCEPTIONS. NO RETALIATION.
NO SHARP-TONGUED SARCASM.
INSTEAD, BLESS—THAT'S YOUR JOB,
TO BLESS. YOU'LL BE A BLESSING
AND ALSO GET A BLESSING.

1 PETER 3:8–12 (MSG)

BLESSING OTHERS
YOUR JOB

ALL PEOPLE DESERVE YOUR MERCY, GENTLENESS, KINDNESS, AND COMPASSION.

You might not think it is your job to bless others. After all, you have enough on your plate to make you feel overwhelmed, stressed, anxious, or frustrated. Life can be a lot. Perhaps your focus is on those urgent issues directly in front of you, and you are blind to the outside world. If so, it is easy to miss what is happening around you or with your loved ones. However, the apostle Paul is asking you to put aside all of that, because it's your job to bless. Work toward humbly shifting your perspective from inward to outward. Love both the lovable and unlovable. Have compassion for those like you and those unlike you. We are called to do this without any expectations. How? One way is by realizing everyone around you is probably just doing the best they can under their own circumstances. What would this week look like if you went around blessing the socks off people—uplifting them, encouraging them without a judgmental thought, and without wanting anything from them? All people deserve your mercy, gentleness, kindness, and compassion. And by focusing outward, you stop fixating on your own concerns, complaints, and woes. Pivot your perspective, lift your head, and look around to notice ways you can be a blessing. In return, you will feel incredibly blessed all along the way.

———— ONE ————

ONES bless others when they are walking out their lives full of humility and love. They have a very strong moral compass, and consequently people tend to put their trust in them. The more time they spend reading their Bibles and being attuned to what God is saying, the more they are able to be a blessing and in return be blessed.

Awareness for Ones: This week as you meditate on 1 Peter 3:8–12, observe your own thoughts and motives within your relationships. Are you looking at ways in which you can bless others? Write down the ways you have witnessed God blessing you in the same way you have been compassionate toward others.

———— TWO ————

TWOS are a blessing through their generous support of others. They have a superpower that allows them to sense what others need before they even speak it. They are full of love and compassion.

Awareness for Twos: This week as you meditate on 1 Peter 3:8–12, observe your own thoughts and motives as you engage in your relationships. Who in your life can you bless this week by simply just being with them? Write down the names of a few people you are going to intentionally bless this week and watch the ways God is going to bless you in return.

———— THREE ————

THREES bless others with words of encouragement. They are sympathetic and kind, always looking for ways to help the people around them become better and achieve more. Also, when they are spending time reading their Bibles and are attuned to what God is saying, Threes are able to see the many blessings that have been bestowed upon them.

Awareness for Threes: This week as you meditate on 1 Peter 3:8–12, allow yourself to see the many ways you have blessed those around you. Recognize in your own life the many blessings God has given to you because of your lovingkindness toward those in your life. Make a chart by listing all of the important people in your life, and beside each name describe the ways you have impacted their lives by humbly loving them well.

FOUR

FOURS are a blessing to others when they authentically live their lives full of compassion. They are attuned to their emotions and the emotions of others. They desire for all people to be loved just as they are. They are sympathetic and caring.

Awareness for Fours: This week as you meditate on 1 Peter 3:8–12, observe in your own life the way people have blessed you. Are you able to see the ways you have been a blessing to others? Draw a picture that describes how you feel after you have done something for someone that you know was a blessing to them.

FIVE

FIVES bless others with their wisdom and knowledge. They have brilliant minds and see life through a unique perspective. They love to share their research, ideas, and inventions with others.

Awareness for Fives: This week as you meditate on 1 Peter 3:8–12, observe how your own thoughts and motives drive you to bless others with your knowledge. Do you feel blessed when you can gain new insight from the Word of God? Write down what insight you have gained from this week's verse.

SIX

SIXES are a blessing to others through their loyalty and trustworthiness. They take their time and with compassion and understanding look at all circumstances. They care deeply about the people in their lives and want to love and support them.

Awareness for Sixes: This week as you meditate on 1 Peter 3:8–12, allow yourself to see the ways you have cared for others. Can you see how compassion for others leads to a life full of God's blessing? Write down a time in your life when you witnessed God bless someone through your lovingkindness.

Notes

SEVEN

SEVENS spread joy and enthusiasm as they bless others with their loving compassion. They are highly relational, always seeking to put a smile on someone's face. They can rally others and spread the love of God in fresh and unique ways.

Awareness for Sevens: This week as you meditate on 1 Peter 3:8–12, allow yourself to see the blessing you have been to the many lives around you. Now, can you identify a person who has blessed you and shown you the love of Christ? Write down several ways in which God has blessed you throughout your life.

EIGHT

EIGHTS bless others by inspiring them to go after their dreams. They are strategic thinkers who show compassion to those they care for. They want their friends, family, and loved ones to be the best they can be, and they want to help them achieve their aspirations.

Awareness for Eights: This week as you meditate on 1 Peter 3:8–12, allow yourself to see the many ways you have blessed others through your support and care. Are there people in your life you have looked to as inspirations of how to bless others well? Write down their names and a few new ways you can be a blessing to those around you.

NINE

NINES are a blessing to others, as they love wholeheartedly with a compassionate heart. They are easygoing and patient. They long for unity and peace and are willing to walk alongside those in need.

Awareness for Nines: This week as you meditate on 1 Peter 3:8–12, allow yourself to see the many ways you have blessed others through your sympathy and compassion. Can you identify a person in your life who has blessed you unexpectedly? Write down a few words that describe how you feel when you see those around you blessed by your actions.

APPLICATION

In what ways can you identify being a blessing to those around you?

_____

_____

_____

How does it make you feel to accept blessings from other people in your life?

_____

_____

_____

In what ways can you relate to other Enneagram numbers when it comes to being a blessing?

_____

_____

_____

How are you hearing God speak to you about being a blessing?

_____

_____

_____

MEDITATION

Go to page 342 and try Contemplation Meditation exercise.

My prayer this week:

_____

_____

_____

_____

_____

_____

_____

_____

_____

WEEK 9

EVEN YOUTHS GROW TIRED AND WEARY,
AND YOUNG MEN STUMBLE AND FALL;
BUT THOSE WHO HOPE IN THE LORD WILL
RENEW THEIR STRENGTH. THEY WILL
SOAR ON WINGS LIKE EAGLES; THEY
WILL RUN AND NOT GROW WEARY,
THEY WILL WALK AND NOT BE FAINT.

ISAIAH 40:30-31

HOPE
WINGS LIKE EAGLES

"POUND FOR POUND, AN EAGLE WING IS STRONGER THAN A WING OF AN AIRPLANE."

What's the genesis of your hope? Do you begin each morning with a renewed strength? Maybe the source of your hope is the current state of your career, your family, your finances, or popularity. However, you might be sustaining hope from your own abilities, influences, and stamina. Leaning on your own wellspring of hope or—worse yet—leaning on others to sustain it, can be utterly draining and deeply dispiriting. There is great news: you serve God, the maker of heaven and earth! Leaning on God's inexhaustible hope strengthens you, like soaring on the wings of eagles. As a matter of fact, an eagle's wings include 7,000 feathers with interlocking structures to lift heavy prey, climb 10,000 feet in the air, and travel 225 miles in a day effortlessly. No small feat. It is said, "Pound for pound, an eagle wing is stronger than a wing of an airplane." This week, be reminded that through God's hope you will soar on His powerful wings of mightiness, accuracy, and renewal. Your Creator, with exact precision, knows your every breath and every desire of your heart. Rest in His profound truth of His promises and abilities: "I pray that God, the source of hope, will fill you completely with joy and peace because you trust in him. Then you will overflow with confident hope through the power of the Holy Spirit" (Romans 15:13, NLT).

ONE

ONES know they are supposed to hope in the Lord. However, hope requires trust and that is hard for them. Hope feels like vulnerability. Ones feel that there is a right and a wrong way to do everything, so leaving some things to chance doesn't necessarily make a lot of sense.

Awareness for Ones: Learning to hope requires you to release your need for perfection and invite God to renew your strength. This week meditate on Isaiah 40:30-31 and allow it to penetrate your heart. Write down the ways you can release your need for everything to appear perfect. Let God fill you with hope so you can run and not grow weary and walk and not be faint. You are a gift from God to all the people you encounter. Live out this life, renewed daily in His hope.

TWO

Hope in the Lord for **TWOS** comes in their trust that He is going to be with them always. Twos are relational people, and connection is extremely important to them. Knowing they have God on their side and that He is walking with them daily grants them the ability to be their own person. Twos need to stop trying to be what others appear to need, in hopes others will subsequently see and meet their own needs.

Awareness for Twos: When you hope in the Lord, you understand He renews your strength. He will help you when you feel tired and weary and will pick you up when you stumble and fall. He is your source of life, and in Him you find your true self. This week while meditating on Isaiah 40:30-31, write down a few ways God has renewed your strength in Him.

THREE

Hope in the Lord for **THREES** is relinquishing control and allowing God to be in the driver's seat of their lives. Threes have a hard time trusting that God is going to work out all things for their good. They desire to establish and execute the plan, no matter how difficult, because their reputations depend on it. Their drive for success and achievement leaves little room for hope. According to Threes, hope seems weak or even unattainable. Work feels much safer, as they feel as though they are guaranteed achievement if they keep moving forward.

Awareness for Threes: Learning to place your hope in the Lord is the very essence that will renew your strength. It is vital for your spiritual, emotional, and physical health. Understanding by God's strength you are able to "run and not grow weary" and "walk and not be faint" is truly key to your endurance. As you process Isaiah 40:30-31 this week, write down the ways you can put your hope in God.

FOUR

For **FOURS**, hope in the Lord is a beautiful place to rest. They long for the days they feel safe in His arms. They are always a bit cautious to trust Him, for fear He will not love and accept them. They have a unique way of viewing the world—it is full of mystery and wonder. Fours are always walking around feeling slightly "less than" in one way or another. They need to allow themselves to fully embrace hope, as it will bring peace to their troubled souls.

Awareness for Fours: Believing God will fill you with the strength is the first step. Embracing this truth will allow you to soar on wings like eagles. You are chosen by God. He wants to help you walk out your life without feeling faint or wanting to just give up. Embrace His love for you today. This week as you meditate on Isaiah 40:30-31, write down ways you have seen God helping you walk out your life with renewed strength.

FIVE

For **FIVES**, the ability to simply hope and trust in the Lord is difficult. The very definition of hope, which is a feeling of expectation and desire for something to happen, goes against their nature. They like certainty and predictability. They are incredibly pragmatic and have a plan to get what they want and need in this life. Fives need to understand that when they put their hope in God, He will renew their strength. They will no longer have to wear themselves out trying to gather what they need.

Awareness for Fives: You will notice when you put your hope in Him, in return He helps you to "run and not grow weary" and "walk and not be faint." You will find yourself soaring on the wings of eagles because your trust is found in Him. This week as you meditate on Isaiah 40:30-31, ask God to show you ways He is trustworthy. Write down the areas in your life you need to surrender to God so you can be renewed by his strength.

SIX

SIXES want to hope and trust that God is working all things out. However, uncertainty causes them to dig and explore in order to figure out what the best scenario is for every situation. As they begin to understand the beauty in simply trusting God, their ability to hope will grow. They are able to relinquish control and breathe in the sweet aroma of knowing God is on their side.

Awareness for Sixes: All that you're questioning and testing will wear you out, but when you put your hope in the Lord, He will renew your strength. He will give you the ability to "run and not grow weary" and "walk and not be faint." This week as you meditate on Isaiah 40:30-31, breathe in hope and breathe out fear. Write down several ways you can release your fears to the Lord and be renewed by His strength.

SEVEN

SEVENS trust God and put their hope in Him easier than most. They have a cheery disposition and a way of reframing everything into a positive. Sevens, however, have a hard time slowing down because they fear being trapped in a situation or stuck in emotional pain. This can cause them to have unrealistic expectations and at times feel as if they are living in a fairy-tale world. This make-believe state is not placing hope in the Lord; it is their pattern of escapism.

Awareness for Sevens: When you have true hope in the Lord, you can tackle hard situations and face challenges head-on with perseverance rather than yielding to a frantic escape. You can "walk and be not faint." When you soar, you are fully grounded in God, as you are tethered to the source who continues to give you strength to not only dream but also fulfill those dreams. This week as you meditate on Isaiah 40:30-31, write down the ways you notice when a false sense of hope tries to overshadow the perfect hope found only in the Lord.

EIGHT

EIGHTS want to put their hope in the Lord, but for them it is not that easy. Their desire to protect themselves and those they love motivates them to make things happen. They have a hard time leaving anything to chance.

Awareness for Eights: When you can put your hope in the Lord, it does not always turn out the way you thought it would or seem to happen in your time frame. Therefore, you are leery to let go and let God do what He wants to in His time frame. However, when you understand the freedom and peace that comes when you surrender to God and put your hope in Him, then and only then can you breathe easily. This week as you meditate on Isaiah 40:30-31, write down several areas you continue to grip controllingly and release those to God asking to renew your hope in Him.

NINE

For **NINES**, their desire for peace and harmony allows them to lean into hope in a beautiful way. Nines are hopeful others are seen and their voices are heard, people can resolve conflict quickly, and life will be peaceful and easier.

Awareness for Nines: Hope in the Lord is different from hope in your day-to-day life. When you can hope in the Lord, you can trust that when you use your voice, it will be heard. You will learn to assert yourself and chase after your passions because the hope of the Lord renews your strength and pushes you out of a state of complacency. You will soar on wings of eagles, because your hope is found in Christ alone and His strength will sustain you. This week as you meditate on Isaiah 40:30-31, write down the ways you notice areas you are holding yourself back because of fear.

APPLICATION

As you reflect on your Enneagram number this week, how are you able to relate to how you engage with this idea of hope?

_____

_____

_____

How can you embrace hope in a new way as you process your Enneagram reflection?

_____

_____

_____

After reading all the Enneagram reflections, in what ways can you help those around you to see hope in their life in a fresh new way?

_____

_____

_____

How can you better put your hope in the Lord in order to "run and not grow weary"? How are you hearing God speak to you about hope?

_____

_____

_____

MEDITATION

Go to page 332 and try the Box Breathing exercise.

My prayer this week:

_____

_____

_____

_____

_____

_____

_____

_____

_____

_____

WEEK 10

"

LOVE IS *LARGE* AND INCREDIBLY PATIENT. LOVE IS GENTLE AND CONSISTENTLY KIND TO ALL. IT REFUSES TO BE JEALOUS *WHEN BLESSING COMES TO SOMEONE ELSE*. LOVE DOES NOT BRAG ABOUT ONE'S ACHIEVEMENTS NOR INFLATE ITS OWN IMPORTANCE. LOVE DOES NOT TRAFFIC IN SHAME AND DISRESPECT, NOR SELFISHLY SEEK ITS OWN HONOR. LOVE IS NOT EASILY IRRITATED OR QUICK TO TAKE OFFENSE. LOVE JOYFULLY CELEBRATES HONESTY AND FINDS NO DELIGHT IN WHAT IS WRONG. LOVE IS A SAFE PLACE OF SHELTER, FOR IT NEVER STOPS BELIEVING THE BEST FOR OTHERS. LOVE NEVER TAKES FAILURE AS DEFEAT, FOR IT NEVER GIVES UP.

1 CORINTHIANS 13:4-8 (TPT)

LOVE
THE HIGHEST FORM

YOUR LORD'S AGAPE TOWARD YOU IS THE GREATEST EXAMPLE OF AN UNPARALLELED EXPRESSION OF TRUE LOVE.

What is your definition of love? You likely learned the meaning of love at a young age from the example shown by adults in your life, perhaps by your parents or grandparents. Maybe you were exposed to beautiful and healthy affection. Or maybe you experienced a scary and unhealthy representation of love. Either way, right now you can embrace the deepest meaning of love by understanding the way your heavenly Father perfectly and magnificently loves you. In this week's verse, the apostle Paul describes love by using the Greek word *agape*. Agape is the highest form of love and the way in which God loves you unconditionally and in everything He does. This is also an edict for the way in which you should demonstrate love toward others. This week, think about the ways you can display love by showing patience, gentleness, joy, and honesty, and by believing the best in everyone around you. Consider exhibiting a love that is humble, respectful, calm, safe, and enduring, just as God has shown you. Your Lord's agape toward you is the greatest example of an unsurpassed and unparalleled expression of true love—and one you can exemplify.

ONE

ONES long for others who are honest and ethical. They look for people they can trust. They want to be in relationships where they are loved and supported. Ones look for love that "joyfully celebrates honesty." In return, they desire to give love that is a "safe place of shelter."

Awareness for Ones: As you meditate on 1 Corinthians 13:4–8, notice the many positive ways love is expressed. Can you identify one way your heart is longing for love to be expressed in your own personal life? Make a list of the times you have experienced love as it is written in this scripture.

TWO

TWOS long for others who are patient and nurturing. They look for people they can count on being there for them. Twos want to be in relationships where they are loved and wanted. They look for love that is "gentle and consistently kind to all." In return, they desire to show love that is a "safe place of shelter."

Awareness for Twos: As you meditate on 1 Corinthians 13:4–8, allow yourself to feel the emotions that arise as you reflect on what love is. Have you experienced this type of unconditional love in your life? Write down the feelings that surge in you as you process each line in this scripture.

THREE

THREES long for others who are supportive and caring. They look for people who will go along with their ideas. Threes want to be in relationships where they are respected and desired. They look for love that "never stops believing the best for others." In return, they desire to show love that is "gentle and consistently kind to all."

Awareness for Threes: As you meditate on 1 Corinthians 13:4–8, can you identify ways in which you long to be loved? How does reading this scripture validate your need to be loved just as you are? Make a list of the do's and don'ts of unconditional love described in this scripture.

FOUR

FOURS long for others who are interesting and deep. They look for people with whom they can have authentic conversations. Fours want to be in relationships where they are well thought of and cherished. They look for love that is "large and incredibly patient." In return, they desire to give love that "never gives up."

Awareness for Fours: As you meditate on 1 Corinthians 13:4–8, allow yourself to embrace love as it is written. As you read this scripture, does it bring you comfort to see love is kind, patient, and honest? Write down ways you desire to experience love in your life.

FIVE

FIVES long for others who are independent and ethical. They look for people who don't demand a lot of time and attention. Fives want to be in relationships where they are valued and respected. They look for love that is not "easily irritated or quick to take offense." In return, they desire to give love that is a "safe place of shelter."

Awareness for Fives: As you meditate on 1 Corinthians 13:4–8, does it bring you peace, knowing love is not easily irritated or disrespectful? As you reflect on love being a safe place, what thoughts come to your mind? Write down the times in your life you have felt the most loved, cared for, and safe.

SIX

SIXES long for others who are trustworthy and steady. They look for people who have high standards. Sixes want to be in relationships where they are understood and respected. They look for love that is not "easily irritated or quick to take offense." In return, they desire to give love that is a "safe place of shelter."

Awareness for Sixes: As you meditate on 1 Corinthians 13:4–8, embrace all the ways love is meant to be. How have you been able to love others in the ways Scripture teaches you? Write down the ways of love that come easily to you in one color, and in another color write down the ways you are learning to love in a new way.

Notes

SEVEN

SEVENS long for others who are adventurous and trustworthy. They look for people who have a positive view on life and who will go along with their new ideas. Sevens want to be in relationships where they can dream about all the possibilities the future holds. They look for love that is a "safe place of shelter." In return, they desire to give love that "never gives up."

Awareness for Sevens: As you meditate on 1 Corinthians 13:4–8, recognize the many ways love goes against what the world tells us to do. Allow yourself to surrender to God's type of love. Draw a heart and in it put all the ways love can be expressed.

EIGHT

EIGHTS long for others who are trustworthy. They look for people who are driven toward success and integrity. Eights want to be in relationships where they can speak their minds and be challenged, as well. They look for love that "never takes failure as defeat." In return, they desire to give love that "never gives up."

Awareness for Eights: As you meditate on 1 Corinthians 13:4–8, does it bring you a sense of peace to see that love is supposed to cover you and protect you? Can you identify the ways love has been graciously given to you in your relationships? Write down the ways you desire to love others as described in this passage of scripture.

NINE

NINES long for others who are kind and understanding. They look for people who have compassion toward others. Nines want to be in relationships where they are seen as valuable and worthwhile. They look for a love that is "gentle and consistently kind to all." In return, they desire to give love that "never stops believing the best for others."

Awareness for Nines: As you meditate on 1 Corinthians 13:4–8, allow yourself to see the many ways you have followed this scripture in the way you have loved others. Can you identify an area of love that you wish to develop further in your life? Write down ways you can love others and in return receive their love as you process this scripture.

APPLICATION

How can you relate to what it says your number is looking for in a relationship?

_____

_____

_____

How can you allow yourself to show love to others and receive the love for which you are searching?

_____

_____

_____

In what ways can you love those around you in the way they need after reading through the Enneagram reflections?

_____

_____

_____

How has God shown you unconditional love? How are you hearing God speak to you when it comes to love?

_____

_____

MEDITATION

Go to page 334 and try the Concentration Meditation exercise.

My prayer this week:

_____

_____

_____

_____

_____

_____

_____

_____

_____

_____

_____

WEEK 11

"

GOD DIDN'T SET US UP FOR AN ANGRY
REJECTION BUT FOR SALVATION
BY OUR MASTER, JESUS CHRIST. HE
DIED FOR US, A DEATH THAT TRIGGERED LIFE.
WHETHER WE'RE AWAKE WITH THE LIVING
OR ASLEEP WITH THE DEAD, WE'RE
ALIVE WITH HIM! SPEAK ENCOURAGING
WORDS TO ONE ANOTHER. BUILD UP
HOPE SO YOU'LL ALL BE TOGETHER IN THIS,
NO ONE LEFT OUT, NO ONE LEFT BEHIND.
I KNOW YOU'RE ALREADY DOING THIS;
JUST KEEP ON DOING IT.

1 THESSALONIANS 5:9–11 (MSG)

ENCOURAGEMENT
BE A WORD BUILDER

"NO ONE LEFT OUT,
NO ONE LEFT BEHIND."

Continue to speak up! Tell yourself God did not create you to dismiss you. Christ died for you to have eternal life right by His side because He treasures you. You, like all Enneagram numbers, have a difficult time believing certain kind and loving truths about yourselves. Let go of any lies you are speaking over yourself. Exchange them for encouragement, truly knowing you are not a disappointment. Conversely, your words to others matter—they hold more weight than you can measure. Allow His love to shine through you as you lavish praise on others by letting them know they matter. Continue with your kind inspiration, hopeful disposition, and positive words of affirmation for those around you. Keep it up, be a word-builder, as we are all in this together— "No one left out, no one left behind."

ONE

ONES may find "you are good" hard to believe. They might find it hard to accept the love that was poured out for them on the cross.

Awareness for Ones: As you read this passage, let the truth of the Word of God settle inside of your soul. "He died for us," and *us* means YOU. God finds you valuable and worthy of death on the cross, so be kind to yourself this week and allow your life to be a living sacrifice to those around you. Speak with love and compassion. Fill up those around you with words that bring forth life and truth. This week as you meditate on 1 Thessalonians 5:9–11, ask God to show you His thoughts about you. Be open to seeing yourself and those around you through the eyes of Christ.

TWO

TWOS may find "you are wanted" hard to believe. They might always second-guess if they are wanted in a group, relationship, or job. They can get lost trying to be what people need, hoping it will earn them a place in others' lives so the Twos will feel safe.

Awareness for Twos: As you read this scripture, allow yourself to see that Christ loved you so much that he died for you. He didn't want heaven without you. You are excellent at showing kindness and compassion to others, and that is important. But what about for yourself? This week as you meditate on 1 Thessalonians 5:9–11, ask God to remind you of His thoughts toward you. Be open to seeing life in a new way. Explore your relationships with lovingkindness.

THREE

THREES may find "you are loved for simply being yourself" hard to believe. Threes have always felt that they have had to perform to be seen. They have tried to excel in many areas, all the while feeling as if they will be exposed.

Awareness for Threes: As you read this scripture, allow yourself to see the value Christ placed on you. He loved you before you were ever born. He made a way for you to live forever with Him in heaven. His thoughts toward you are kind. He sees the person He created and He loves you for simply being you. This week as you meditate on 1 Thessalonians 5:9–11, allow God to reveal the truth of who you are. You are created in the image of Christ, meaning you are perfect just the way you are. Be open to feeling more settled in who you are behind the mask and loving yourself the way you try to love others.

FOUR

FOURS may find "you are seen for exactly who you are" hard to believe. They might feel that no one really gets them. They may struggle with other people accepting them for being authentically themselves.

Awareness for Fours: As you read this scripture, allow God to show how important you are to Him. He loves your uniqueness and He has a purpose for you on this earth. Practice speaking kind words to yourself and to those around you. Your words are like medicine to your soul. This week as you meditate on 1 Thessalonians 5:9–11, allow God to breathe life back into the places you have closed off, and open up to new ideas and thoughts. Be mindful of how you are speaking to yourself and others.

FIVE

FIVES may find that "your needs are not a problem" is hard to believe. They most likely learned how to navigate life in a way that allowed them not to have to ask for help. They may struggle with allowing people into their inner world.

Awareness for Fives: As you read this scripture, allow God to show you how much He loves and cares for you. You are never a burden to God. His ear is always bent toward you. He tells us that "we're *alive* with Him." This week as you meditate on 1 Thessalonians 5:9–11, allow Him to speak to your heart. Be open to what feelings arise and share them with one person close to you.

SIX

SIXES may find that "you are safe" is hard to believe. They have a mind that goes to the worst-case scenario every time. They want to believe that they can trust what Christ says yet they wonder if it is true. They understand the sacrifice that was made on the cross and they want to encourage those around them with the truth. However, they get stuck in overthinking and second-guessing while losing sight of the power that took place at the cross.

Awareness for Sixes: As you read the scripture this week, allow the truth of who God is to settle into your soul. Notice your words to yourself and those around you. Let them be life-giving. This week as you meditate on 1 Thessalonians 5:9–11, ask God to be your protector. Be aware of the people He has placed in your life to care for you and keep you safe.

Notes

SEVEN

SEVENS may find that "you will be taken care of" is hard to believe. This is scary for Sevens because they don't know exactly whom they can trust. Sevens are known as adventurers, enthusiastic, the life of the party, and optimistic. Yet deep down there is a fear of truly trusting anyone, out of a fear of being abandoned. When they begin to understand that their eternity is secure with Christ in heaven, they can begin to live a life much more in the present.

Awareness for Sevens: As you read this scripture, allow God to show you that you are better when moving through life with trusted friends and loved ones. Let your words be life to you and those around you. This week as you meditate on 1 Thessalonians 5:9–11, allow yourself to be aware of the many ways Christ has taken care of you through the years.

EIGHT

EIGHTS may find that "you will not be betrayed" is hard to believe. They like to be in control so they know the outcome. If they don't let many people into their inner circle, there is a lower chance of hurt and betrayal. Eights are always on guard, but this is exhausting.

Awareness for Eights: As you read the scripture this week, allow God to speak right to your wounds. He took all the sin, hurt, and betrayal to the cross. He wore it all so that you can live a life full of love and abundance. This week as you meditate on 1 Thessalonians 5:9–11, lean into these words, allowing truth to be spoken to your heart. Letting others in and loving them well is part of this journey. Sharing the love you have found in Christ is the greatest gift you can give anyone. Allow yourself to love this week in a deeper, more connected way.

NINE

NINES may find "your presence matters" hard to believe. They are caring and observant. They are great listeners, but often don't feel heard themselves. They wonder, "Does my voice matter? Do people even see the real me?" They have mastered the skill of conflict avoidance because chaos is unsettling.

Awareness for Nines: Can you see how important you are to God? He sent His one and only Son to die for you. Your thoughts, voice, opinions, and feelings matter to the King of kings. God's desire for you is to love and be loved. He wants to use your voice to share the love of Christ and to build up those around you. He wants you fully awake to what He has in store for your life. Allow God to whisper truths to you. Open your eyes with childlike wonder to the world in which you live. This week as you meditate on 1 Thessalonians 5:9–11, don't suppress your voice. Allow space for your thoughts and feelings. Love yourself the way Christ loves you and that love will flow through you to others.

APPLICATION

How does your Enneagram reflection resonate with you, regarding what you have a hard time believing?

_____

_____

_____

How can you process your Enneagram reflection and embrace who you are in a new way?

_____

_____

_____

In what way can you identify with another person's Enneagram number as you process what her or his heart longs to hear?

_____

_____

_____

What are some of the beautiful ways in which God sees you? How are you hearing God speak to you about encouragement?

_____

_____

_____

MEDITATION

Go to page 336 and try the Reflection Meditation exercise.

My prayer this week:

_____

_____

_____

_____

_____

_____

_____

_____

_____

_____

_____

WEEK 12

"

TRUST IN THE LORD WITH ALL YOUR
HEART AND LEAN NOT ON YOUR OWN
UNDERSTANDING; IN ALL YOUR
WAYS SUBMIT TO HIM, AND HE WILL
MAKE YOUR PATHS STRAIGHT.

PROVERBS 3:5-6

TRUST
A STRAIGHT PATH

THE SCRIPTURES ARE NOT SIMPLY A MANUSCRIPT; RATHER THEY ARE FULL OF HIS PROMISES CERTAINLY WORTH YOUR TRUST.

Are you struggling with any trust issues currently? You might be apprehensive about trusting a certain situation, trusting a person, or perhaps trusting yourself. Being vulnerable and opening your heart can sometimes make you feel uneasy because misplaced trust often results in pain and disappointment. Fortunately, you can lay down your life on this one unwavering fact: The Word of God is truth. The Scriptures are not simply a manuscript; rather they are full of His promises certainly worth your trust. You can trust you are never alone, He's right there listening and loves you deeply and dearly. This week start each morning by opening your mind to His promises and His Word. Know that even when you don't understand your current circumstances, God gets them. Even when you don't understand recent outcomes, God comprehends them. Even when you don't understand yourself, God grasps your deepest unspoken concerns. This week, work on vulnerability by submitting yourself, your cares, and your heart's desires to Him and trust He fully realizes how to nurture every need. "He will make your paths straight" even when the view seems wobbly, shaky, or off balance. Trust His direction with all your vigor and strength.

ONE

For **ONES**, putting their trust in this type of faith can be challenging. When they feel exposed and fearful that others are seeing their less-than-perfect selves, Ones become hypercritical and demand perfection from themselves and others. Recognizing this pattern of behavior will allow Ones to surrender it to Christ. When they are secure in their relationship with Christ, trust becomes easier.

Awareness for Ones: You believe God's promises and are willing to submit to His authority. The beauty in cultivating a relationship with Him is you no longer have to fight for your place in this world, because you know who you are and where your place is. This week as you meditate on Proverbs 3:5–6, take time to ask yourself this question: "Do I trust the Lord?" Write down the areas in which you find it hard to release your grip. Pray He will help you submit your ways to Him and make your paths straight.

TWO

TWOS have a natural desire to trust God because they are highly relational. However, when they are not at their best, they fear losing connection with the people they care about and with Christ. Twos can become clingy, feeling they need others to need them in order to be loved. Recognizing this pattern of behavior will allow Twos to surrender it to Christ.

Awareness for Twos: When you are secure in your relationship with Christ, you believe His promises and are willing to submit to His authority. The beauty in cultivating a relationship with Christ is you no longer have to try to figure out your place in this world. This week as you meditate on Proverbs 3:5–6, take time to ask yourself this question: "Do I trust the Lord?" Pray He will help you submit your ways to Him and make your paths straight.

THREE

For **THREES**, putting their trust in this type of faith can be challenging. When they feel exposed and fearful that others are seeing their less-than-perfect selves, Threes begin to feel as if they no longer have value. They start chasing after success, hoping to mask their vulnerabilities instead of trusting their worth in Christ. Recognizing this pattern of behavior will allow them to surrender it to Christ.

Awareness for Threes: When you are secure in your relationship with Christ, trust and vulnerability become easier. You believe His promises and are willing to submit to His authority. The beauty in cultivating a relationship with Christ is you no longer have to strive for your place in this world. This week as you meditate on Proverbs 3:5–6, take time to ask yourself this question: "Do I trust the Lord?" Write down the moments you find it hard to trust others. Pray He will help you submit your ways to Him and make your paths straight.

FOUR

For **FOURS**, putting their trust in this type of faith can be challenging. They long to be loved and accepted just as they are. However, when they make mistakes and fear rejection, they become self-indulgent and try to gratify and protect themselves instead of trusting Christ's love. Recognizing this pattern of behavior will allow them to surrender it to Christ.

Awareness for Fours: When you are secure in your relationship with Christ, fear no longer has control over you. You believe His promises and are willing to submit to His authority. The beauty in cultivating a relationship with Christ is you no longer have to justify yourself to try to find your place in this world. This week as you meditate on Proverbs 3:5–6, take time to ask yourself this question: "Do I trust the Lord?" Write down the circumstances you find it difficult to surrender to Christ. Pray He will help you submit your ways to Him and make your paths straight.

FIVE

For **FIVES**, putting their trust in this type of faith can be challenging. They want to trust, but they have a hard time believing they can count on anyone in this way. Their need to be competent causes them to gather useless information and collect items in hopes of keeping themselves safe. Recognizing this pattern of behavior within themselves will allow them to surrender it to Christ.

Awareness for Fives: When you are secure in your relationship with Christ, trust becomes easier. You believe His promises and are willing to submit to His authority. The beauty in cultivating a relationship with Christ is you no longer fear you will not have what you need in this world. This week as you meditate on Proverbs 3:5–6, take time to ask yourself this question: "Do I trust the Lord?" Note the parts of your life that you feel God may not help you with. Pray He will help you submit your ways to Him and make your paths straight.

SIX

For **SIXES**, putting their trust in this type of faith can be challenging. When they feel like their security is slipping, they cling to ideas, facts, and belief systems in an attempt to reestablish order. Recognizing this pattern of behavior allows them to surrender it to Christ.

Awareness for Sixes: When you are secure in your relationship with Christ, you can trust He is your protector and you no longer have to be on guard, because you are able to find peace in this world. This week as you meditate on Proverbs 3:5–6, take time to ask yourself this question: "Do I trust the Lord?" Write down the areas you find it hard to surrender to God trusting He will protect you. Pray He will help you submit your ways to Him and make your paths straight.

Notes

_____

_____

_____

_____

_____

_____

_____

_____

_____

_____

_____

_____

_____

_____

_____

_____

_____

_____

_____

_____

SEVENS don't like to be limited or to focus on past mistakes. When they feel restricted, they may dream about escaping relationships, a job, a friendship, or their relationship with Christ so they can get back to the freedom they long for. Recognizing this pattern of behavior will allow them to surrender it to Christ.

Awareness for Sevens: When you are secure in your relationship with Christ, you no longer try to escape your circumstance. You believe His promises and are willing to submit to His authority. The beauty in cultivating a relationship with Christ is when you realize you are safe and loved. This week as you meditate on Proverbs 3:5–6, take time to ask yourself this question: "Do I trust the Lord?" Write down the situations in your life that cause you to feel trapped and release them to God. Pray He will help you submit your ways to Him and make your paths straight.

EIGHT

For **EIGHTS**, putting their trust in this type of faith can be challenging. When they feel exposed, they become hypersensitive, leading them to bicker and fight in order to protect themselves. Recognizing this pattern of behavior will allow them to surrender it to Christ.

Awareness for Eights: When you are secure in your relationship with Christ, trust becomes easier. You believe His promises and are willing to submit to His authority. The beauty in cultivating a relationship with Christ is you no longer have to fight for your place in this world because you know who you are. This week as you meditate on Proverbs 3:5–6, take time to ask yourself this question: "Do I trust the Lord?" Write down the situations in which you find it hard to release your desire to defend yourself. Pray He will help you submit your ways to Him and make your paths straight.

NINE

NINES desire to put their trust in this type of faith. But when their peace is disturbed, they retreat, neglecting themselves and their responsibilities. Recognizing this pattern of behavior will allow Nines to surrender it to Christ.

Awareness for Nines: When you are secure in your relationship with Christ, you no longer feel the need to withdraw. You believe His promises and are willing to submit to His authority. The beauty in cultivating a relationship with Christ is you become more confident in your own abilities and willing to share your thoughts and ideas with the world. This week as you meditate on Proverbs 3:5–6, take time to ask yourself this question: "Do I trust the Lord?" Write down the situations keeping you from speaking what is on your mind and heart. Pray He will help you submit your ways to Him and make your paths straight.

APPLICATION

As you reflect on your Enneagram number, in what way does it resonate with you?

_____
_____
_____

How do you recognize when you are not at your best?

_____
_____
_____
_____

After reading your Enneagram reflections, how are you able to see those closest to you in new ways?

_____
_____
_____
_____

In what ways have you trusted in the Lord with all of your heart, even when you did not understand? How are you hearing God speak to you when it comes to trust?

_____
_____
_____
_____

MEDITATION

Go to page 342 and try the Contemplation Meditation exercise.

My prayer this week:

_____
_____
_____
_____
_____
_____
_____
_____
_____

WEEK 13

"

HE HAS TOLD YOU, O MAN, WHAT IS GOOD;
AND WHAT DOES THE LORD REQUIRE
OF YOU BUT TO DO JUSTICE, AND TO LOVE
KINDNESS, AND TO WALK HUMBLY
WITH YOUR GOD?

MICAH 6:8 (ESV)

COMPASSION
TO BE FAIR

TREATING OTHERS RESPECTFULLY, HONORABLY, AND WITH EMPATHY.

This passage is from the prophet Micah, clarifying to the people that animal sacrifices, a common practice at the time, do not cancel their sin. The prophet teaches that God is not looking for an outside offering, but a sacrifice from inside the heart. God is emphasizing a matter of your heart. Take a moment to do a heart check, since it is good for your soul to take inventory. How is your heart feeling today? Any issues you need to reconcile? Any resentment you need to release? Any regrets or shame you need to lay at the foot of the cross? The way God wants you to live is not complex. It is simply treating others respectfully, honorably, and with empathy. Most people have *sympathy* for those who are hurting in some way, but *empathy* is often more difficult to grasp. Sympathy is feeling sorry for someone going through a hard time, whereas empathy is being with the person in their pain. Empathy moves you toward compassion for those in difficult situations. Compassion is care in action. And to be in love with the commitment of caring and kindness is to embrace what it means to live with a narrative of selflessness—a life engaged with your heart extended toward others while humbly and graciously walking alongside others and the Lord.

Notes

_____

_____

_____

_____

_____

_____

_____

_____

_____

_____

_____

_____

_____

_____

_____

_____

_____

_____

ONE

When **ONES** don't take themselves too seriously, they have compassion and empathy for people. They allow others to have different points of view without passing judgment. Ones can see people as they truly are and, with care and concern, help them out of difficult situations without feeling the need to fix them.

Awareness for Ones: You are most open-minded when you listen without passing judgment. As you meditate on Micah 6:8, take note on how you should live: do what is right, be compassionate and loyal, and do not take yourself too seriously. This week write down when you have witnessed the effects of lovingkindness being extended to you in your own life.

TWO

When **TWOS** have compassion for others, they accept them just as they are. They no longer try to influence others to do what *they* think is best. Twos spend time with others and truly listen and care about their situation and circumstances.

Awareness for Twos: When you don't try to persuade others to choose your ideas, you find peace within yourself. As you meditate on Micah 6:8, embrace your natural ability to show compassion and understanding to others. This week, journal how it felt for you to have someone listen intently as you shared a difficult situation.

THREE

When **THREES** have compassion for people, they are present in conversations and are willing to be with others even during uncomfortable situations. They extend kindness through godly love and mercy as they comfort them in their pain.

Awareness for Threes: When you are authentic in relationships and care about speaking truth to others, your humility is on display. As you meditate on Micah 6:8, recognize the importance of walking humbly with the Lord. This week write down what it feels like to extend compassion and empathy to others.

FOUR

When **FOURS** show compassion, they can put aside their own feelings and understand others' points of view without internalizing them or taking them personally. They can be with people in their deep personal trauma and extend empathy without feeling overwhelmed.

Awareness for Fours: Because of your depth of emotional awareness, when you see injustices happening, you extend kindness because you care deeply that all humanity is respected. As you meditate on Micah 6:8, continue to embrace the importance of kindness and compassion. This week write down your feelings that surface when you think about a time in your life when you were present with someone in their pain.

FIVE

When **FIVES** have compassion for people, they acknowledge another's emotions and concerns without personally withdrawing or retreating. They become patient and listen while they allow others to form their own conclusions and opinions.

Awareness for Fives: When you extend kindness to others, you resist the urge to try to solve their problems, while still staying emotionally connected. As you meditate on Micah 6:8, notice the importance of extending empathy to others. This week write down how you can practice compassion and offer kindness toward others.

SIX

When **SIXES** have compassion for people, they cast aside their strong opinions and care for others with love and concern. Because of their display of loyalty to those they trust, they desire that those they care deeply about be treated justly and fairly.

Awareness for Sixes: Your desire to be loyal and supportive in relationships motivates you to extend kindness and compassion. As you meditate on Micah 6:8, be mindful that you are asked to live humbly and do what is right. This week as you reflect on what it has felt like to share your deep feelings with others, write down what emotions arise.

SEVEN

When **SEVENS** have compassion for people, they are patient and show concern by helping them through their difficult situations. With humility and kindness, they can be fully present and listen intently without always needing to offer a response.

Awareness for Sevens: You display kindness to and support for others as you encourage them to see the positive. As you meditate on Micah 6:8, notice how humility plays a vital role in your kindness. Write down when you have shown compassion to others in their time of need.

EIGHT

When **EIGHTS** have compassion for people, they no longer think others should "just get over it." They listen intently to people's different points of view and focus on others' issues and concerns without turning the topic back on themselves.

Awareness for Eights: When you extend kindness through humility, you genuinely care about other people's feelings and emotions. As you meditate on Micah 6:8, how can you extend kindness without being judgmental? This week write down the ways you are expressing kindness while you are interacting with others.

NINE

For **NINES**, having compassion for others comes naturally. They see the beauty in people and work toward understanding others' perspectives. They are full of understanding and empathy as they desire to create harmony in all their relationships.

Awareness for Nines: You are gifted with the ability to see all sides of a situation and react in a way that brings about peace and unity. As you meditate on Micah 6:8, embrace the kindness that you often exude. This week write down a few ways you can speak up for injustices, knowing God desires you to use your voice for the good of others.

APPLICATION

How can you identify how you respond to others through your own lens of empathy and compassion?

_____

_____

_____

How does the information about your number help you to move toward empathy for others and to "care in action"?

_____

_____

_____

In what ways can you see how all five Enneagram numbers you use (your number, wings, and the numbers you go to in stress and health) impact how you display empathy and compassion for others?

_____

_____

_____

How has walking humbly with the Lord allowed you to care for others with empathy and kindness?

_____

_____

_____

MEDITATION

Go to page 332 and try the Box Breathing exercise.

My prayer this week:

_____

_____

_____

_____

_____

_____

_____

_____

_____

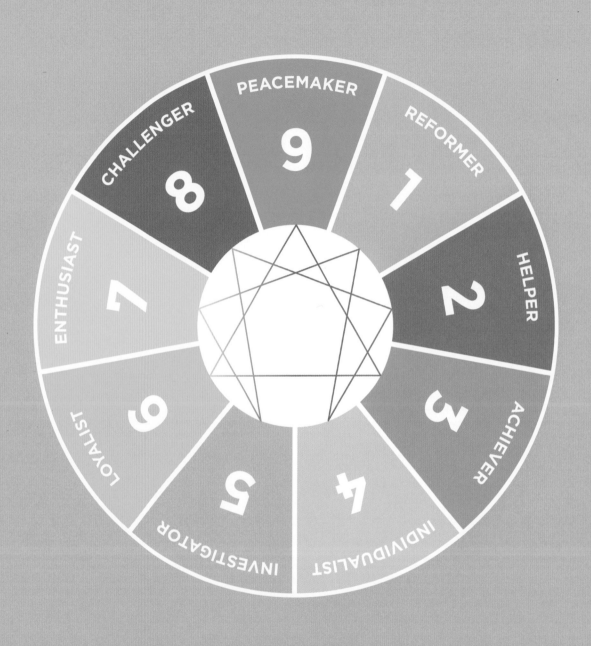

QUARTER TWO

YOUR PROTECTOR

Our Heavenly Father is our ultimate Protector and whom we turn to for security, trust, and freedom. Each Enneagram personality desires to feel known and protected regardless of our current season—whether it's before the storm, in the midst of one, or following the tempest.

WEEK 14

"

SO, WHAT DO YOU THINK? WITH GOD ON OUR SIDE LIKE THIS, HOW CAN WE LOSE? IF GOD DIDN'T HESITATE TO PUT EVERYTHING ON THE LINE FOR US, EMBRACING OUR CONDITION AND EXPOSING HIMSELF TO THE WORST BY SENDING HIS OWN SON, IS THERE ANYTHING ELSE HE WOULDN'T GLADLY AND FREELY DO FOR US? AND WHO WOULD DARE TANGLE WITH GOD BY MESSING WITH ONE OF GOD'S CHOSEN? WHO WOULD DARE EVEN TO POINT A FINGER? THE ONE WHO DIED FOR US—WHO WAS RAISED TO LIFE FOR US! — IS IN THE PRESENCE OF GOD AT THIS VERY MOMENT STICKING UP FOR US. DO YOU THINK ANYONE IS GOING TO BE ABLE TO DRIVE A WEDGE BETWEEN US AND CHRIST'S LOVE FOR US? THERE IS NO WAY! NOT TROUBLE, NOT HARD TIMES, NOT HATRED, NOT HUNGER, NOT HOMELESSNESS, NOT BULLYING THREATS, NOT BACKSTABBING, NOT EVEN THE WORST SINS LISTED IN SCRIPTURE.

ROMANS 8:31–39 (MSG)

THE PROTECTOR
NO WEDGE BETWEEN US

GOD'S PROMISE THAT THERE IS NOTHING HE WOULD NOT "GLADLY AND FREELY" DO FOR YOU.

There will be days you are weary, and the world seems to be a constant battle. When your heart is heavy and your joy is smothered, it's comforting to read this message in Romans in which Paul reminds you of God's promise that there is nothing He would not "gladly and freely" do for you. He will protect you from anyone trying to steal your joy. He will fight against any bullies coming against you. He conquered the grave for you by sending His son, Jesus, to die and be raised to life for you. No matter if you feel worthless or useless, or if you believe you are insignificant or invisible, God chooses you. He is on your side and is your shield. He will not leave you during the darkest days of your life. He will not abandon you regardless of the demons you face from your past. Absolutely nothing you have done nor anything that has ever been said about you—even in the worst ways—can diminish His promise. There simply isn't a way to separate you from God's love.

ONE

For **ONES**, the fear of being bad, corrupt, or even defective can be crippling. Their desire to hide this part of themselves can cause them to suppress their true feelings about the situation or perhaps even the person involved.

Awareness for Ones: As you read this scripture, take heart that nothing you do, think, or even say can separate you from the love of God. When things don't go the way you think they should or when accusations are made against you, learning to trust the truth laid out in this passage will be the catalyst to change. This week as you meditate on Romans 8:31-39, allow God to reveal where you have kept your true thoughts and feelings at bay for fear of people thinking poorly of you. Let the love of God fill you up this week. Write down truths you know about who you are in Christ.

TWO

The fear of being unlovable can feel so overwhelming that **TWOS** may try to earn love by being what they think other people need them to be. This feeling can keep them isolated and alone in their own shame. When people do not treat Twos the way they think they should or when others say things about Twos that are untrue, it can truly be debilitating.

Awareness for Twos: As you read this passage, know Jesus loves you so much that He is in heaven at this moment fighting for you. This week as you meditate on Romans 8:31-39, allow these words to settle over you, "Do you think anyone is going to be able to drive a wedge between us and Christ's love for us? There is no way!" Write down the ways this truth brings a sense of peace to your soul.

THREE

The fear of being worthless has **THREES** doing everything in their power to show the world that they have value. It can cause them to become someone other than who God created them to be. Threes fear that if they don't show up the way other people expect them to, they will be seen as "less than."

Awareness for Threes: As you read this passage, allow the truth of what Christ has done for you to settle into your soul. He has taken all your sin and shame to the cross. God's love for you is never-ending. And no matter what people say or do, *nothing* can keep His love from you. Your worth is found in Christ alone. This week as you meditate on Romans 8:31-39, allow yourself to release the shame you are carrying. God is not afraid of your past. He already washed you clean, and all your sins are buried beneath the depths of the ocean floor. Write down truths you know about who you are in Christ.

FOUR

The fear of being insignificant can have **FOURS** chasing many different things. They can get lost in feeling they are not enough. They can get trapped in the comparison game that will swallow them. Constantly trying to find their place in this life leaves them feeling exhausted and misunderstood.

Awareness for Fours: When the lies of the Enemy start to sound louder than Christ's truth, remember that Jesus is in heaven fighting for you. He is always on your side. You are unique and creative. This week as you meditate on Romans 8:31–39, allow yourself to know *you* are a gift to this world. What thoughts are you carrying or what words that you have heard about yourself do you need to release this week? Write down truths you know about who you are in Christ.

FIVE

The fear of being useless or incompetent has the potential to keep **FIVES** constantly consuming information. It also has the potential to keep them withdrawn from deep personal connections. This fear can drive them away from a relationship with God for fear of not measuring up.

Awareness for Fives: As you read the scripture, can you see that you are loved for simply being yourself? No matter how far you run or how high you climb, God is always there fighting for you. He has your back. Even when people accuse you or say things about you that are not true, God is in heaven fighting for you. This week as you meditate on Romans 8:31–39, allow yourself to see your value in Christ. He is fighting the battle for you and nothing can ever keep Him from loving you. As you process this truth, allow God to reveal the areas of your life you need to release to Him and let Him love you through all of it. Write down truths you know about who you are in Christ.

SIX

For **SIXES**, the fear of being without support can be scary. Going through life not knowing whom they can count on exhausts them. Always scanning their environment for possible threats is not a peaceful way to live.

Awareness for Sixes: As you read the scripture, can you see how God is your protector? Don't you love that He is fighting your battles for you? He will not let anything or any person come between you and His love for you. This week as you meditate on Romans 8:31–39, allow yourself to feel the safety and security that comes as you read, "The One who died for us—who was raised to life for us!—is in the presence of God at this very moment sticking up for us." Draw a picture of what you think this looks like.

SEVEN

The fear of being trapped in emotional pain is one of the scariest things **SEVENS** can imagine. They do their best to keep their thoughts moving toward positive things. Even when words are said against them or something happens to them, oftentimes they put it out of their minds and run toward something fun and exciting.

Awareness for Sevens: As you read the passage, can you see that you don't have to be afraid of being trapped? What Christ did on the cross has given you a life free from eternal torment. Allow this to settle into your soul: There is nothing that God will not do for you. He desires that you know Him and love Him as much as He knows and loves you. This week as you meditate on Romans 8:31–39, allow yourself time to see where you have pushed God to the side for fear of being trapped. Write down truths you know about who you are in Christ.

EIGHT

The fear of being controlled by others can keep **EIGHTS** in a defensive posture. This leads to many negative comments said about them and to them. However, you are strong and powerful, and God created you just that way to accomplish what He has set out for you to do here on earth.

Awareness for Eights: As you read the passage, can you see that you have a mighty God fighting to protect you on your behalf? Lean into God and allow Him to soften you in this area. This week as you meditate on Romans 8:31–39, be reminded Jesus is in heaven fighting on your behalf, even when you sleep. You are so loved. You are fiercely protected. Write down truths you know about who you are in Christ.

NINE

The fear of losing connection with others in their life keeps **NINES** closed off from fully showing up in the way they would like. They care about keeping the peace and avoiding conflict because separation is scary and lonely.

Awareness for Nines: As you read the scripture, do you see that God has promised you that *nothing* can separate you from His love? Allow these words to penetrate your heart, giving yourself space to show up truly just as you are. You matter. Your thoughts and ideas matter. Regardless of what words come against you or what conflict arises, you have a heavenly Father fighting for you. This week as you meditate on Romans 8:31–39, allow yourself space to create—whether that's in the form of painting, writing, exercising, being in nature, rearranging furniture, or anything that allows you the freedom to be fully present in yourself. Write down truths you know about who you are in Christ.

APPLICATION

After you've read each Enneagram number, which fear do you resonate with the most?

_____

_____

_____

How can you see that particular fear at play in your relationships, work environments, and home?

_____

_____

_____

In what way can you see another person's fear being displayed?

_____

_____

_____

What situations are you currently facing where you desire God to have your back? How are you hearing Him speak to you when it comes to your strengths?

_____

_____

_____

_____

MEDITATION

Go to page 334 and try the Concentration Meditation exercise.

My prayer this week:

_____

_____

_____

_____

_____

_____

_____

_____

_____

WEEK 15

"

MY CHOICE IS YOU, GOD, FIRST AND
ONLY. AND NOW I FIND I'M *YOUR* CHOICE.
YOU SET ME UP WITH A HOUSE AND YARD.
AND THEN YOU MADE ME YOUR HEIR!

PSALM 16:5 (MSG)

GODLY DISPLAY
YOU'RE HIS HEIR

YOU ARE HIS HEIR, A MEMBER
OF HIS ROYAL FAMILY, AND HIS
CHOICE IS YOU, ALWAYS.

In your current season of life, with whom are you surrounding yourself? After all, your friendship tribe is a reflection of you and has a strong influence on your life decisions. Can you connect your healthy seasons with the times you chose to be with healthier people? Do your unhealthy moments reflect the times when you let unhealthy influences into your life? Your draining "friends" are the ones who have a negative influence, always trying to push your boundaries or bail as soon as the going gets rough. Relationship choices matter because you are the sum of those around you. Discern wisely while keeping in mind that one of your biggest and best relationship choices is building intimacy with Yahweh and picking Him first. As far as God's choice, this scripture makes one irrevocable promise: you are His heir, a member of His royal family, and His choice is you, always. He never bails on you, even when you're in a mess or mess up—you are still His choice, His heir. Following a fall from grace or failure in judgment, you are still His choice, His heir. It makes choosing a relationship with God your natural and most beautiful friendship choice.

ONE

ONES display goodness to the world. They look for purity in their environment and their relationships. They long to see God's masterpiece displayed with awe and wonder. They show everyone who Christ is through their integrity and through their desire for excellence while using their energy and resources to make this world better.

Awareness for Ones: Knowing God has chosen you brings you a sense of grounding and peace. This week as you meditate on Psalm 16:5, embrace being chosen by God, who loves you just as you are. Write down ways you show Christ to the world through goodness.

TWO

TWOS display love and nurturing to the world. They look for ways to care for and love others well. They long to see a place full of people who are all connected and have their needs met. They show everyone who Christ is through their kindness, love, and desire to help.

Awareness for Twos: Allow yourself to embrace the love of Christ because He chooses you freely and not because of anything you have done. He simply chooses you because he loves you. This week as you meditate on Psalm 16:5, write down what it feels like to be loved and chosen by God. Reflect on how Christ's love for you impacts the way you show the world love and nurture.

THREE

THREES display hope to the world. They desire to see all people shine, and they believe everyone plays a role in the unfolding of something greater. Threes show the world who Christ is through their never-ending hope of what can be accomplished in life.

Awareness for Threes: You may have a hard time believing that God would choose to love you without any strings attached. But as you begin to trust Him and allow yourself to embrace how deeply you are loved, your soul will feel complete. This week as you meditate on Psalm 16:5, express your love to Christ. Write down how you believe you have shown Christ to the world through the hope you display.

———— FOUR ————

FOURS display creativity and depth to the world. They long for people to be authentic and accepted just as they are. Fours show the world who Christ is through their creativity and uniqueness.

Awareness for Fours: Being in a relationship with Christ and knowing He chooses you is simply the most comforting feeling you could ever experience. This week as you meditate on Psalm 16:5, reflect on how your life has changed since you accepted Christ as your savior. Write down the ways His love for you allows you to express your creativity to the world.

———— FIVE ————

FIVES display wisdom and truth to the world. They can bring understanding to complex situations. They long to see perspective through God's eyes, which helps make sense of everything. Fives show the world who Christ is through their keen understanding, depth, and insight.

Awareness for Fives: Knowing that God not only chooses you but also wants to provide, protect, and love you brings comfort to your mind and heart. This week as you meditate on Psalm 16:5, allow yourself to embrace God's unconditional love for you. Write down how your relationship with God affects how you display wisdom and truth to the world.

———— SIX ————

SIXES display loyalty and courage to the world. They desire faithfulness and security. Sixes long to see God's love displayed through relationships. They show the world who Christ is through their commitment to others and their determination to follow through on those commitments.

Awareness for Sixes: Having a relationship with Christ and knowing you are not only chosen but also taken care of allows you to feel safe and secure. This sense of security enables you to embrace life and know you are loved and cared for well. This week as you meditate on Psalm 16:5, allow yourself to see the impact that your relationship with God has had on your life. Write down ways you can display Christ to the world through loyalty and courage because of your relationship with Him.

Notes

SEVEN

SEVENS display joy to the world. They desire to live in a world free of heartache and suffering. They long to see God's masterpiece displayed with awe and wonder. Sevens show everyone who Christ is through their enthusiasm and excitement.

Awareness for Sevens: You have longed to be cared for and loved. Knowing that God not only chooses you but also desires to care for you as His heir is comforting. This week as you meditate on Psalm 16:5, embrace what it feels like to be chosen by God. Write down the ways His love for you has helped you show joy to the world.

EIGHT

EIGHTS display protection and strength to the world. They live full of passion and have grand ideas of what the world could be like if everyone had a fair chance. Eights long to see justice displayed throughout the earth. They show everyone who Christ is through their ability to empower others and protect those treated unfairly.

Awareness for Eights: Knowing you are in a relationship with God and that He chooses you gives you a sense of feeling established. This week as you meditate on Psalm 16:5, praise God for not only choosing you but also for providing for you. Write down the ways His love for you has allowed you to show the world protection and strength.

NINE

NINES display peace to the world. They desire to see harmony displayed through the earth. Nines long to see all people living together in one accord. They show everyone who Christ is through unconditional love and unity.

Awareness for Nines: Having a relationship with Christ and knowing that not only have you chosen Him but He has also chosen you allows you to feel settled within yourself. This week as you meditate on Psalm 16:5, reflect on His love for you. How has knowing you are loved and chosen by God allowed you to show Christ to the world through being understanding and fighting for unity?

APPLICATION

As you reflect on your Enneagram number this week, how do you resonate with the attributes you display to the world?

_____

_____

_____

How do you relate to the attributes of your wings?

_____

_____

_____

After reading the Enneagram reflections, can you recognize how your friendship circle displays specific attributes?

_____

_____

_____

How does it make you feel to truly understand God chooses you? How are you hearing God speak to you about being His heir?

_____

_____

_____

MEDITATION

Go to page 336 and try the Reflection Meditation exercise.

My prayer this week:

_____

_____

_____

_____

_____

_____

_____

_____

WEEK 16

"

TROUBLE AND SUFFERING HAVE COME
UPON ME, YET YOUR WORD IS MY
JOY. YOUR LAW IS RIGHT FOREVER. GIVE
ME UNDERSTANDING AND I WILL LIVE.
I CRIED WITH ALL MY HEART. ANSWER ME,
O LORD! I WILL KEEP YOUR LAW.

PSALM 119:143-145 (NLV)

STRESS
TRUSTING DURING TROUBLE

GOD IS YOUR UNFAILING SOURCE OF STRENGTH AND YOUR UNWAVERING COMFORTER.

There is no escaping trouble. It is a natural part of our fallen world and imperfect human race. While often you can't control your stressful circumstances, you can control your reaction to such trouble. Spinning your concerns out of control can lead to unhealthy behaviors that make you feel irritable, numb, depressed, critical of yourself and others, fearful, or even paranoid. When you are under extreme stress, a physical reaction occurs in your nervous system that leads to the release of stress hormones. This places your weary body on guard and causes it to react as if it is in a state of emergency. When you are feeling anxious, your body sends warnings: your heart pounds faster, muscles tense up, blood pressure rises, and breathing becomes irregular. Calling out to God in prayer to release your burdens on Him is a cathartic and calming practice. He is your unfailing source of strength and your unwavering comforter. Cry out to Him, as He can handle your frustration and every other deep emotion. He hears you, He sees you. When you feel your body physically reacting—try to deeply breathe in His Word of truth: "Your Word is my joy." His promises are mighty, and His love and peace can overcome your circumstances, "Cast all your anxiety on him, because he cares for you" (1 Peter 5:7).

———— ONE ————

When **ONES** are under stress, they go to a type Four. They begin to feel annoyed that their expectations are not being met. They internalize their anger about the situation and neglect processing it in a healthy way.

Awareness for Ones: When you are in a lower emotional state, you can begin feeling depressed when things are not going the way you desire them to go. This often causes you to lose sight of what really matters in life. This week as you meditate on Psalm 119:143–145, remind yourself of all the ways that God has been faithful to you. Write down the times He has provided for you without your intervention.

———— TWO ————

When **TWOS** are under stress, they go to a type Eight. They tend to become irritable, assertive, controlling, and even demanding. They can get caught up in blaming other people for their problems, while only seeing their own intentions as good.

Awareness for Twos: Stress is a big trigger for you. You are naturally a loving and caring person, but when stress enters the picture, you almost feel as if you are losing yourself. This week as you meditate on Psalm 119:143–145, take the time to allow the words to penetrate your heart. Ask God to show you where you get caught up in the stress cycle. Take some time to write down all the ways that God has provided for you and showed up.

———— THREE ————

When **THREES** are under stress, they go to a type Nine. They become disconnected from what is happening around them. They tend to neglect themselves and their personal care.

Awareness for Threes: You escape into your own world by numbing yourself and doing mindless things. The stress of always feeling as though you have to be "on" is debilitating. You will run yourself ragged until your body physically shuts down. Allowing God to take control of your life is not easy for you. Allowing Him to take over for you feels like you are giving up too much control. After all, what if He chooses a different path or time frame than you had hoped? This week as you meditate on Psalm 119:143–145, thank God for His understanding of how you are wired. Thank Him for helping you slow down, and begin to trust Him. Life lived in the presence of God is peaceful and is truly what your heart is longing for. Take some time to write down all the ways that God has provided for you.

FOUR

When **FOURS** are under stress, they go to a type Two. Fours are typically independent, but under stress they become over-involved and clingy. They tend to manipulate others into loving them. They often feel that getting attention from others will help fill the feelings of emptiness and loneliness inside.

Awareness for Fours: Stress truly brings out your fear of not being accepted and loved. This week as you meditate on Psalm 119:143–145, pray God helps you see the pattern you have created. Ask Him to meet your needs. Allow Him to show you the ways in which He has been providing for you all along. Write down a few ways where you can clearly see God has taken care of you.

FIVE

When **FIVES** are under stress, they go to type Seven. They are typically cool and collected, but under stress they suddenly become scattered and busy. Fives tend to take on new projects impulsively and are easily distracted and unfocused.

Awareness for Fives: You care greatly about taking care of yourself and having enough resources to avoid asking for help. This week as you meditate on Psalm 119:143–145, write down a few words that describe how you are feeling. Do you feel relieved? Do you feel anxious? Do you feel sad? As you become more aware of the truth about yourself, you are able to see the whole picture. Take some time to write down all the ways that God has provided for you.

SIX

When **SIXES** are under stress, they go to a type Three. They are typically compliant and grounded. When stress enters the picture, they tend to get competitive and arrogant. Sixes busy themselves, trying to calm the anxiety rising within them.

Awareness for Sixes: You are less likely to try something new for fear of failure. Also, you like to problem-solve and have a plan for all things, which helps you feel in control. As you read the scripture for this week, notice it says, "Don't fuss." How often do you find yourself fussing over what could happen? This week as you meditate on Psalm 119:143–145, allow God to reveal the areas in your life where you are unwilling to release your grip of control. Write down how He has provided and cared for you through the years.

Notes

SEVEN

When **SEVENS** are under stress, they go to type One. They are typically free-spirited and energetic. But, when they become stressed, they retreat into themselves and become perfectionistic.

Awareness for Sevens: When you feel limits are being forced upon you, you become hypercritical of others, trying to change them to be who you think they should be. You can also quickly blame others for preventing you from having fun. This week as you meditate on Psalm 119:143-145, see how much God loves you and desires to take care of you. Take some time to write down all the ways God has proven that He cares for you.

EIGHT

When **EIGHTS** are under stress, they go to a type Two. Eights are confident by nature—able to move with force through the world, gathering and grabbing what they desire. When stress rises in them, the fear of being betrayed causes Eights to retreat inwardly. They tend to become more secretive and fearful.

Awareness for Eights: You are not typically a fearful person. However, when this feeling arises, it causes you to push your emotions down so they don't overpower you. This week as you meditate on Psalm 119:143-145, notice how stress and fear cause you to try to do it all on your own. Allow God to show you the areas where you are having a difficult time trusting that He will take care of you. Write down these areas and commit them to prayer. God desires for you to trust that He cares for you in all areas of your life.

NINE

When **NINES** are under stress, they go to a type Six. Nines are typically laid back and at peace. When they are faced with a stressful situation, they tend to become worried and anxious, which then leads to defensiveness and edginess. Their minds go into overdrive, which is the very feeling they try to avoid at all costs.

Awareness for Nines: You desire to live in a harmonious state. Therefore, when stress arises, it causes you to shut down and retreat. This week as you meditate on Psalm 119:143-145, how are you able to find joy as you spend time in the word of God? How does this make you feel? Can you see the ways that He cares for you? Write down a few words to describe the peace you feel when you can trust God is there to care for you.

APPLICATION

As you reflect on your Enneagram number this week, how can you identify times you have gone to your stress number?

_____

_____

_____

How do you react in moments, seasons, or situations that cause you stress?

_____

_____

_____

In what way can you begin to see why each Enneagram number reacts differently in stress?

_____

_____

_____

What fears can God quiet in your heart, as you put your trust in Him during times of trouble? How are you hearing God speak to you about stress?

_____

_____

_____

♥ **MEDITATION**

Go to page 342 and try the Contemplation Meditation exercise.

My prayer this week:

_____

_____

_____

_____

_____

_____

_____

_____

_____

_____

_____

WEEK 17

"

UNDERSTAND THIS, MY DEAR BROTHERS AND SISTERS: YOU MUST ALL BE QUICK TO LISTEN, SLOW TO SPEAK, AND SLOW TO GET ANGRY. HUMAN ANGER DOES NOT PRODUCE THE RIGHTEOUSNESS GOD DESIRES. SO GET RID OF ALL THE FILTH AND EVIL IN YOUR LIVES, AND HUMBLY ACCEPT THE WORD GOD HAS PLANTED IN YOUR HEARTS, FOR IT HAS THE POWER TO SAVE YOUR SOULS. BUT DON'T JUST LISTEN TO GOD'S WORD. YOU MUST DO WHAT IT SAYS. OTHERWISE, YOU ARE ONLY FOOLING YOURSELVES. FOR IF YOU LISTEN TO THE WORD AND DON'T OBEY, IT IS LIKE GLANCING AT YOUR FACE IN A MIRROR. YOU SEE YOURSELF, WALK AWAY, AND FORGET WHAT YOU LOOK LIKE. BUT IF YOU LOOK CAREFULLY INTO THE PERFECT LAW THAT SETS YOU FREE, AND IF YOU DO WHAT IT SAYS AND DON'T FORGET WHAT YOU HEARD, THEN GOD WILL BLESS YOU FOR DOING IT.

JAMES 1:19–25 (NLT)

ANGER

THE FREE LIFE

DISCOVER A MORE COMPLETE FREEDOM
AND A HEART THAT GROWS MORE HUMBLY
TOWARD GOD'S PEACE AND COMFORT.

Although anger is a normal emotion—especially in moments we cannot control, such as during pandemics, isolation, unforeseen interruptions in our routine, and unprecedented circumstances—frustrations and exasperations are inevitable and often unanticipated. However, when you are tempted, as we all are from time to time, to fill your spirit with rage, this scripture encourages you to refrain from being angered quickly and to throw out all the spoiled pollution and unnecessary noise that can take over your thought process. This act of purging leads to freedom, meaning you will be embraced in delight and immensely blessed by this discipline. When you allow God to prune these unhealthy tendencies from your life, you will discover a more complete freedom and a heart that grows more humbly toward God's peace and comfort.

ONE

ONES deal with feelings of frustration and dissatisfaction with themselves and others. This stems from repressed anger. They don't want to appear angry, because they think that is a negative emotion; therefore, they turn their anger onto themselves. They may not be aware of this pattern of behavior. But holding on to anger only keeps them from being set free.

Awareness for Ones: When you lean into Scripture and allow God to speak to your heart, you will be able to recognize more easily when anger and bitterness begin to take root. Allow God to tenderly care for you as you make room for Him to plant the word of truth in your life. This week as you meditate on James 1:19–25, allow yourself to notice the roots that have taken hold in your heart. Begin to release them to God and ask Him to fill the holes with His Word.

TWO

TWOS love to help others, but they don't want others to see their needs. When they're in a give-to-get pattern of behavior, Twos tend to hope others fulfill their needs without having to ask for their help. This conduct is a slippery slope for Twos' emotional health. When they don't get their needs met, they become angry and feel unseen.

Awareness for Twos: Recognize this pattern bubbling to the surface in your life, then call out to God, the Father. Allow the feelings or emotions to surface, because giving them a voice will help you to process them with God. He is a kind and just God. Go to Him with your feelings, and He will speak truth to you through His Word. This week as you meditate on James 1:19–25, speak truth to yourself about your needs. Allow all your emotions to surface and place them at the cross. Visually do this or perhaps write them down and place them on a table as you pray, asking God to reveal Himself to you in this process.

THREE

THREES can get caught up in *becoming* and lose sight of *just being*. They have a hard time seeing themselves apart from what they do or how others see them. They tend to rise up in anger if someone comes between them and what they are trying to achieve.

Awareness for Threes: Letting go of the titles, labels, stages, platforms, and people as a form of identity feels scary. However, as you do this, you will find that your gifts and talents no longer control you. You no longer compromise your true character to make others happy. This week as you meditate on James 1:19–25, allow yourself to choose an activity you enjoy doing that doesn't garner any praise from others. Do not post about it on socials or even share it with friends. Allow God to be with you in this process and try to get in touch with what you like personally.

FOUR

FOURS struggle with feeling complete. While looking around at others, Fours feel that something is missing inside of them, making them wish they had what others have. Often, they miss the very blessings right in front of them. They want to listen better and speak kind words. Because of the brokenness and the envy Fours feel, they often lash out in anger or harsh judgment.

Awareness for Fours: As you become more aware of your brokenness, invite God, the Father, into your world. He will show you who you are through His Word and how uniquely He created you. He pours His love over you, and your brokenness becomes the catalyst for blessing others. Don't allow the shame of not being enough hold you back anymore. This week as you meditate on James 1:19–25, allow God to show you your many gifts and talents. Allow Him to expose the lies of the Enemy that have held you back in anger and shame. Say "NO MORE" and walk this life, knowing that God delights in you and affirms you.

FIVE

FIVES fear being overtaken by people and expectations. They feel taken advantage of if people invade their space. Fives are excellent at listening and giving advice; however, they become angry or disinterested in those who don't see it their way. Reading this passage may leave Fives feeling ambivalent. They don't like to rely on others or even say they need help, because they prefer to handle their business themselves.

Awareness for Fives: As you read this passage, you may ask, "What do I need to give up?" and "How long is this process?" These and your other questions are fair. Being set free in Christ is more about trusting that He is taking care of you and less about controlling your environment. It is hard to let go of patterns of behavior. This week as you meditate on James 1:19–25, allow God to reveal His desire for you to trust that your needs are not too much and that you are loved.

SIX

To **SIXES**, the world feels like a scary place. They feel apprehensive about the future. Very often, anxiety lies underneath all their fears. This triggers anger within them as they try to gain control of their situation or their environment. However, at times they move toward their fears in the hopes of conquering them and proving to themselves they are strong and courageous.

Awareness for Sixes: As you read this scripture, how badly do you desire to be set free from worry, free from fear, free from the "what if's" that plague your mind? This week as you meditate on James 1:19–25, allow God to show where you have replaced truth with the lies of the Enemy. Take time this week to process the lies from which your fears and anxieties are stemming.

SEVEN

SEVENS love new experiences. They chase new ideas. They are constantly looking for positive stimulation, all in the hopes of finding a way to fill themselves. However, anger arises anytime they feel abandoned, neglected, or made to feel less than. It is in those moments when anger rises and explosive responses happen. Keep in mind, Sevens are ready to move on much quicker than the other party, who may be shaken by surprise.

Awareness for Sevens: You do not want to feel like an inconvenience. Nor do you want to be trapped in an inescapable emotional whirlwind or to be left without support. Knowing you are loved and wanted by your heavenly Father helps you combat this fear that triggers your anger. This week as you meditate on James 1:19–25, allow God to bring you comfort in all areas of your life. Take in your surroundings and discover the beauty of being fully present in and cared for unconditionally by your heavenly Father.

EIGHT

EIGHTS go into the world with purpose and passion. They see all the possibilities and desire to make things happen. They move with intensity, pushing people and things forward, asserting their authority. Often, they speak what is on their minds, and they can sometimes let anger take control. They have a hard time preventing anger from becoming the strangler. Anger often leads, and because of Eights' need for justice, they tend to take matters into their own hands.

Awareness for Eights: Living a life that is set free in Christ is everything you hope for and desire. Letting Him bring awareness to the areas in your life which trigger anger can help soften you and allow you to love others well. This week as you meditate on James 1:19–25, try releasing your grip slightly and see how it feels. The more you release your life to God, the freer you begin to live.

NINE

NINES have a hard time fully engaging in their lives. They prefer to go through life unaffected, because they desire peace and tranquility. They listen to others and weigh their words carefully as they will go along to get along; however, this is not always what they truly want to do. They actually can become quite frustrated and angry when they feel as if they are not seen and do not matter.

Awareness for Nines: As you read the scripture, allow God to reveal the areas in your life where anger has taken root. You often suppress anger as a way of coping, but this can lead to resentment. He desires to set you free through the truth of His Word. This week as you meditate on James 1:19–25, embrace the feelings sitting just below the surface. Breathe in the peace of God and breathe out feelings of anger and resentment. A life fully lived in Christ is worth showing up for.

APPLICATION

As you read the Enneagram numbers this week, how do you resonate with your specific number's struggle with anger?

_____

_____

_____

After reading your number, how can you become more aware of how anger shows up in your life?

_____

_____

_____

With the knowledge of how other numbers deal with anger, how can you extend grace to them?

_____

_____

_____

In what areas of your heart do you need to release anger to God and be set free? How are you hearing God speak to you when it comes to your anger?

_____

_____

_____

MEDITATION

Go to page 332 and try the Box Breathing exercise.

My prayer this week:

_____

_____

_____

_____

_____

_____

_____

_____

_____

WEEK 18

"

"DO NOT JUDGE, OR YOU TOO WILL BE JUDGED.
FOR IN THE SAME WAY YOU JUDGE OTHERS,
YOU WILL BE JUDGED, AND WITH THE MEASURE
YOU USE, IT WILL BE MEASURED TO YOU.
"WHY DO YOU LOOK AT THE SPECK OF SAWDUST
IN YOUR BROTHER'S EYE AND PAY NO ATTENTION
TO THE PLANK IN YOUR OWN EYE? HOW CAN
YOU SAY TO YOUR BROTHER, 'LET ME TAKE THE
SPECK OUT OF YOUR EYE,' WHEN ALL THE TIME
THERE IS A PLANK IN YOUR OWN EYE? YOU
HYPOCRITE, FIRST TAKE THE PLANK OUT OF YOUR
OWN EYE, AND THEN YOU WILL SEE CLEARLY TO
REMOVE THE SPECK FROM YOUR BROTHER'S EYE."

MATTHEW 7:1-5

JUDGMENT

GOD IS THE JURY

GOD WILL TAKE CARE OF INJUSTICES ONE WAY OR ANOTHER BECAUSE HE IS JURY, JUDGE, AND PROSECUTOR.

Judgment is universal. There is not a race, gender, or socioeconomic group of people who have the monopoly on judgment. Every person gets trapped in patterns of judgment throughout their lifetime. You are probably familiar with the popular words Jesus exclaimed as people gathered around the woman who was accused of adultery—a crime punishable by death—and then tossed in the streets to be stoned. He urged, "Let the one who has never sinned throw the first stone!" (John 8:7, NLT). Those words were revolutionary two thousand years ago, and they are still relevant for us today. After all, do you ever judge others and put them down? It is especially tempting to make a judgment call on others who struggle with sins that do not tempt you. Focus this week on stopping your unfair actions, unpleasant thoughts, and unkind words. Each time you find yourself wanting to toss stones, take a step back and remember that you, like everyone else, certainly have heavy dark planks and challenges in your own life. Let God take control. He is omnipotent—all-powerful. He is omniscient—all-knowing. And He is omnipresent— present at all times. Therefore, God will take care of injustices one way or another because He is jury, judge, and prosecutor. When you start to feel judgmental, pivot and remember to follow the greatest commandment in the law: love the Lord with all of your heart and love your neighbor as yourself (Luke 10:27).

--- **ONE** ---

ONES tend to use their own standards to judge others. They think people should do things their way because it is "the right way." They have a strong desire to do what is right at all times.

Awareness for Ones: When you find yourself judging, perhaps it is because you are feeling inadequate in some way. Scripture gives you a clear order, "Do not judge, or you too will be judged." As you become more aware of the areas in your life where you find yourself looking at others through a judgmental lens, ask yourself what it is that is causing you to feel the need to judge. This week take some time to meditate on Matthew 7:1–5. Ask God to show you what it is about yourself that you are trying to ignore or justify. Write down what He reveals to you and ask Him to help you release it to Him.

--- **TWO** ---

TWOS tend to judge others by thinking others should be more nurturing and willing to help. After all, Twos believe people should do things just as they do them. If others are unwilling to help the way Twos think they should, Twos tend to judge them for not being compassionate or understanding.

Awareness for Twos: If you find yourself passing judgment on others, try asking yourself, "What is it about them that I see in myself?" Matthew 7:1–5 gives you a very clear order, "Do not judge, or you too will be judged." As you become more aware of the areas in your life where you tend to pass judgment, remind yourself others are people just like you, trying their best. This week take some time to meditate on Matthew 7:1–5. Ask God to reveal areas in your life that cause you to compare yourself to others. Write down a few sentences about how you have used comparison to help you feel better about yourself.

--- **THREE** ---

THREES tend to judge others who are not as driven as they are. They can't understand why people are not willing to do what it takes to succeed and achieve. They see so much untapped potential in the people all around them and wish others would see it in themselves, too.

Awareness for Threes: When you realize that you are judging others, evaluate your true feelings, and think about the possibility that they are gaining momentum in areas you wish you were. Matthew 7:1–5 gives you a clear order, "Do not judge, or you too will be judged." This week take some time to meditate on Matthew 7:1–5. Ask God to reveal to you the ways in which you have been judging other people. Write a letter to God asking Him to forgive you for judging others.

— FOUR —

FOURS tend to judge others who seem inauthentic. They believe people are frauds if they act differently in front of others than they act in more private settings. Fours pride themselves on being exactly who they are in front of people as they are behind the scenes, and they want to be accepted just for being their true selves.

Awareness for Fours: When you find yourself judging others, try to recognize what is causing you to do so. Are you feeling inadequate or insignificant in some way? Try seeing people through a different perspective as you will grow in empathy and compassion for all humankind. This week take some time to meditate on Matthew 7:1–5. Ask God to reveal to you why you tend to pass judgment on other people. Write a few sentences about how you imagine you make people feel when you judge them.

— FIVE —

FIVES tend to judge others who do things differently than they do, which tends to cause them to withdraw. They think people should do things their way because it is the best way, and they have little tolerance for people who think differently. Even though they have strong opinions, they don't always voice them.

Awareness for Fives: When you find yourself judging others, take some time to reflect on why you are passing judgment in the first place. Understanding and accepting that all people have different ways of viewing the world, including various cultures and ways of expression, will allow you to appreciate people and their unique qualities. This week take some time to meditate on Matthew 7:1–5. Allow yourself to see areas where you have been judging others. Write down a few sentences about how judging others has caused you to withdraw from relationships.

— SIX —

SIXES tend to judge others by their standards. Sixes think people should do things their way because they explored all the options and came up with the best plan. They have little tolerance for people who make quick decisions and spontaneous plans.

Awareness for Sixes: When you find yourself judging others, ask yourself, "Am I doing this as a way of protecting myself?" As you explore your motivation for judging others, allow yourself to recognize just how detrimental this practice is to not only others but also toward yourself. When you can see people through a different perspective, you will grow in empathy and compassion for all humankind. This week take some time to meditate on Matthew 7:1–5, write down a few sentences about how this has been a way for you to protect yourself.

─────── SEVEN ───────

SEVENS tend to judge others who are too rigid and unwilling to look at life as an adventure. They can't understand why people would want to limit themselves when life has so many possibilities. Sevens often think other people are missing out on life.

Awareness for Sevens: When you find yourself judging others, try to identify what is truly bothering you about the person or situation. Do you feel you are being compared to that person in some way? As you become more aware of this temptation and find yourself looking at others through a judgmental lens, ask yourself, "What is really bothering me?" This week take some time to meditate on Matthew 7:1–5. Ask God to reveal to you the ways you have been judging other people. Write down a few sentences about how this makes you feel.

─────── EIGHT ───────

EIGHTS tend to judge others who don't take life seriously. They think people should figure out what they care about in life and go after it with gusto. Eights do not respect those who appear to be underachievers.

Awareness for Eights: When you find yourself judging others, take a good look at yourself. Are you feeling inadequate or envious? As you become more aware of the areas in your life where you tend to pass judgment on others, change your perspective and recognize the beauty of all people who have different ways of thinking and living in the world. This week take some time to meditate on Matthew 7:1–5. Ask God to reveal to you why you tend to pass judgment on other people. Write down a few sentences about how having compassion and love for others can make a bigger impact on your life than passing judgment.

─────── NINE ───────

NINES tend to judge others who are overbearing and boisterous. They don't like conflict or chaos, and they can't understand why people feel the need to go into the world with such force. Nines view people who have strong personalities as overconfident.

Awareness for Nines: When you start to judge others, you tend to feel angry with yourself for feeling that way. You are generally caring for others, accepting of all people as they are, and truly appreciative of them. You mostly abide by this order in Matthew 7:1–5; "Do not judge, or you too will be judged" as you strive to live a life full of empathy and compassion for all humankind. Therefore, when you display your rarely seen judgmental side, it makes you feel bad and guilty. This week take some time to meditate on Matthew 7:1–5. Ask God to fill you with a continued appreciation of others. Write down a few sentences about how judging others in the past has made you feel.

APPLICATION

As you reflect on your Enneagram number this week, in what ways did you find it eye-opening to see the ways you judge others?

_____

_____

_____

How can you bring more awareness to yourself in your daily life as it pertains to the way you judge others?

_____

_____

_____

In what ways can you see how the judgment of others can limit the way we allow people to show up as their authentic selves?

_____

_____

_____

How can you show others more empathy? How are you hearing God speak to you when it comes to judgment?

_____

_____

_____

MEDITATION

Go to page 334 and try the Concentration Meditation exercise.

My prayer this week:

_____

_____

_____

_____

_____

_____

_____

_____

_____

WEEK 19

"

MY FLESH AND MY HEART MAY FAIL,
BUT GOD IS THE STRENGTH OF MY HEART
AND MY PORTION FOREVER.

PSALM 73:26

SECURITY POINTS
YOUR PERFECT PORTION

LEAN ON YOUR HEAVENLY FATHER, FOR HE IS THE ONE IN WHOM YOU CAN ALWAYS PLACE YOUR TRUST AND FIND YOUR STRENGTH.

Although you desire to feel safe and secure like everyone else, you have weaknesses in mind, body, and heart that often keep you from being vulnerable and trusting in others. It's perfectly normal to falter and fail and feel unsafe with a posture of self-reliance. Nevertheless, lean on your heavenly Father, for He is the One in whom you can always place your trust and find your strength, even when you are at your lowest point. He will meet you exactly where you are, while understanding each one of your feelings and apprehensions, because He designed you. The Lord, the Creator of heaven and earth, already knows what your heart is wrestling with and thinks you are fabulous anyway. He fights for you mightily despite your mistakes and missteps. He celebrates your successes. He empathizes with your struggles. He recognizes your impulses. He is your perfectly prepared portion now and into eternity. God is your strength, for His love, grace, and compassion are sufficient for you.

ONE

When **ONES** feel safe, they go to a type Seven. They become much more playful, can express the silly side of themselves, and experience a fuller range of emotion.

Awareness for Ones: When you feel safe with Christ, you can lean into Him, knowing He loves you despite your mistakes and failures. He is your strong tower. He is the One you can always turn to. This week as you meditate on Psalm 73:26, let the words "God is the strength of my heart and my portion forever" sink in. Can you see yourself letting your guard down in His presence? Can you identify how you allow Christ to see you in a way you most often don't share with other people? This week, thank God for His never-ending love and write down the ways He has shown it to you.

TWO

When **TWOS** feel safe, they go to a type Four. They tend to openly show their emotions, needs, and darker feelings. They also can become moodier and more temperamental.

Awareness for Twos: Treating yourself to special gifts or goodies is a way you tell yourself you're worth it. However, when you feel safe with Christ, you can share your true feelings about life. Your struggles and disappointments are no longer yours to carry alone. He is your strong tower where you can always run. This week as you meditate on Psalm 73:26, let the words "God is the strength of my heart and my portion forever" sink in. Speak these words aloud. Can you allow yourself to embrace this scripture, knowing that God adores you? Thank God for His never-ending love and write down the profound ways He has shown it to you.

THREE

When **THREES** feel safe, they go to a type Six. They tend to share their frustrations and anxieties. They keep a positive, upbeat persona for the world to see, and they can let down their guard with others with whom they feel safe.

Awareness for Threes: You will share your struggles, fears, and even anger with your safe people. Feeling safe enough to express your true feelings with Christ, however, is hard for you. You often think, "He will only love me if I perform." This thought process makes it difficult for you to let down your guard and allow Christ into your life. This week as you meditate on Psalm 73:26, let the words "God is the strength of my heart and my portion forever" sink in. Can you see how beneficial it is for you to let down your guard in His presence? Can you see the love Christ has for you for simply just being "you"? Allow yourself to embrace your relationship with Him. Thank God for His never-ending love and write down the ways He has shown it to you.

FOUR

When **FOURS** feel safe, they go to a type One. They may be more controlling and critical of others, but they are also more willing to show their demanding, nitpicky, and impatient side with those they trust.

Awareness for Fours: Your relationship with Christ can be hard for you. You want to be authentic to who you are, and your hope is that Christ will love and accept you this way. This week as you meditate on Psalm 73:26, let the words "God is the strength of my heart and my portion forever" sink in. Can you see yourself letting down your guard in His presence? What feelings and emotions are emerging? How can you allow Christ into this space? Write down the ways you can trust Him to handle what you are feeling and still know that He is your strength and portion even in the difficult times?

FIVE

When **FIVES** feel safe, they go to a type Eight. They tend to be more forceful and vocal about what displeases them. They can even become argumentative and aggressive instead of being quiet and withdrawn.

Awareness for Fives: When you feel you can be honest in your relationship with Christ and willing to allow your emotions to surface, you will express your disappointments and questions. This week as you meditate on Psalm 73:26, let the words "God is the strength of my heart and my portion forever" sink in. Can you see how He desires to be all that you need? How can you allow yourself to be vulnerable with Christ this week? Can you see the benefit in expressing to Him how you really feel? Thank God for His never-ending love and write down the ways He has demonstrated it to you.

SIX

When **SIXES** feel safe, they go to a type Nine. They tend to shut down and retreat. They begin to numb themselves and feel they have worked hard enough to deserve a break.

Awareness for Sixes: As you think about your relationship with Christ, can you see how you might at times pull away and just go through the motions, instead of leaning in and cultivating a relationship with Him? This week as you meditate on Psalm 73:26, let the words "God is the strength of my heart and my portion forever" sink in, and try to identify the ways you have fallen asleep in your relationship with Him. Can you draw closer to Him this week by seeking to be in His presence? Thank God for His never-ending love and write down the ways He has demonstrated it to you.

SEVEN

When **SEVENS** feel safe, they go to a type Five. They tend to retreat, looking for a quiet space to just be themselves.

Awareness for Sevens: You no longer need to be the life of the party or upbeat all the time, because those who know you best accept you for who you are. This week as you meditate on Psalm 73:26, let the words "God is the strength of my heart and my portion forever" sink in. Can you see how beneficial it is for you to seek a quiet space? When you can slow down and are comfortable in the quiet, you will find that God will meet you there. He will give you the strength and comfort your heart longs for. Find a quiet space this week and invite God into it. Thank Him for His never-ending love and write down the ways He has shown you His love.

EIGHT

When **EIGHTS** feel safe, they go to a type Two. They tend to show their more vulnerable side to those they trust. They long to hear others thank them for all they do for them. Eights want to know they are needed.

Awareness for Eights: In your relationship with Christ, you desire the same thing. You want to know you are important to God and that He sees your sacrifices. This week as you meditate on Psalm 73:26, let the words "God is the strength of my heart and my portion forever" sink in. Can you see how He desires to be your comforter? He longs for you to know He will always be by your side and see all you do. Rest in the fact that God is your source of strength and He is your strong tower. You can run to Him and find all you need. Thank Him for His never-ending love and write down the ways He has shown you His love.

NINE

When **NINES** feel safe, they go to a type Three. They tend to be more vocal about their accomplishments. They can get caught up doing busywork instead of the very things they are supposed to be doing.

Awareness for Nines: When you feel safe and secure in your relationship with Christ, you can see yourself as He sees you. You acknowledge the gifts and talents He has given to you. This week as you meditate on Psalm 73:26, let the words "God is the strength of my heart and my portion forever" sink in. Can you see how beautiful it is for you to be able to express your thankfulness to Christ for who you are? This week take a little time to write down your strengths and thank God for your many gifts and talents.

APPLICATION

Identify times in your life when you have gone to your "security" number?

_____

_____

_____

How would you describe what trust and vulnerability look like for you?

_____

_____

_____

In what ways can you see how those whose Enneagram numbers are closest to yours function differently when they feel safe and secure?

_____

_____

_____

In what ways do you feel that God is your strength and portion? How are you hearing Him speak to you about your sense of security?

_____

_____

_____

♡ MEDITATION

Go to page 336 and try the Reflection Meditation exercise.

My prayer this week:

_____

_____

_____

_____

_____

_____

_____

_____

_____

_____

WEEK 20

"

THEREFORE, SINCE WE ARE SURROUNDED
BY SUCH A HUGE CROWD OF WITNESSES
TO THE LIFE OF FAITH, LET US STRIP OFF
EVERY WEIGHT THAT SLOWS US DOWN,
ESPECIALLY THE SIN THAT SO EASILY TRIPS
US UP. AND LET US RUN WITH ENDURANCE
THE RACE GOD HAS SET BEFORE US.

HEBREWS 12:1 (NLT)

SELF-AWARENESS
TRIP US UP

"HIS MERCIES NEVER COME
TO AN END; THEY ARE NEW
EVERY MORNING."

You likely have issues tripping you up and sin slowing you down. Whatever it is, release all of the extra dead weight and surrender it to God. As you have learned more about yourself through spiritual disciplines and Enneagram exposure, you have started recognizing patterns of behavior that are not serving you well. You are self-aware and no longer enslaved to your old way of thinking because your mind has been continually renewed by the Word of God. It is a new day. Get up and run the race that He has set before you with a pace filled with tenacity. When you run with perseverance, grit, and grace, you will enjoy a strengthening of your soul and unequivocal peace in your spirit. You already have what it takes to brave all obstacles that try to slow you down, because you are who God says you are. When you stumble, as we all do, get back up and start running again. "His mercies never come to an end; they are new every morning" (Lamentations 3:22–23, ESV). This race is free, your debt is paid, your life is priceless. All the while, God is sprinting right toward you and cheering you on along the way. His love for you and belief in you are limitless.

ONE

Healthy **ONES** are able to acknowledge their emotions and express them without shame or guilt. They are also able to express themselves creatively without self-doubt and can tap into their passions with comfort and ease.

Awareness for Ones: As you become more self-aware, you find yourself more at ease because you know you are found in Christ. This week as you meditate on Hebrews 12:1, allow God to reveal the areas in your life where you have experienced freedom from the weight of your sin. Take some time to write down the anger you are able to release as a result. Praise God for the strength to run this race with the endurance He is giving you as you learn and grow every day.

TWO

Healthy **TWOS** are able to own their strength. They also have the ability to make decisions that move their lives forward in a positive manner, because they feel comfortable taking up space in the world.

Awareness for Twos: As you become more self-aware, you find yourself in a place where you no longer need outside validation, because you know you are found in Christ. This is truly living. This week as you meditate on Hebrews 12:1, allow God to show you the areas of growth you have had. Take some time to write down the worry you can release as a result. Praise God for the strength to run this race with the endurance He is giving you as you learn and grow every day.

THREE

Healthy **THREES** are able to be exactly who they are. They are comfortable being seen as their authentic selves, without feeling the need to perform. They also become relaxed and enjoy life.

Awareness for Threes: As you become more self-aware, you find yourself able to show up just as you are, because your self-worth is found in Christ. This week as you meditate on Hebrews 12:1, allow God to show you the beauty that happens when you strip off the pressure of "people pleasing." Take some time to write down the fears you are able to release. Praise God for the strength to run this race with the endurance He is giving you as you learn and grow every day.

FOUR

Healthy **FOURS** are able to love and accept themselves. They see their uniqueness as a gift to the world, instead of a curse. Furthermore, they put others' needs above their own.

Awareness for Fours: As you become more self-aware, you find yourself able to trust that those around you love and accept you, because you know you are fearfully and wonderfully made. This week as you meditate on Hebrews 12:1, allow God to show you the growth you have had in the area of shame. Take some time to write down the emotions you are able to release. Praise God for the strength to run this race with the endurance He is giving you as you learn and grow each and every day.

FIVE

Healthy **FIVES** are able to see life as joyful and exciting. They trust God to provide for them and to replenish their resources and energy.

Awareness for Fives: As you become more self-aware, you no longer minimize your wants and desires for fear of being too "needy," because you are confident in who you are in Christ. This week as you meditate on Hebrews 12:1, allow God to show you the areas of growth you have had in living a life built on faith. Write down the insecurities you are able to release. Praise God for the strength to run this race with the endurance He is giving you as you learn and grow every day.

SIX

Healthy **SIXES** are able to value themselves. Their self-worth is no longer dependent on other people's opinions of them. They are confident and take actions that lead to results.

Awareness for Sixes: As you become more self-aware, you find yourself no longer needing outside validation because you know you are found in Christ. This week as you meditate on Hebrews 12:1, allow God to reveal to you the areas in your life where you no longer feel slowed by the weight of your worry. Take some time to write down the concerns you are able to release to the Lord. Praise God for the strength to run this race with the endurance He is giving you as you learn and grow every day.

Notes

SEVEN

Healthy **SEVENS** are able to acknowledge the importance of structure. Finishing what they started is important to them. Also, they become more grounded in who they are because they understand God's calling and purpose for their lives.

Awareness for Sevens: As you become more self-aware, you find yourself able to follow through and finish tasks because you are no longer distracted by trying to find ways to feel satisfied. This week as you meditate on Hebrews 12:1, allow God to show you the areas of growth you have had by letting go of business in your life. Take some time to write down what it feels like to be at peace within yourself because you are rooted in Christ. Praise God for the strength to run this race with the endurance He is giving you as you learn and grow every day.

EIGHT

Healthy **EIGHTS** are able to become more humble. Their focus shifts from protecting themselves to walking out their purpose. They grow in empathy and compassion toward themselves and others.

Awareness for Eights: As you become more self-aware, you find yourself needing to control less because you feel safe in your relationship with Christ. This week as you meditate on Hebrews 12:1, allow God to show you how releasing your grip of control has allowed you to live more freely. Write down the ways you feel more content in your life. Praise God for the strength to run this race with the endurance He is giving you as you learn and grow each day.

NINE

Healthy **NINES** become more vocal in their opinions and ideas. They are willing to have hard conversations without suppressing how they really feel. They trust their instincts.

Awareness for Nines: As you become more self-aware, you are more comfortable speaking up while sharing your thoughts and ideas with others, because you know who you are in Christ. This week as you meditate on Hebrews 12:1, allow yourself to feel the pressure that has been lifted off you as you continue to surrender your life to the Lord. Write down the insecurities you are able to release. Praise God for the strength to run this race with the endurance He is giving you as you learn and grow each day.

APPLICATION

In light of this week's Enneagram reflection, how do you see some of your behaviors changing when you feel "healthy"?

_____

_____

_____

How are you able to express yourself differently from when you first started this devotional?

_____

_____

_____

In what ways have you become more aware of your patterns of behavior as you read your wings and the Enneagram numbers you go to in health and stress?

_____

_____

_____

How can you run your God-given race with endurance? How are you hearing God speak to you about your self-awareness?

_____

_____

_____

MEDITATION

Go to page 342 and try the Contemplation Meditation exercise.

My prayer this week:

_____

_____

_____

_____

_____

_____

_____

_____

_____

_____

_____

_____

WEEK 21

"

THIS IS MY COMMAND— BE STRONG
AND COURAGEOUS! DO NOT BE AFRAID
OR DISCOURAGED. FOR THE LORD YOUR
GOD IS WITH YOU WHEREVER YOU GO.

JOSHUA 1:9 (NLT)

YOUR HEART LONGS TO HEAR
STRONG AND COURAGEOUS

GOD IS YOUR MASTER PLANNER, DIRECTING YOUR JOURNEY, LAYING DOWN THE PAVEMENT FOR YOUR FUTURE STEPS.

No matter our Enneagram numbers, all of our hearts long to hear a message of affirmation reminding us that our worth is priceless and precious to God and others. Take heart in this—the Lord your God is always available. When you are feeling weak, do not fear. You are strong because God is near. If you are undone or over it, do not fear. You are strong because God is near. If you are feeling discouraged or depressed, full of anxiety or angst, do not fear. You are strong because God is near. He is your Pathfinder who goes ahead of you and directs your way when you are lost or headed in the wrong direction. He is your Rainmaker during your seasons of drought when you are emotionally or physically empty and dried up. He is your Master Planner, directing your journey, laying down the pavement for your future steps, and preparing your path. After each fall, when you get back up with all the will and might you can muster, you will know Who lifted you, carried you, and was with you all along. "Do not be afraid or discouraged." If you are currently climbing challenging hills, or resting amid peace and certainty, get down on your knees in praise and thanksgiving because God is near.

ONE

ONES' hearts long to hear, "You are good." As they go through life, they have developed patterns of behavior that position them to hear those words of affirmation. Ones will weigh every decision they make through the lens of how they will be perceived by others.

Awareness for Ones: As you embrace Christ's love for you, find comfort in knowing your heavenly Father thinks you were worth sending His Son to die on the cross so you can have eternal life with Him. Let this be your prayer from Psalm 17:8, "Keep me as the apple of your eye; hide me in the shadow of your wings." Always remember how important you are to your heavenly Father. God tells you in Joshua 1:9 that He is with you wherever you go. Let this scripture settle into your heart this week. You are good and you are loved. You are the apple of God's eye just for being yourself.

TWO

TWOS' hearts long to hear, "You are wanted." They navigate life through the lens of other people's wants, needs, and desires, hoping to find the love and acceptance their hearts have longed for all their lives.

Awareness for Twos: As you embrace Christ's death on the cross, you will see just how loved and wanted you have always been. Reflect on 1 John 3:1, "See what great love the Father has lavished on us, that we should be called children of God! And that is what we are!" Can you see the ways in which God has walked alongside you all your life? God tells you in Joshua 1:9 that He is with you wherever you go. Let this scripture settle into your heart this week. You are loved and wanted. You are a child of God.

THREE

THREES' hearts long to hear, "You are loved for being yourself." They have tried all their lives to be what other people deem as "accomplished." The thought of others seeing them as less than admirable leaves them feeling alone and exposed.

Awareness for Threes: As you embrace your identity in Christ, you no longer need to look to others, hoping they see you as valuable, because you know your worth is in Christ Jesus. Try to embrace His love for you by letting this be your prayer, from Jeremiah 29:11: "'For I know the plans I have for you,' declares the LORD, 'plans to prosper you and not to harm you, plans to give you a hope and a future.'" Lean into knowing you are loved just for who you are, not what you do. God has His hand on you, guiding your steps and paving the way. Always remember how loved you are by your heavenly Father. God tells you in Joshua 1:9 that He is with you wherever you go. Let this scripture settle into your heart this week. You are enough just as you are.

FOUR

FOURS' hearts long to hear, "You are seen for who you are." They desire desperately to be accepted just as they are, yet they have a hard time believing this is possible because they feel as if there is something missing inside of them.

Awareness for Fours: Grasping the love that was shed for you on the cross and believing you are still loved now in that exact same way is what you need to remember when you feel "less than." Allow this passage in Psalm 139:13–14 to help you see just how special you are to God: "For you created my inmost being; you knit me together in my mother's womb. I praise you because I am fearfully and wonderfully made; your works are wonderful, I know that full well." Always remember Christ made you unique and special. He took His time creating you, and you are His masterpiece. God tells you in Joshua 1:9 that He is with you wherever you go. Let this scripture settle into your heart this week. You are His masterpiece.

FIVE

FIVES' hearts long to hear, "Your needs are not a problem." They try hard to gather all the resources such as money, food, and shelter. This helps them feel comfortable in this world and at ease, without feeling the need to rely on anyone.

Awareness for Fives: Knowing that your heavenly Father desires to walk alongside you and provide for you can be a source of comfort to your soul. Take hold of Philippians 4:19 and claim it as yours, for this is a promise God wants to fulfill in your life: "And my God will supply all your needs according to His riches in glory in Christ Jesus." Find strength in Christ as you see the ways God is holding out His hand to help you. God tells you in Joshua 1:9 that He is with you wherever you go. Let this scripture settle into your heart this week. You are not a burden to the Lord. You are His treasure.

SIX

SIXES' hearts long, "You are safe." They have a hard time trusting themselves to make decisions, for fear of making the wrong choice. This can leave them feeling alone and without support.

Awareness for Sixes: You want to believe you can trust God. You desire to let down your guard, yet there is always this little ping of doubt that rises in your mind. You can take hold of this scripture in Nahum 1:7 and claim it as yours. This is a promise God wants to fulfill in your life: "The LORD is good, a refuge in times of trouble. He cares for those who trust in him." Always remember how loved and wanted you are by your heavenly Father. He is always right by your side, guiding and directing your steps. He wants to be your source of strength and your protector. God tells you in Joshua 1:9 that He is with you wherever you go. Let this scripture settle into your heart this week. You are safe in the arms of the Lord.

SEVEN

SEVENS' hearts long to hear the words "You will be taken care of." They have a fear that they can never rely on people, yet their desire is to be in relationships with others they can trust and lean on for support.

Awareness for Sevens: You have a strong desire to let others become close to you, yet there is always a fear of abandonment and rejection. As you hear Matthew 11:28 (NKJV), embrace it as yours: "Come to me, all you who labor and are heavy laden, and I will give you rest." God wants to take care of you and wants you to remember always how loved and wanted you are by Him. He tells you in Joshua 1:9 that He is with you wherever you go. Find comfort in knowing you are never alone and that He desires to care for you.

EIGHT

EIGHTS' hearts long to hear the words "You will not be betrayed." They never want to feel exposed, nor made to look foolish by another person. They are strong and competent, always ready to stand their ground.

Awareness for Eights: As you continue to put your trust in God, you will find your strength is in Him. Take hold of this scripture in Psalm 91:2 and claim it as yours, "I will say of the LORD, 'He is my refuge and my fortress, my God, in whom I trust.'" God wants to be your hiding place. He longs for a relationship with you. He wants to be your source of strength and your courage. God tells you in Joshua 1:9 that He is with you wherever you go. Let this passage settle into your heart this week. You are defended by God.

NINE

NINES' hearts long to hear, "Your presence matters." They have gone through much of their life believing it was not okay to give their opinion or share their thoughts.

Awareness for Nines: As you continue to grow in your relationship with Christ, you will feel more confident in knowing He has created you with a purpose and that your ideas are important and valid. He wants you to value yourself enough to use your voice and know your worth. Take hold of this scripture in Philippians 4:13 and claim it as yours: "I can do all things through him who gives me strength." God wants you to stand firm, knowing your strength and confidence is in Him. God tells you in Joshua 1:9 that He is with you wherever you go. Let this scripture settle into your heart, knowing today and every day that you matter.

APPLICATION

As you reflect on your Enneagram number this week, how do you resonate with what your heart longs to hear?

_____

_____

_____

How can you write what your heart longs to hear in your own words after reading this week's reflection?

_____

_____

_____

After reading the other Enneagram reflections, in what ways do you feel like you understand those in your life better, with more insight into what their hearts long to hear?

_____

_____

_____

How does it bring your heart comfort when you hear, "The Lord your God is with you wherever you go"? How are you hearing God speak to you about what your heart longs to hear?

_____

_____

_____

MEDITATION

Go to page 332 and try the Box Breathing exercise.

My prayer this week:

_____

_____

_____

_____

_____

_____

_____

_____

_____

_____

WEEK 22

"

THE THIEF COMES ONLY TO STEAL
AND KILL AND DESTROY; I HAVE
COME THAT THEY MAY HAVE LIFE,
AND HAVE IT TO THE FULL.

JOHN 10:10

YOUR UNIQUE BATTLE
LIFE TO THE FULLEST

"PUT ON THE FULL ARMOR OF GOD,
SO THAT YOU CAN TAKE YOUR STAND
AGAINST THE DEVIL'S SCHEMES."

What has Satan stolen from you? Your childhood, innocence, or financial stability? Maybe he has destroyed one of your closest relationships, your health, or your dreams. Perhaps the Enemy is killing your joy or robbing your spirit. Regardless, remember Jesus is the one who gives you life in abundance. Our Savior doesn't give you half of life, three-quarters, or even 99.9 percent—He has come so that you will have life to the FULLEST. The past doesn't define your future. You will be returned everything the Enemy takes, because there is nothing that cannot be redeemed, resurrected, or restored by the blood of Jesus. Though you might feel as though you have a bull's-eye on your back, know God is protecting you, and there is "no weapon forged against you that will prevail" (Isaiah 54:17). Each morning, begin your day by praying His shield of protection over you and your loved ones: "Put on the full armor of God, so that you can take your stand against the devil's schemes" (Ephesians 6:11). At the same time, He orders the angels to be in charge, "For it is written: 'He will command his angels concerning you to guard you carefully'" (Luke 4:10). You know the ending of this story. You are on the winning team of this battle and you will spend eternity—warzone free—in the presence of the Glory of God.

ONE

ONES often battle with resentment. They have high morals and don't want to appear judgmental. They often put on a smile or keep quiet instead of sharing their true thoughts and feelings, an action that eventually leads to anger and resentment. This pattern allows the Enemy to steal their voice, preventing them from loving people the way Christ desires.

Awareness for Ones: God tells us He has come to give us life. How do you get rid of the trap set by the Enemy and fully live in Christ? Awareness and surrender are the answers. When you begin to see the patterns of judgment arising, take them captive and place them in God's hands. This week as you meditate on John 10:10, pray your eyes are opened to the ways anger has taken root and turned into resentment in your heart. Journal the ways you can release them all to God, inviting Him into the situations to bring you healing and peace.

TWO

TWOS battle with pride. This pride is different from that of those who have an inflated view of themselves. Twos want to be the support system for others; however, when they have a need of their own, they don't want to share it with others for fear of appearing "needy." This pattern allows the Enemy to steal their self-esteem and confidence.

Awareness for Twos: When you recognize that your patterns of trying to earn love are rising, take them captive by placing them in God's hands. This week as you meditate on John 10:10, pray your eyes are opened to the way in which the Enemy has caused you to believe people will only love you if you do something for them. Journal the ways you have tried to please others, hoping to be loved in return. Then, ask God to give you a peace that surpasses all understanding as you release your written words to Him.

THREE

THREES battle with deceit, either on a large or small scale. Threes often deceive themselves by believing they have worth only if other people see them as valuable. The Enemy enjoys constantly whispering to them, "You are not worth loving." He can get them twisted and confused, resulting in them making destructive decisions, all the while looking for affirmation and approval from others.

Awareness for Threes: As you become more aware of the way the Enemy tries to deceive you, you will be able to recognize his schemes and no longer get caught up in them. When you begin to see the patterns of destructive decision-making in your life, take this habit captive and place it in God's hands. This week as you meditate on John 10:10, pray for insight as you take inventory of your life. Journal about the ways in which the Enemy has continually ensnared you.

FOUR

FOURS battle with envy. Envy is not just about wanting what others have, but about looking at other people and wishing life could be as easy or successful as theirs is. Fours also wish they had other gifts and talents so they could achieve more. This pattern allows the Enemy to steal Fours' self-worth, preventing them from loving people and themselves the way Christ desires.

Awareness for Fours: God tells us He has come to give us life. This message can feel as if it were written for everyone else but you. As you become more aware of the way the Enemy tries to get you off track by telling you the lie that everyone else has it better than you, remember you have been given unique gifts and talents for a specific purpose and plan. When you begin to see the patterns of jealousy arise, take these thoughts captive by placing them in God's hands. This week as you meditate on John 10:10, pray for compassion and understanding for yourself. Journal ways you can celebrate the many gifts and talents you have been given.

FIVE

FIVES battle with greed, but not necessarily in terms of gathering wealth. Fives do not like to ask others for help, so they gather resources to make sure they always have what they need. This pattern allows the Enemy to steal Fives' ability to be generous, preventing them from loving people the way Christ desires.

Awareness for Fives: God tells us He has come to give us life. Does this give you a sense of peace? Becoming aware of the way the Enemy tries to convince you that no one wants to meet your needs will allow you to overcome this lie. When you see yourself fall into a pattern of gathering and storing resources, take this habit captive by placing it in God's hands. This week as you meditate on John 10:10, pray for God to show you the many ways He has not only given you life, but life to the fullest. Journal the many blessings God has bestowed upon you.

SIX

SIXES battle with fear. They are in a constant state of hypervigilance, anticipating the worst to happen. Sixes want to believe the best, but they are keenly aware of all that can go wrong. This pattern allows the Enemy to steal their peace of mind, preventing them from living and enjoying life the way Christ desires.

Awareness for Sixes: God tells us He has come to give us life. Knowing you have a heavenly Father who desires for you to live a life full of joy and peace gives you comfort as you surrender to His will and plans. When you begin to feel the patterns of thinking about worst-case scenarios, take these thoughts captive by placing them in God's hands. This week as you meditate on John 10:10, ask God to reveal the many ways He has filled your life with joy. Journal your feelings as you process God's desire for you to live a life that is full of love.

Notes

SEVEN

SEVENS battle with gluttony. *Gluttony* refers not only to food and drink but also to the endless need for experiences and intensity while trying to fill a void. This pattern allows the Enemy to steal Sevens' ability to feel content, preventing them from loving people and themselves the way Christ desires.

Awareness for Sevens: God tells us He has come to give us life. Do those words fill you with hope? As you become more aware of the ways the Enemy tries to make you feel that you will never have enough, displace this lie with God's truth. When you begin to see the pattern of overindulgence arise, take this habit captive by placing it in God's hands. This week as you meditate on John 10:10, pray for God to help you feel fully satisfied in your life. Journal the ways you have experienced fulfillment in your life.

EIGHT

EIGHTS battle with lust. This lust is not just a sexual lust, but also more about a struggle with a desire for intensity, control, and self-extension. This pattern allows the Enemy to steal Eights' satisfaction, preventing them from feeling at peace in the way Christ desires.

Awareness for Eights: God tells us He has come to give us life. Embracing this truth will allow you to live out your life secure in Christ. The Enemy tells you lies to make you chase after things of this earth with intensity, only to find they leave you empty. The more aware you are of these lies, the less you will fall prey to them. When you begin to see the patterns of discontentment arise, take these thoughts captive by placing them in God's hands. This week as you meditate on John 10:10, pray for humility and grace to be at the center of your life. Write down the ways you can recognize when the Enemy tries to make you believe you need "more" in your life.

NINE

NINES battle with sloth. They can fall into a state of being unaffected by life. They prefer a harmonious environment and become very content in their day-to-day routines. This pattern allows the Enemy to steal their energy and purpose, preventing them from being present in their life the way Christ desires.

Awareness for Nines: God tells us He has come to give us life. Does this fill your heart and mind with peace? As you recognize the ways the Enemy has been at work in your life, are you able to see the patterns of apathy arise? This week as you meditate on John 10:10, ask God to take this habit captive. Journal the ways you have found yourself "checking out" and losing your zest for life.

APPLICATION

Reflecting on your Enneagram number this week, what have you discovered about your battle?

_____

_____

_____

How can you see that particular issue play out in your life?

_____

_____

_____

In what way has reading all of the Enneagram reflections given you a different perspective about the issues that other people battle?

_____

_____

_____

Give an example of a time in your life you witnessed God fighting your battle. How are you hearing God speak to you when it comes to your unique battles?

_____

_____

_____

MEDITATION

Go to page 334 and try the Concentration Meditation exercise.

My prayer this week:

_____

_____

_____

_____

_____

_____

_____

_____

_____

WEEK 23

"

I HAVE SET THE LORD CONTINUALLY
BEFORE ME; BECAUSE HE IS AT MY RIGHT
HAND, I WILL NOT BE SHAKEN.

PSALM 16:8 (NASB)

GRIEF
DON'T BE SHAKEN

CONTINUALLY SET THE LORD BEFORE
YOU. HE IS ALONGSIDE YOU FOR
YOUR ENTIRE JOURNEY.

Loss is an inevitable part of life. You might be grieving the loss of a job, a
relationship, or a dream. Worse, you could be in the midst of the loss of a loved
one—the finality making it feel like the most difficult loss of all. Grief is a difficult
emotion to reconcile because you can't build a system around it, can't always
predict it, and certainly can't control it. Know the Lord meets your tears with
empathy. This is evident in John 11:33–35 when Jesus went to see sisters Mary and
Martha following the death of their brother, Jesus' dear friend Lazarus: "When
Jesus saw [Mary] weeping, and the Jews who had come along with her also
weeping, he was deeply moved in spirit and troubled. 'Where have you laid him?'
he asked. 'Come and see, Lord,' they replied. Jesus wept." Verse 35, "Jesus wept,"
is the shortest verse in the Bible yet it speaks extensively. Even though Jesus
knew He was going to raise Lazarus from the dead, He grieved alongside Mary
and the others. When you grieve, He grieves. Continually set the Lord before you.
He is alongside you for your entire journey, even in your grieving. Because of this,
you will not be shaken.

───── ONE ─────

When **ONES** encounter grief and loss, they have a hard time processing their emotions because they often view them as a weakness and something they need to improve. They suppress their feelings, trying to move forward while keeping up the appearance of emotional stability.

Awareness for Ones: Allowing your emotions to surface without feeling the need to hide them is how you can heal. Inviting God into the process is the true healing balm that will bring you comfort. This week as you meditate on Psalm 16:8, allow yourself to see that God has been with you always. Write down a few ways God has shown you He is always by your side.

───── TWO ─────

When **TWOS** encounter grief and loss, they feel an overwhelming surge of emotion. They tend to try to meet the needs of others around them instead of dealing with their own emotions, because they think focusing on their needs is selfish.

Awareness for Twos: You try to keep upbeat and positive, never wanting to appear needy. Letting down your walls and inviting God into your pain will bring healing. This week as you meditate on Psalm 16:8, reflect on the times you have gone before God and shared your pain. Write down the ways He has shown you comfort in these times.

───── THREE ─────

When **THREES** encounter grief and loss, they detach themselves from their emotions. They avoid hard conversations and ignore their current state of reality. They tend to busy themselves by creating a new narrative, hoping this keeps their feelings at bay.

Awareness for Threes: Allowing yourself to stay present will help you process your pain. This week as you meditate on Psalm 16:8, be reminded of the importance of keeping God at the center of what you are doing. Write down the ways God has proven His faithfulness to you when you have gone to Him with your emotions.

FOUR

When **FOURS** encounter grief and loss, their emotions can consume them. They can find themselves overwhelmed and unable to accomplish their day-to-day tasks. They feel their emotions so deeply, they can spiral into a dark place spiritually.

Awareness for Fours: Inviting God into the situation and asking Him to carry your pain will bring healing and peace of mind. This week as you meditate on Psalm 16:8, allow God to reveal areas in your life where you need healing. Draw a picture of how you feel when you allow yourself to invite God into your pain.

FIVE

When **FIVES** encounter grief and loss, they detach themselves from their emotions. They seek out information to try to understand how it happened. They need to make sense of the loss before they can move forward.

Awareness for Fives: You desire to grieve alone. However, allowing God into your grief is where you will find true and lasting healing. This week as you meditate on Psalm 16:8, thank God for always being quietly by your side. Praise him for helping you process your pain.

SIX

When **SIXES** encounter grief and loss, they spend time processing what is happening. It can leave them feeling fearful and anxious. They need to make sense of the loss before they can move forward.

Awareness for Sixes: Allowing yourself to stay present by inviting God into your pain will bring healing and comfort. This week as you meditate on Psalm 16:8, allow yourself to see the ways God has been present with you the whole time. Write down a few ways you have felt God's comfort and love amid your pain.

SEVEN

When **SEVENS** encounter grief and loss, they suppress their emotions for fear of being overtaken by them. They busy themselves with new ideas and adventures to escape the feelings of sadness and pain. They have a hard time staying in touch with feelings of sadness or grief.

Awareness for Sevens: When you can process your emotions, you are able to move forward in a much healthier way. When you invite God into your pain, you will no longer be alone. The great and mighty comforter will be by your side. This week as you meditate on Psalm 16:8, praise God for always being next to you. Write down the feelings that come to mind when you think about Him being present in your pain.

EIGHT

When **EIGHTS** encounter grief and loss, their initial response is denial. They tend to take charge in the moment and do what needs to be done, all the while detaching from their own emotions because they have a desire to fix the situation.

Awareness for Eights: By inviting Christ into your pain and allowing yourself to be in the moment, it will produce lasting healing and peace. This week as you meditate on Psalm 16:8, allow God to reveal times in your life where you have tried to deal with loss all by yourself. Write down what it feels like to invite Christ into your grief.

NINE

When **NINES** encounter grief and loss, they mentally block out their pain and emotions by seeking out activities that bring them comfort. They desire harmony and peace in their relationships and environments; therefore, when loss happens, they feel unstable and scared.

Awareness for Nines: You feel deeply, and grief and loss can become overwhelming for you to carry alone. Allowing God into your pain will bring you comfort and peace. This week as you meditate on Psalm 16:8, allow yourself to relax, knowing God is by your side. Take a walk and allow yourself to feel God's presence all around you.

APPLICATION

As you reflect on your Enneagram number this week, how do you see yourself experiencing a sense of feeling known?

_____

_____

_____

How can you allow yourself to process grief and pain in a new way?

_____

_____

After reading all the Enneagram reflections, in what ways can you allow those closest to you to process their grief and loss in an authentic way?

_____

_____

When has God helped you not feel shaken? How are you hearing God speak to you about your grief?

_____

_____

MEDITATION

Go to page 336 and try the Reflection Meditation exercise.

My prayer this week:

_____

_____

_____

_____

_____

_____

_____

_____

_____

_____

WEEK 24

"

PUT ON GOD'S COMPLETE SET OF ARMOR PROVIDED
FOR US, SO THAT YOU WILL BE PROTECTED
AS YOU FIGHT AGAINST THE EVIL STRATEGIES
OF THE ACCUSER! YOUR HAND-TO-HAND COMBAT
IS NOT WITH HUMAN BEINGS, BUT WITH THE HIGHEST
PRINCIPALITIES AND AUTHORITIES OPERATING
IN REBELLION UNDER THE HEAVENLY REALMS.
FOR THEY ARE A POWERFUL CLASS OF DEMON-GODS
AND EVIL SPIRITS THAT HOLD THIS DARK WORLD
IN BONDAGE. BECAUSE OF THIS, YOU MUST WEAR
ALL THE ARMOR THAT GOD PROVIDES SO YOU'RE
PROTECTED AS YOU CONFRONT THE SLANDERER,
FOR YOU ARE DESTINED FOR ALL THINGS
AND WILL RISE VICTORIOUS.

EPHESIANS 6:11-13 (TPT)

YOUR ARMOR
THE REAL ENEMY

GUARD YOURSELF EACH MORNING
WITH GOD'S PROTECTIVE SHIELD.
PUT ON YOUR SUIT OF ARMOR.

You might be headed into a relational storm, be in the midst of the storm, or just coming out of one. When another person's actions or words hurt you, it is tempting to take it personally. If you are attacked, you likely respond by going into either fight, flight, or freeze mode. Oftentimes, you, like all people, use defense mechanisms to protect yourself when you feel threatened or ambushed. These are normal reactions, but they are often counterproductive. Instead, if someone is mean-spirited or takes a cruel shot at you, respond by rising above it. When you disengage from earthly warfare, you are choosing peace. You are also recognizing whom you are truly battling, because it's not the people around you. The true Enemy is the evil accuser who wants to keep you in a stronghold of bondage. Starting this week, guard yourself each morning with God's protective shield. Put on your suit of armor. Read His trusting Word and become a prayer warrior. And when the true Enemy tries to enter your battlefield again, you will rise victorious every time, as there is no match for your Lord of lords.

——— ONE ———

ONES' defense mechanism is reaction formation. They use this strategy to help them deal with uncomfortable and difficult situations. They try to reduce or eliminate anxiety caused by their underlying emotion of anger. They do not believe anger is an appropriate emotion to express; therefore, they suppress their true feelings and respond in a manner that is the exact opposite of how they actually feel. These suppressed emotions often lead to bitterness and resentment.

Awareness for Ones: When you recognize the emotions of anger and rage bubbling under the surface, take a minute to reflect on this verse in Ephesians. You are able to use the Word of God as your weapon to fight against the lies of the Enemy. As you meditate on Ephesians 6:11–13 this week, ask God to give you a new understanding of the ways the Enemy has been attacking you. Write down a few strategies you could use to combat these attacks on your mind.

——— TWO ———

TWOS' defense mechanism is repression. They use this strategy to help them keep the feelings of jealousy and hurt at bay. They do not want to face what is really going on inside themselves. They attempt to hide their true feelings, thoughts, and desires from themselves. In other words, they focus on other people's needs instead of acknowledging their own needs.

Awareness for Twos: When you recognize the emotions of jealousy and hurt sitting below the surface of your reaction, remind yourself of what is written in Ephesians. As you meditate on Ephesians 6:11–13, ask God to reveal to you the ways that the Enemy has continually trapped you into believing you are not enough.

——— THREE ———

THREES' defense mechanism is identification. They take on other people's behaviors by copying their characteristics and beliefs as a way of avoiding possible feelings of shame and rejection. They can even go as far as adopting others' ideas, hobbies, and interests as their own. This is not something they overtly do, but it's more likely a coping strategy they picked up early in life to keep their unwanted feelings at bay.

Awareness for Threes: When you feel yourself trying to become something other than who you truly are for fear of shame and rejection, remind yourself that you are a child of God. You will no longer feel the need to smooth over situations and relationships in the hopes of not being rejected, because you are able to use the Word of God as your weapon. As you meditate on Ephesians 6:11–13 this week, write down ways you have been unknowingly let the Enemy have a foothold.

FOUR

FOURS' defense mechanism is introjection. They struggle with feelings of worthlessness and shame. They take criticism personally and internalize their feelings of inadequacy. They get stuck in negative thought patterns and begin to believe they are the cause of all the problems. They disregard any positive feedback given to them because they feel broken inside.

Awareness for Fours: As feelings of worthlessness and shame surface, be reminded of God's shield over you to combat the lies of the Enemy. You will no longer allow other people's opinions to control you, because you are able to use the Word of God as your weapon. As you meditate on Ephesians 6:11–13 this week, put on the full armor of God. Pray your mind would be renewed.

FIVE

FIVES' defense mechanism is isolation. They tend to withdraw from others, hoping to minimize their feeling of being a burden on anyone. They can easily be overtaken by feelings of anxiety. They believe isolating themselves is the best form of self-protection.

Awareness for Fives: When you feel yourself retreating and isolating from others, ask yourself, "Is this the Enemy causing me to believe I am being a burden?" You have God's armor to combat these lies the Enemy tries to trick you into believing. As you meditate on Ephesians 6:11–13, remember the power of the Word of God. Write down a scripture you can use to remind yourself of what God thinks of you.

SIX

SIXES' defense mechanism is projection. They use this strategy to quiet the fears and anxiety they are feeling inside. They subconsciously make up stories in their own minds and then project these thoughts and opinions onto others. As a result, they often become increasingly anxious even though they believe this strategy is going to bring them a sense of safety and comfort.

Awareness for Sixes: The constant struggle of an underlying sense of fear and anxiety can be crippling at times. Allow yourself to recognize the many tools you have to help you. Be reminded you are really fighting against the Enemy, not the people or situations in your life. You will no longer feel the need to be in a state of hypervigilance, fearful of what might happen, because you are able to use the Word of God as your weapon to combat the lies of the Enemy. As you meditate on Ephesians 6:11–13 this week, pray for a better understanding of the feelings of anxiety that arise in you. Write down the ways the Enemy has continually tormented you with feelings of fear.

SEVEN

SEVENS' defense mechanism is rationalization. They do this by using positive reframing of situations. The fear of abandonment is a huge source of anxiety in their lives. As a result, they constantly look for positivity in all situations to avoid feeling sad, guilty, lonely, and even unloved by others. This keeps them from truly feeling the consequences of their actions or acknowledging the devastating effects of other people's actions in their lives.

Awareness for Sevens: When you feel anxiety rising in your body, remind yourself that you are loved and cherished by your heavenly Father. Use the shield of armor to combat the lies the Enemy is trying to whisper in your mind. As you meditate on Ephesians 6:11–13 this week, put on the full armor of God. Pray your mind would be renewed.

EIGHT

EIGHTS' defense mechanism is denial. They do not want to be overtaken by their emotions or left feeling exposed by anyone. They protect themselves by subconsciously negating anything that makes them feel anxious by acting as if it never happened. There are several ways they use denial. First, they might deny the reality of unpleasant information. Or, they might acknowledge the information but deny the severity of it. Or, they could acknowledge the information and the severity of it but deny their own involvement in it altogether.

Awareness of Eights: When you feel anger overshadowing your thoughts, take a minute and discern if it is coming from a fear of being betrayed or exposed in some way. Understanding who you are really fighting against will help you to no longer take control of the situation and plead your case. As you meditate on Ephesians 6:11–13 this week, write down the tools that help you stand firm against the Enemy.

NINE

NINES' defense mechanism is narcotization. They desperately want to keep feelings of anger and hostility in the distance and buried internally. They numb themselves to avoid situations that are too painful, overwhelming, difficult, or uncomfortable to handle. They will also avoid their circumstances by performing routines that are rhythmic, habitual, and familiar—all of which require little attention. This brings them comfort and helps to create a calm environment.

Awareness for Nines: When you feel the desire to numb yourself, first ask yourself, "Do I want to withdraw because I am feeling anger or hostility about a situation or toward a particular person?" Don't fear speaking up for what you need, because you're able to use the Word of God as your weapon. As you meditate on Ephesians 6:11–13 this week, write down the ways you can combat the lies with which the Enemy plagues your mind.

APPLICATION

As you reflect on your Enneagram number this week, how do you find the information regarding your defense mechanism eye-opening?

_____

_____

_____

How has reading about your Enneagram type helped you notice areas in your life when you have reacted instead of listened?

_____

_____

_____

How can this new awareness of your Enneagram number help you recognize the schemes of the Enemy?

_____

_____

_____

In what areas of your life do you need to pray for the full armor of God's protection? How are you hearing God speak to you about your hurt feelings?

_____

_____

_____

 MEDITATION

Go to page 342 and try the Contemplation Meditation exercise.

My prayer this week:

_____

_____

_____

_____

_____

_____

_____

_____

_____

_____

WEEK 25

"

DO NOT CONFORM TO THE PATTERN
OF THIS WORLD, BUT BE TRANSFORMED
BY THE RENEWING OF YOUR MIND.
THEN YOU WILL BE ABLE TO TEST AND
APPROVE WHAT GOD'S WILL IS— HIS GOOD,
PLEASING AND PERFECT WILL.

ROMANS 12:2

QUESTIONING BEHAVIOR
NONCONFORMITY

MAKE A COMMITMENT TO LOOK AT YOUR DAY LIKE NEVER BEFORE.

You have patterns of behavior that are second nature because you have been developing them since you were around the age of two. You have learned to navigate the world by using these patterns as a way of trying to gain love and acceptance and to keep yourself safe from harm and hard times. As you begin to uncover these cycles, ask yourself, "Are these patterns serving me well in my current situation?" It is certainly a daily decision each morning to make positive choices. But you live in a busy world and are bombarded with messages from everyone around you every day. When you are tired, you can begin putting your decisions on autopilot and either just do what everyone around you is doing or the same thing you have always done. If you are feeling apathetic or are just following the crowd, the outcome may not be the one God has in mind for you. When writing a letter to the Romans, Paul knew that God has a better plan for you, if only you focus on what He wants for you rather than what our world says is acceptable. You are called to break your unhealthy behavioral cycles and watch his pleasing and perfect will for your life to unfold. This week make a commitment to look at your day like never before. Write down some of the ways you can choose loving words and be patient, humble, and kinder, while also finding ways you can rest and care for your health and well-being, too. Perhaps the first question you can ask each morning this week is, "What can I do today that will make it better than yesterday?" Focus on making the best choices you can and watch what God can do.

ONE

ONES have developed patterns of behavior that keep their internal selves consistent and orderly to appear as if they have it all together. This can cause them to be judgmental and rigid in their thinking.

Awareness for Ones: As you reflect on Romans 12:2, can you see the importance of questioning your patterns? Renewing your mind in Christ is a daily practice that you, as well as all people, must do. This way you can clearly see the ways your old patterns of behavior may be hindering your relationship with Christ. This week ask yourself if being too rigid and unwilling to see other people's points of view could be hurting your relationships and your role as a Christian witness. Write down the areas in your life you wish to surrender to Christ and pray He will reestablish new patterns that are healthier and more authentic.

TWO

TWOS seek relational security. This pattern they have developed makes them feel safe and secure. Developing these types of relationships is a way they have learned to meet their needs.

Awareness for Twos: Recognizing your patterns of behavior will allow you to have a better understanding of the ways you try to create a sense of security in your relationships to feel safe. As you reflect on Romans 12:2, allow yourself to explore the patterns you have built in your life. Are these patterns serving you well in your current circumstances? This week write down the areas in your life that you would like God to help transform. Put your trust in Him and watch what He will do.

THREE

THREES are high-energy and incredibly driven people. They have learned early in life that changing their personality depending on the current environment is a way to earn acceptance and favor.

Awareness for Threes: This week, ask God to search your heart. As patterns begin to reveal themselves to you through prayer and meditation, reflect on Romans 12:2. Do you find yourself being superficial and unwilling to be authentic for fear of exposure? Write down all the behaviors you wish to change. Allow God to renew your mind and help set your feet on solid ground so you can run after His will for your life with clarity.

FOUR

FOURS often feel misunderstood. This causes them to develop patterns of behavior to protect themselves from the disapproval of others by putting on a hard outer shell and avoiding close relationships.

Awareness for Fours: When you feel yourself putting up walls of protection to avoid disappointment, remind yourself of what is written in Romans 12:2. You do not go to war against people but against the evil one. This week, ask God to help you overcome the patterns of behavior keeping you from going deeper in a relationship with Him. Write down any behaviors you are aware of within yourself that are keeping you from surrendering your life fully to Christ. Pray He will renew your mind, so you are able to walk out your calling with clarity.

FIVE

FIVES prefer a lot of alone time. They do not like to have expectations placed on them. Over time, they have developed patterns of behavior that keep others at bay as a way of self-protection. They prefer to do life solo or with just a few trusted loved ones and friends.

Awareness for Fives: When you feel yourself needing to retreat and withdraw from the outside world, look to Romans 12:2. Be reminded of the importance of renewing your mind in Christ. This week ask God to help you be open to the wisdom of others as you seek His will and purpose for your life. Write down thoughts that keep you from sharing your needs with others. Ask God to show you how He will meet those needs and become your ultimate protector as you chase after your calling according to His will and purpose for your life.

SIX

SIXES often second-guess themselves and their decision-making. They have developed this pattern throughout their lives because they learned not to trust their own thoughts and ideas. They are concerned with making the wrong choice and jeopardizing their comfort and safety.

Awareness for Sixes: As you find yourself getting caught up in worry and fear, look at Romans 12:2. Be encouraged by renewing your mind in Christ. You will find purpose and direction and will no longer feel stuck out of a fear of making the wrong move. Instead, you will move forward in your calling. This week ask God to reveal His plan for you. Write down the ways you can move forward and establish healthy patterns in your life.

Notes

SEVEN

SEVENS possess a high energy and are always thinking of new ideas and plans. They have developed patterns of behavior to keep them busy and distracted to ward off feelings of loneliness and abandonment. They have a hard time being fully present in any situation, because they are fearful of missing out on something better.

Awareness for Sevens: When your mind starts racing and you can't seem to keep yourself present in the moment, remember Romans 12:2. You have to take every thought captive and ask God to renew your mind. This week, as you pray and seek God, ask Him to reveal the areas in your life that have kept you aimlessly running forward, unable to focus on the path God has for you. Write down areas in your life you wish to surrender to God. Praise Him for always being by your side.

EIGHT

EIGHTS are strong and independent. They like to be in control. They developed this pattern early on in life. They do not like to feel vulnerable in any situation and very rarely let their guard down in front of anyone. Eights don't want to be taken advantage of under any circumstance.

Awareness for Eights: When you feel yourself trying to control a situation, ask, "Why do I feel the need to be in control?" As you reflect on Romans 12:2, can you see the importance of questioning your patterns? At times, your patterns can get in the way of God's purpose for your life. This week ask God to search your heart and reveal any areas that are hindering you from pursuing life the way God intended. Write down the areas in your life where you are having a hard time releasing control to God. Thank Him for meeting you right where you are in this moment.

NINE

NINES are often unsure of how they should show up in a situation. They have developed patterns that keep them from speaking how they truly feel. They learned early on it was safer, easier, and better for them to shrink back and make themselves small so others can get their way. This is how they learned to keep the peace.

Awareness for Nines: When you feel yourself shrinking back, afraid to say what you are truly thinking, look at Romans 12:2. Can you see how your patterns have kept you a prisoner by preventing you from speaking your truth and being your true self in your own life? This week ask God to renew your mind so you can have the understanding of just how important your voice and presence is to the world. Write down ways you can begin to value your voice. Thank God for the many gifts and talents He has placed inside you.

APPLICATION

As you reflect on your Enneagram number this week, what patterns of behavior do you remember forming from an early age?

_____

_____

_____

How can you see the patterns of behavior you have created throughout your life hindering you from moving forward?

_____

_____

_____

After reading the Enneagram reflections, in what way can you see how your wings have impacted your personality and behavior patterns?

_____

_____

_____

How is God renewing your mind in this season? How are you hearing God speak to you about your conviction?

_____

_____

_____

♥ MEDITATION

Go to page 332 and try the Box Breathing exercise.

My prayer this week:

_____

_____

_____

_____

_____

_____

_____

_____

_____

WEEK 26

"

WHEN I AM AFRAID, I PUT MY TRUST IN YOU.
IN GOD, WHOSE WORD I PRAISE—IN GOD
I TRUST AND I AM NOT AFRAID. WHAT CAN
MERE MORTALS DO TO ME?

PSALM 56:3-4

CORE FEAR
IN GOD WE TRUST

*"IN GOD, WHOSE WORD I PRAISE—IN GOD
I TRUST AND I AM NOT AFRAID."*

Fear. It's a debilitating feeling that can seemingly appear out of nowhere. You might fear losing money, your job, health, influence, or loved ones. Fear can also trigger many deep emotions, such as feeling overwhelmed or ashamed, or it can even whirl you into a cycle of anxiousness or anger. Consequently, God peacefully encourages us to "fear not" 365 times in the Bible—one reminder for each day of the year. Our heavenly Father, in his beautiful grace and kind affinity, understands this battle and gently encourages us to move forward daily in trust—the antithesis of fear. Instead of allowing fear to freeze your dreams, rob your joy, and squander your hope and creativity, allow your trust to build on the foundation of God's Word. When the vicious four-letter word of fear rears its deceitful head and makes you afraid, pause and lean on your steadfast faith in the Lord of all creation. He has you covered. Remember His promises and declare them, "In God, whose word I praise—in God I trust and I am not afraid." Rest assured, with every ounce of your heart, "If God is for us, who can be against us?" (Romans 8:31)

ONE

The fear of being perceived as bad, dishonest, or imperfect in some way is very real to **ONES**. They strive for order and perfection as a way to combat these fears. But, when they embrace Christ and His sacrifice on the cross, they understand all of their imperfections have been washed away.

Awareness for Ones: Understanding the role that fear plays in your life allows you to begin to live with more freedom. Allowing yourself to lean on Christ in times of fear will not only grow you as a person but will also help mute your inner critic. Speaking aloud, "In God I trust and am not afraid," can help to calm the fears trying to overpower you. This week as you meditate on Psalm 56:3–4, write your fears down, release them to Christ, and trust that He is working out all things on your behalf.

TWO

The fear that stirs inside of **TWOS** is feeling unworthy of being loved. This fear causes Twos to try to meet the needs of others, hoping others will love and need them in return. As they embrace the love of Christ through salvation, they are able to realize they no longer need to chase after love.

Awareness for Twos: When you begin to recognize this fear, combat it with the Word of God. You no longer have to fear being unworthy because you are a child of God. Understand your self-worth is not dependent on another person, but rather is found in Christ Jesus. Speaking aloud, "In God I trust and am not afraid," can help to calm the fears trying to overpower you. This week as you meditate on Psalm 56:3–4, write down your patterns, release them to Christ, and trust that He is working out all things on your behalf.

THREE

THREES fear being seen as worthless unless they are performing and pleasing others. This fear causes them to shape-shift to be what they think others need or want them to be, all the while losing their true selves. As they are able to embrace the love of Christ, they let down their guard, becoming more vulnerable.

Awareness for Threes: Invite God into your battle with fear, because He has the power to validate who you truly are. Begin to view yourself as His chosen masterpiece. Then your fear of what others might think of you will begin to melt away. God is the only one who can calm your struggle with feeling worthless. He desires you to know and understand your true identity. Speaking aloud, "In God I trust and am not afraid," can help to calm the fears trying to overpower you. This week as you meditate on Psalm 56:3–4, write down your patterns, release them to Christ, and trust that He is working out all things on your behalf.

FOUR

For **FOURS**, the fear of being seen as inadequate, plain, or even flawed is a huge struggle. They have dealt with the feelings of "something is missing inside of me" all their lives. They are afraid others will not see them as valuable or special. However, as they embrace their salvation through Christ's death on the cross, they see just how important and special they are to God.

Awareness for Fours: When you begin to understand Christ made you unique and there is no lack of anything within you, you will be able to calm the fear that stirs inside. You are exactly the person God created you to be. Speaking aloud, "In God I trust and am not afraid," can help to calm the fears trying to overpower you. This week as you meditate on Psalm 56:3-4, write down your patterns, release them to Christ, and trust that He is working out all things on your behalf.

FIVE

For **FIVES**, the fear of being engulfed by other's expectations of them can be overwhelming. Not having enough resources or time for themselves plays a big part in what causes them to withdraw and keeps them from truly showing up. However, when they can cultivate a relationship with Christ, they can begin letting go of control and trusting in Him.

Awareness for Fives: When you begin to understand God will supply all your needs according to His riches and glory, there is a part of you able to breathe more easily. Allowing yourself time to read the Bible and recharge can teach you to calm the fear of being overtaken by others. This week as you meditate on Psalm 56:3-4, write down your patterns, release them to Christ, and trust that He is working out all things on your behalf.

SIX

Anxiety overwhelms **SIXES** in many ways, and that fear can be crippling. Sixes fear the uncertainty of life, in general. However, as they live out their life tethered to Christ, it brings a sense of peace to their very being.

Awareness for Sixes: When you begin to understand you can give God all your concerns, you can breathe more easily. It is incredibly important for you to grab hold of this scripture and allow it to be a mantra you use in your daily life. Speaking aloud, "In God I trust and am not afraid," can help to calm the fears trying to overpower you. This week as you meditate on Psalm 56:3-4, write down your patterns, release them to Christ, and trust that He is working out all things on your behalf.

SEVEN

Fear stirs inside of **SEVENS** in a different way. Their fear arises when limits are placed on them. They also fear getting caught up in emotional pain. They try to push the boundaries in their lives in hopes of finding freedom and fulfillment. However, as they develop a relationship with Christ, they can embrace the beauty in boundaries and a life lived in order.

Awareness for Sevens: You will begin to understand limits and boundaries are not to be feared but rather embraced, because they guide you toward wise decisions and good judgment. Fear has no place in your life. Speaking aloud, "In God I trust and am not afraid," can help to calm the fears trying to overpower you. This week as you meditate on Psalm 56:3–4, write down your patterns, release them to Christ, and trust that He is working out all things on your behalf.

EIGHT

For **EIGHTS**, the fear of being powerless or manipulated causes them to build walls to defend and protect themselves. When they read a scripture that refers to fear, their first reaction oftentimes is, "I don't struggle with fear." In the typical sense of the word, they are right. Eights are not fearful people; however, they have certain fears just like all humans. Learning to recognize when these fears arise and how they react to them is key for their personal growth. When their relationship grows with Christ, they can better cast their anxiety to Him.

Awareness for Eights: True freedom is found in Christ alone. Inviting Him into your most vulnerable places helps you grow in strength deep within your soul. Speaking aloud, "In God I trust and am not afraid" can help to calm your fears. This week as you meditate on Psalm 56:3–4, write down your patterns, release them to Christ, and trust that He is working out all things on your behalf.

NINE

For **NINES**, the fear of losing connection with those they care about causes them to willingly conform, hoping this will keep the peace in their relationships. As a result, they ignore their own needs, desires, and wants, believing theirs are not as important as others'. However, as they lean into their relationship with Christ, they understand their self-worth.

Awareness for Nines: Claim the scripture above as truth and find the freedom in Christ for which your heart longs. Discover your true value and self-worth as you draw closer to the Lord. Replace your fear of not being loved for who you are with the knowledge that you are found in Christ and you matter. This week as you meditate on Psalm 56:3–4, write down your patterns, release them to Christ, and trust that He is working out all things on your behalf.

APPLICATION

As you reflect on your Enneagram number this week, can you identify ways you have a hard time trusting in people and in the Lord?

_____

_____

_____

How have you found true freedom after processing the Enneagram reflections?

_____

_____

_____

In what way can you relate to another Enneagram number in dealing with fear?

_____

_____

_____

What are your current fears that you need to turn over to God as you trust in Him? How are you hearing God speak to you when it comes to your fears?

_____

_____

_____

MEDITATION

Go to page 334 and try the Concentration Meditation exercise.

My prayer this week:

_____

_____

_____

_____

_____

_____

_____

_____

_____

_____

_____

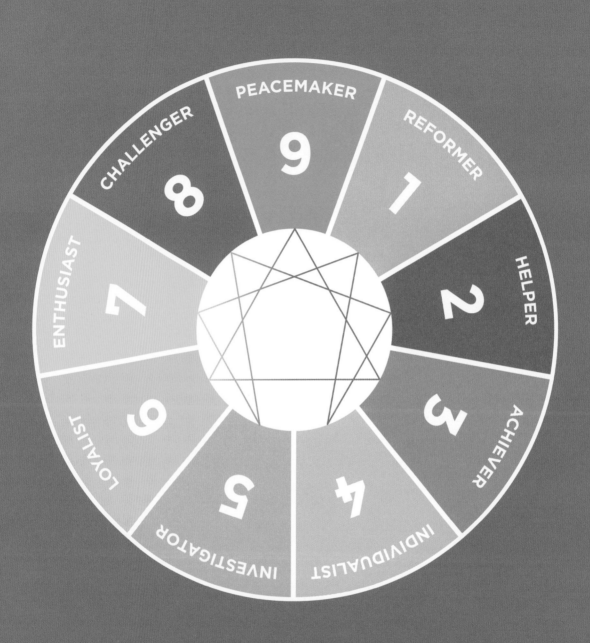

QUARTER THREE
YOUR PURPOSE

The Creator made you on purpose, for a purpose, with a purpose—and that's a promise! No matter your personality type, He magnificently custom-crafted you and gave you a unique set of divine attributes with specific gifts and talents to fulfill your purpose.

WEEK 27

"

AND WE KNOW THAT GOD CAUSES EVERYTHING
TO WORK TOGETHER FOR THE GOOD
OF THOSE WHO LOVE GOD AND ARE CALLED
ACCORDING TO HIS PURPOSE FOR THEM.

ROMANS 8:28 (NLT)

YOUR CALLING
ANSWERING GOD

KNOW THAT GOD DESIGNED YOU EXACTLY THE WAY HE INTENDED, WITH UNIQUE TALENTS.

You have a true desire for significance. You want to understand why you are here on earth and that you have a meaningful purpose. While you are seeking your calling, know God designed you exactly the way He intended, with unique talents. You have deep significance already because your Creator believes in your abilities beyond your wildest expectations. Tap into your God-given gifts because He is the One orchestrating your life to work in harmony for His purpose. Perhaps your gifts are the dreams you feel deep within your soul and the fire that fuels your heart toward making a difference for the greater good. Ask yourself, "What passions do I have? What dreams would I want to pursue if there were no issues holding me back and if I were guaranteed not to fail?" Chase that calling! Sprint toward it and don't look back, regardless of the noise of naysayers on the sidelines. If you stumble, get back up. The God of the universe is not disappointed in you or discouraged by your pitfalls.

ONE

ONES don't want to make mistakes. They are rule followers and want to be seen as "good." When they are trying to find their calling here on earth, they can feel overwhelmed by the many paths available for them to choose.

Awareness for Ones: Understand that God created you in the very image of Christ and has placed gifts and talents in you that He desires you to use in this world. God causes everything you do to work together for good because you love Him. As you seek your purpose, lean into what you know about yourself. Write down what you like to do and what is life-giving to you. This week as you meditate on Romans 8:28, pray for God to continue to help you walk out your purpose here on earth, and ask Him to open your eyes to the gifts you have within you. Allow yourself to express your many talents, as they display the goodness of God.

TWO

TWOS have a natural ability to take care of people. Because they are incredibly attuned to the needs of others and sense what others need before they speak it, Twos have a superpower that no other Enneagram number has. Knowing they love and deeply care for others helps them figure out their calling here on earth.

Awareness for Twos: God is going to work out all things because you love and serve Him. This can help set your mind at ease. As you ponder your calling, pray about what you are supposed to be doing and lean into the gifts already within you. Write down what you like to do and what is life-giving to you. This week as you meditate on Romans 8:28, ask God to help you know what direction is best for you based on your gifts and talents. Dream big and allow God to direct your steps.

THREE

THREES can read a situation and adapt to become what is needed in the moment. Because they are fast-paced and strategic, they are not afraid to chase after their calling by taking risks and trying new things.

Awareness for Threes: Allowing yourself to get in touch with your true self is key to discovering your calling here on earth. God will use everything you do for good because you love Him; therefore, no more striving to earn your place! Write down what you like to do and what is life-giving to you. This week as you meditate on Romans 8:28, breathe in His grace and mercy as you seek purpose in what you are doing. Allow God to direct your steps according to His will and plan for your life.

FOUR

FOURS are acutely aware of the emotional tone in their environment. They see the world through a creative lens and want their uniqueness to be recognized and appreciated. It is easier for them to run after their calling when they accept that something is not missing within them, since they already have what it takes.

Awareness for Fours: God knows you already have everything you need. He has placed gifts and talents within you for a calling only you can fulfill. As you seek your purpose, find comfort in knowing God is going to work out all things because you love Him. Write down what you like to do and what is life-giving to you. This week as you meditate on Romans 8:28, allow God to show you how valuable you are to His Kingdom. Ask Him to reveal something new about you.

FIVE

FIVES are investigators. They are naturally curious. They have a way of looking at the world differently than other people. Fives see possibilities and pathways to make things happen, and they often answer their calling to use their sharp mind as a gift to the world.

Awareness for Fives: Because you prefer to work independently, finding your calling can get a little wobbly as you realize you must engage with people, sometimes on their terms. For you, privacy is a must. However, when you submit yourself to the Lord and begin to understand He has placed unique qualities in you for a purpose, you are then able to release your grip of control and collaborate with others. Write down what you like to do and what is life-giving to you. This week as you meditate on Romans 8:28, ask God to give you discernment about decisions you are making.

SIX

SIXES are great problem solvers and incredibly wise and discerning. They are often called to use their ability to look at the whole picture and see what others may be missing.

Awareness for Sixes: At times, this gift can make it difficult for you to move forward and trust yourself to make decisions about your future, since you fear making the wrong choice. You can become frozen and unable to move forward. Therefore, it's essential to understand your heavenly Father has you in the palm of His hands and is with you. Trusting that God is by your side will give you the ability to lean into your calling and take the next steps without feeling paralyzed. Write down what you like to do and what is life-giving to you. This week as you meditate on Romans 8:28, ask God to comfort you as you seek His will for your life.

Notes

Notes

SEVENS are excellent visionaries. They see potential around every corner. They are fast movers and great gatherers of people. Therefore, when they aren't getting caught up with their need to plan exciting opportunities, they are able to focus and set their sight on their calling.

Awareness for Sevens: It is critical to slow down and refocus often. The real beauty lies in your connection to Christ, where your dreams and His calling on your life intersect. What an amazing outcome when you can slow down and stay focused on the task until its completion! Write down what you like to do and what is life-giving to you. This week as you meditate on Romans 8:28, allow God to quiet your racing mind. Ask Him to guide your thoughts and settle you.

————————— **EIGHT** —————————

Fear is not something that often grips **EIGHTS**. They are strong, independent, and fierce leaders. They go after what they want and don't let anything get in their way. They pursue their calling best when they can stay on track without distraction and not get ahead of themselves.

Awareness for Eights: You can accomplish a lot, but this doesn't always coincide with your calling. Slowing down and making sure God is at the center of your decisions is going to be important for you. Inviting Him into the process may bring clarity and direction you did not notice on your own. This week as you meditate on Romans 8:28, allow God to open your eyes to His ways and His plans and write down what you feel is life-giving to you. Ask Him for patience and understanding as you pursue your purpose.

————————— **NINE** —————————

NINES are peacemakers. They can see all sides of a situation. They don't like to assert themselves, but they do want their voice and ideas to matter. When they allow themselves to think, feel, and say what is in their heart, they can move forward and pursue their calling.

Awareness for Nines: Allowing yourself to express yourself is key to chasing after your purpose. No more making yourself small so others have room to shine. It is okay for you to take up space and use the gifts and talents God has gifted you. He will use all the things you have been a part of for good because you love and serve Him. He also wants to use you specifically for a purpose that is set aside just for you. Don't shy away from your dreams or passions. This week as you meditate on Romans 8:28, ask God to reveal the gifts and talents hidden inside of you. Write down your gifts that show the love of Christ.

APPLICATION

How can you identify the challenges that arise when you're trying to find your unique calling in your life?

_____

_____

_____

How can you identify your unique gifts and talents as you process your Enneagram reflection?

_____

_____

_____

In what ways can you better see the gifts and talents of your loved ones as you read about each of their Enneagram numbers?

_____

_____

_____

How can you use your immense God-given gifts and talents to help you find your purpose? How are you hearing God speak to you about your calling?

_____

_____

_____

MEDITATION

Go to page 336 and try the Reflection Meditation exercise.

My prayer this week:

_____

_____

_____

_____

_____

_____

_____

_____

_____

_____

_____

WEEK 28

"

I PRAY THAT HE WOULD UNVEIL WITHIN YOU
THE UNLIMITED RICHES OF HIS GLORY
AND FAVOR UNTIL SUPERNATURAL STRENGTH
FLOODS YOUR INNERMOST BEING WITH HIS
DIVINE MIGHT AND EXPLOSIVE POWER.

EPHESIANS 3:16 (TPT)

GROWTH
HIS STRENGTH AND FAVOR

YOU SERVE THE KING OF KINGS
AND ARE A RIGHTFUL HEIR TO THE
KINGDOM OF GOD.

We have all developed unhealthy patterns that often spin us on a perpetual cycle of struggle and dysfunction. However, know that where you are weak, God floods you with His supernatural strength and power. It is during these times when things do not look or feel the way they should that God is at work trying to teach you and move you toward Him. Ask Him, "What do You want me to learn and how do You want me to rise above my current situation?" When you are feeling depleted, remember who you are and whose you are. When you are feeling less than, not enough, or worse off than others, remember who you are and whose you are. You serve the King of kings and are a rightful heir to the kingdom of God. Take hold of Ephesians 3:16, which is the apostle Paul's prayer on behalf of the Christians of Ephesus. Now, this is a proclamation worth declaring and decreeing over your life. This is your time; this is your battle cry! Speak this gospel of unwavering favor over your life, for it is a gift presented to you by Jehovah Jireh, God the provider. The power of the God of all creation is at work within you, filling you with His infinite riches of divine glory through the Holy Spirit.

ONE

As **ONES** become aware of the patterns of behavior they have created over their lifetime, they can begin to identify with some of the struggles they have in trying to get their needs met by being good. As Ones move toward the healthy traits of the Enneagram Seven, they can extend grace and patience to themselves and others. They can live with more freedom.

Awareness for Ones: When you begin to understand you are created perfectly in His image, you can find peace within yourself as you embrace the love of God and the grace He has given you freely. This week as you meditate on Ephesians 3:16, in what ways can you begin to see how precious you are to God and that you have His favor? As you find joy and relaxation, write down the ways you are embracing who you are in Christ, knowing you are chosen by a God who loves you.

TWO

TWOS strive to be self-sufficient and avoid their emotional needs. As they become more aware of the patterns of behavior they have created to appear less "needy," they can identify when they are holding back from expressing their true feelings and needs to others. However, as they move toward the healthy traits of the Enneagram Four in growth, they become more transparent and honest. They can express their emotions and are willing to share their needs with others openly.

Awareness for Twos: While you strive to get your own needs met, can you see how being authentic and truthful with your emotions can bring you feelings of freedom? This week as you meditate on Ephesians 3:16, embrace who you are and grasp on to His strength. You are God's child! You are loved and wanted. Write down the ways you feel that you have come alive in your own life as you embrace your emotions and welcome close friends into them with you.

THREE

As **THREES** ground themselves in the Word of God, they can identify the pattern of striving for attention and affirmation, hoping to get their needs met in this way. As they move toward the healthy traits of the Enneagram Six, they become more truthful and trustworthy. They no longer feel it necessary to be what people need them to be, because they are secure in who they are.

Awareness for Threes: Pay attention when you are tempted to strive for the approval of others as a way of getting your needs met, since this will only lead to loneliness and disappointment. This week as you meditate on Ephesians 3:16, allow yourself to embrace who you are in Christ. Write down what it has been like for you as you have learned to live your life knowing you are loved, favored, and chosen by your heavenly Father.

FOUR

As **FOURS** become more grounded in who they are in Christ, they can recognize the pattern of unrealistic expectations of others and turbulence in their emotional reactions. As they move toward the healthy traits of the Enneagram One, they become self-accepting, honest, flexible, and more respectful of others' opinions and differences.

Awareness for Fours: You feel offended and hurt when people tell you that your feelings, thoughts, and ideas are "extra" or overdramatic, since you want people to accept you just as God created you. This week as you meditate on Ephesians 3:16, praise God for His infinite power and strength. You are His child, so allow yourself to feel joyful and content, knowing you are chosen. Write down the ways you are finding gratitude and contentment in Christ as you continue to cultivate a relationship with Him.

FIVE

As **FIVES** continue to cultivate a relationship with Christ and embrace who He has created them to be, they will be able to recognize the patterns of withdrawal and isolation they have developed in hopes of keeping themselves safe. Fives move toward the healthy traits of the Enneagram Eight, becoming more generous with their time and willing to be a part of a community. They can see the needs of those around them and the importance of relationships.

Awareness for Fives: Your patterns have kept you withdrawn and self-sufficient, hoping not to have to ask anyone for anything. But you and your needs are not a burden to God or anyone else, for He gives you His divine might. This week as you meditate on Ephesians 3:16, embrace your value and worth as a child of God. Write down the ways you have grown in generosity and compassion for others as you have drawn closer to the Lord.

SIX

As **SIXES** embrace who they are in Christ, they can let go of the patterns of behavior that have kept them hypervigilant and suspicious. They move toward the healthy traits of the Enneagram Nine and become rooted in truth and at peace within themselves.

Awareness for Sixes: When you begin to understand your identity is in Christ, you will be able to cast your cares on Him because you are confident that He loves you. This week as you meditate on Ephesians 3:16, thank God for His love and explosive power. Write down the ways you have seen growth in your life as you confidently pursue Him with passion.

SEVEN

As **SEVENS** begin to understand they are created perfectly in God's image, they can see their behavior patterns of busyness and distraction that are keeping them from living truly free in Christ. As the Seven moves toward the healthy traits of the Enneagram Five, they become more disciplined and orderly. They become settled as they seek truth through the Word of God.

Awareness for Sevens: Always feeling like you must be enthusiastic and busy is exhausting. When you are connected to the Lord and His Word, you begin to desire peace and enjoy a slower pace in your daily routine. This week as you meditate on Ephesians 3:16, allow yourself to see how cherished and favored you are as a child of God. Write down the benefits you have experienced in your life as you have created order and embraced discipline.

EIGHT

EIGHTS have created patterns of behavior throughout their life that help them appear strong and assertive. As they move toward the healthy traits of the Enneagram Two, they become more tenderhearted. They can extend mercy and grace because they have experienced the love of Christ in their own life.

Awareness for Eights: As you embrace who you are in Christ, you become less cynical and can trust in Him and those around you. You understand you are deeply cared for by your heavenly Father and your loved ones. This week as you meditate on Ephesians 3:16, give thanks to God, praising Him for the many ways He has cared for you and given you His might and power. Write down the ways your life has changed as you have learned to extend tenderness and grace to those around you.

NINE

As **NINES** begin to embrace the way Christ made them, they no longer feel the need to use the patterns of behavior that have kept them from speaking up and being fully present. As they move toward the healthy trait of the Enneagram Three, they find the freedom to use their voice and realize the importance of living their life as well as using their gifts to honor Christ.

Awareness for Nines: You no longer feel the need to shy away from speaking your mind or sharing your ideas, because you are confident in who you are in Christ. You accept that God created you perfectly in the image of Christ and He has made you strong. This week as you meditate on Ephesians 3:16, praise God for the beautiful creation you are. Write down the ways using your voice and valuing yourself has impacted those around you for Christ.

APPLICATION

As you reflect on your Enneagram number this week, how can you identify the areas in your life where you desire to see growth?

_____

_____

_____

How can you begin to change the situations and obstacles that are getting in the way of your Enneagram number's growth track?

_____

_____

_____

How can you have more empathy and compassion for others as you read about how each Enneagram type works toward growth?

_____

_____

_____

What can you celebrate about yourself, knowing God created you in His very image? How are you hearing God speak to you about your journey toward growth?

_____

_____

MEDITATION

Go to page 342 and try the Contemplation Meditation exercise.

My prayer this week:

_____

_____

_____

_____

_____

_____

_____

_____

_____

_____

WEEK 29

"

"FOR I KNOW THE PLANS I HAVE FOR YOU,"
DECLARES THE LORD, "PLANS TO PROSPER
YOU AND NOT TO HARM YOU, PLANS TO GIVE
YOU HOPE AND A FUTURE."

JEREMIAH 29:11

YOUR LONGING
HIS PLANS FOR YOU

YOUR GOD OF THE UNIVERSE IS CUSTOM CRAFTING YOUR FUTURE PLANS.

Do you ever wish you could travel back in time to change something? Maybe you waste time playing the "would have, should have, could have" game. Perhaps you want a do-over for the painful moments, a restart for the heartbreaking times, or a chance to say yes to any missed opportunities. Unfortunately, the simple law of physics prevents you from traveling back in time to change anything, or traveling to the future to control anything. Although you can't change your circumstances, you can change your point of view by turning previous poor decisions into wise teachable moments. This practice keeps you from a hangover of remorse and motivates you to embrace an appreciation for the present. This week fill your days with this declaration of scripture from the Lord. His promises are never empty; they are full of plenty. Plenty of peace in the anxious days, light in the darkest days, safety in the fearful days, joy in the despairing days, and heart in the disheartening days. Your God of the universe is custom crafting your future plans, because He understands your heart's desire for a bright future void of harm and full of His promises of hope.

ONE

ONES desire to hear, "You are good," because these words help them feel safe, secure, accepted, and loved. They spend a lot of time ensuring they are perceived as good to those around them, but this can be exhausting.

Awareness for Ones: As you meditate on Jeremiah 29:11 this week, write down, "You are good," and allow God to speak those words directly to your heart. You matter to God and He has a plan for your life. Embrace this truth, allowing it to bring peace to your days.

TWO

TWOS desire to hear, "You are wanted," because knowing this brings a sense of peace to them. They care for others with a hope and desire that they will be loved and cared for in return. This can cause them to fear rejection is around every corner.

Awareness for Twos: As you meditate on Jeremiah 29:11 this week, can you see just how loved and cared for you are by your heavenly Father? Write down, "You are wanted," and allow yourself to recognize the many ways God has shown you this through His Word and through your life experiences. Embrace God's love for you knowing He has a plan for your life.

THREE

THREES desire to hear, "You are loved for simply being yourself," since hearing these words allows them to stop striving to achieve out of a desire to gain love and acceptance from others. So much of their time and energy is spent trying to figure out how to position themselves to be seen as valuable and worthwhile.

Awareness for a Three: As you meditate on Jeremiah 29:11 this week, embrace the words and claim them for yourself. Write down, "You are loved for simply being you," and embrace this truth, allowing it to bring peace to you as you put your trust in God, knowing He desires to give you a hope and a future.

FOUR

FOURS desire to hear, "You're accepted just as you are." Their feelings of being misunderstood or being called "oversensitive" have caused them to build a hard shell of protection around themselves. Knowing they can be exactly who they are without being judged, ridiculed, or belittled allows them to embrace the way Christ made them.

Awareness for a Four: As you meditate on Jeremiah 29:11 this week, allow yourself to embrace the plans God has for you. Write down, "You are accepted just as you are," and embrace the unique way God made you and His desire for you to prosper in all you do.

FIVE

FIVES desire to hear, "Your needs are not a problem." They often feel the world is unsafe, and therefore, they choose to isolate as a way of self-protection. However, knowing someone cares about their thoughts, desires, hopes, and dreams allows them to live more confidently and comfortably in the world.

Awareness for a Five: As you meditate on Jeremiah 29:11 this week, can you see how much Christ desires to care for you? Write down the words, "Your needs are not too great," and allow God to speak them directly to your heart. His desire is not only for you to prosper in all you do but also He desires to give you hope and a future.

SIX

SIXES desire to hear, "You are safe and protected." Because they can easily detect danger or problems, they stay on high alert, questioning people's motivations and intentions. When they can trust others and know they can count on people, organizations, and institutions, they get a sense of peace and relief.

Awareness for a Six: As you meditate on Jeremiah 29:11 this week, allow yourself to seek the plans God has for you. Write down, "You are safe and protected," and embrace God's Word in the knowledge that he will protect you.

SEVEN

SEVENS desire to hear, "You will be taken care of." When they feel like they don't hear this message, Sevens become fearful of abandonment and tend to keep people at arm's length. Being able to trust that someone will love, protect, and care for them is what they are looking for in their relationships.

Awareness for a Seven: As you meditate on Jeremiah 29:11 this week, recognize that God not only has a plan for you but He also desires to care for you as you pursue your calling. Write down, "You will be taken care of," and write down the ways you desire the Lord to show you He cares for you.

EIGHT

EIGHTS desire to hear, "You will not be betrayed." At times, it can be hard for them to grasp God's desire to protect them. It is important for them to know they can trust in Christ and those close to them and that they will not be made to look like a fool, incompetent, or stupid.

Awareness for an Eight: As you meditate on Jeremiah 29:11 this week, can you see He has a plan for you to prosper in all areas of your life? Write down, "You will not be betrayed," and in your own words elaborate on the many ways God has shown you He is trustworthy in this way.

NINE

NINES desire to hear, "Your presence matters." They struggle with valuing themselves enough to speak up and make their thoughts, ideas, and desires known to others. Knowing they are wanted and that their voice matters to those around them is important.

Awareness for a Nine: As you meditate on Jeremiah 29:11 this week, can you see that God has a purpose and a plan for you? Write down, "Your presence matters," and then elaborate on the ways you can begin to walk out this phrase with confidence knowing God desires to give you a bright future filled with hope.

APPLICATION

As you reflect on your Enneagram number this week, how can you resonate with what your heart longs to hear?

_____

_____

_____

As you begin to understand your Enneagram personality, what are some of the ways you are reassured in knowing God understands the desires of your heart?

_____

_____

_____

_____

In what ways can you relate to some of the other Enneagram reflections this week? Which ones and why?

_____

_____

_____

In what ways do you see your future being filled with God's truth? How are you hearing God speak to you about the plans for your future?

_____

_____

_____

MEDITATION

Go to page 332 and try the Box Breathing exercise.

My prayer this week:

_____

_____

_____

_____

_____

_____

_____

_____

_____

WEEK 30

"

WHATEVER GOD HAS PROMISED GETS STAMPED
WITH THE YES OF JESUS. IN HIM, THIS IS WHAT
WE PREACH AND PRAY, THE GREAT AMEN, GOD'S
YES AND OUR YES TOGETHER, GLORIOUSLY
EVIDENT. GOD AFFIRMS US, MAKING US A SURE
THING IN CHRIST, PUTTING HIS YES WITHIN US.
BY HIS SPIRIT HE HAS STAMPED US WITH HIS
ETERNAL PLEDGE— A SURE BEGINNING OF WHAT
HE IS DESTINED TO COMPLETE.

2 CORINTHIANS 1:20–22 (MSG)

PROMISES
YES, AND AMEN

GOD IS AFFIRMING AN AGREEMENT
WITH YOU—AN "ETERNAL PLEDGE"
MAKING YOU A "SURE THING IN CHRIST."

Yes, and Amen! God's yes and your yes dance together in celebration of all the promises completed and carried out by your heavenly Father who sacrificed His only Son, Jesus. God is affirming an agreement with you—an "eternal pledge" making you a "sure thing in Christ." Your Amen is lifted to the heavens as you give Him the glory and honor for giving you a purposeful life here on earth and the promise of eternity in heaven. Standing on God's promise allows you to take a deep breath and release the pressure of trying to figure out life on your own. When you understand that God's promises have been fulfilled by Christ's death on the cross, you can release the grip of fear the Enemy uses to try to control you. All that is required from you is aligning your life with the Word of God and acting in obedience to His Word, for this is your "Amen" lifted to heaven. This week think about all that your Provider has given you that is worth celebrating! "Shout to the LORD, all the earth; break out in praise and sing for joy!" (Psalm 98:4, NLT)

ONE

When **ONES** are spiritually connected to the promise of God's eternal salvation, they can live a principled life. They are hardworking and ethical while looking out for the well-being of others.

Awareness for Ones: You will find joy in the process, along with a feeling of freedom, as you no longer feel the weight of the world on your shoulders. This week as you meditate on 2 Corinthians 1:20–22, pray for guidance and wisdom as you seek to align yourself with the Word of God. Write down how God's promise of eternal salvation has impacted your life.

TWO

When **TWOS** are spiritually connected to the promise of God's agape love, they are affirming, supportive, and openhearted. Once they are confident of God's care for others, they will no longer feel the need to rescue others from their circumstances.

Awareness for Twos: When you take the time to nurture yourself, you can embrace yourself and better care for others. This week as you meditate on 2 Corinthians 1:20–22, pray for your heart to continue to be supportive of others as you seek God's grace and validation through His Word. Write down how God's unconditional love has reshaped your life.

THREE

When **THREES** are spiritually connected to God's promise of hope, they know they are beloved. They are optimistic, energetic, and empowering. They have a desire to be a person of integrity and strong character.

Awareness for Threes: You can embrace your leadership abilities when you put your hope in God. This week as you meditate on 2 Corinthians 1:20–22, pray for vision and direction as you passionately pursue your purpose. Write down a few ways in which putting your hope in the Lord has allowed you to find freedom in your life.

FOUR

When **FOURS** are spiritually connected to the promise of God's compassion, they live more sincerely. As they embrace their originality, expressiveness, and creativity, they truly come alive.

Awareness for Fours: You can find freedom as you embrace the rise and fall of your emotions. This week as you meditate on 2 Corinthians 1:20–22, pray for empathy and sincerity as you are reminded of God's kindness. Draw a picture that expresses how you feel as you embrace the life of love and compassion the Lord has for you.

FIVE

When **FIVES** are spiritually connected to the promise of God's provision, they are insightful and sensitive. They rest in knowing their security comes from the Lord.

Awareness for Fives: You can continue to build trusting relationships even if you don't know the outcome. This week as you meditate on 2 Corinthians 1:20–22, pray for perseverance as you are reminded of God's sufficiency. Write down the many ways God has provided for you during seasons of difficulty.

SIX

When **SIXES** are spiritually connected to the promises of God's protection, they can trust that God covers all contingencies. They are responsible and determined and no longer allow fear to cause them stress.

Awareness for Sixes: As you trust that God will take care of you and all the details happening in your life, you feel relaxed and settled in your spirit. This week as you meditate on 2 Corinthians 1:20–22, pray for courage and strength. Place both feet on the floor and draw in deep breaths; as you slowly exhale, also release any worry and tension you are carrying in your body.

_____

_____

_____

_____

_____

_____

_____

_____

_____

_____

_____

_____

_____

_____

_____

_____

_____

_____

_____

SEVEN

When **SEVENS** are spiritually connected to the promises of God's joy, they find contentment in their day-to-day life. They embrace the simplicity around them and bless others with their zest for life.

Awareness for Sevens: You are highly aware of how your life experiences tie directly to the Creator of the universe. This week as you meditate on 2 Corinthians 1:20–22, pray for clear vision as you seek to align yourself with God's limitless possibilities for your life. Write down how embracing God's joy enables you to reclaim your ability to find wonder in the simple pleasures of life.

EIGHT

When **EIGHTS** are spiritually connected to the promises of God's strength, they find freedom in expressing their struggles, knowing others will appreciate their vulnerability. They are also empowering, inspiring, and willing to stand up against injustice.

Awareness for Eights: You can encourage others to rise up and not let anyone or anything hold them back from their calling and passion. This week as you meditate on 2 Corinthians 1:20–22, pray for wisdom and compassion as you empower others around you. Write down how God's strength has given you the courage to be fully known.

NINE

When **NINES** are spiritually connected to the promises of God's unity, they are content, receptive, and unpretentious. They live their lives in harmony with all and value the point of view of others as well as their own.

Awareness for Nines: You are diplomatic and open-minded. You see the value and self-worth of others and respect their different perspectives. This week as you meditate on 2 Corinthians 1:20–22, pray for patience as you are reminded of God's solidarity. Head outdoors in nature and allow yourself to see the many ways God is orchestrating unity in every living thing around you.

APPLICATION

As you reflect on your Enneagram number this week, can you see how embracing God's promises for your life allows you to live with joy and freedom?

_____

_____

_____

How are you able to activate what you have read in your Enneagram reflection as you move forward with a clearer vision and purpose?

_____

_____

_____

In what ways can you encourage those in your life to become more spiritually connected after reading the Enneagram reflections?

_____

_____

_____

What does it mean to you that God's promise has been fulfilled by Christ's death on the cross? How are you hearing God speak to you when it comes to His promises?

_____

_____

_____

MEDITATION

Go to page 334 and try the Concentration Meditation exercise.

My prayer this week:

_____

_____

_____

_____

_____

_____

_____

_____

_____

_____

_____

_____

WEEK 31

"

NOW GLORY BE TO GOD, WHO BY HIS
MIGHTY POWER AT WORK WITHIN US IS ABLE
TO DO FAR MORE THAN WE WOULD EVER
DARE TO ASK OR EVEN DREAM OF—INFINITELY
BEYOND OUR HIGHEST PRAYERS, DESIRES,
THOUGHTS, OR HOPES.

EPHESIANS 3:20 (TLB)

YOUR MOUNTAINTOP
BEYOND YOUR DREAMS

GOD'S MIGHTY POWER IS WORKING INSIDE YOU, AND HIS SPIRIT WITHIN YOU IS STRONGER THAN YOU CAN IMAGINE.

In this moment of your life, whether you are feeling weak beyond words or filled with strength beyond measure, be assured that when you lift your voice to God, you can humbly ask Him to accomplish anything you desire! Your Jehovah Jireh, God your Provider, is accomplishing far more for you than even your heart can fathom, surpassing the indescribable. Why? Because God's mighty power is working inside you, and His spirit within you is stronger than you can imagine. When you seek the King of kings first, your life aligns with Him because it is found in His truth as it is written in the Scriptures. When you ground yourself in His truth through the Word of God, you will find that no matter your current season, God can do the unstoppable with you and through you. This week as you are reading the Word and praying in accord with the spirit of God, dare to dream as high as you can conceive, "Now glory be to God." And when you get to that point on the mountaintop, dream even higher. His miracles are happening in your life, right here, right now. Watch as He performs mountain-moving moments through His mighty power.

ONE

When **ONES** grow in spiritual awareness toward their personal mountaintop, they desire to experience excellence in life. They envision an ideal world in which there is no brokenness or sickness. They use their energy and resources to make the world a better place.

Awareness for Ones: When you find your identity in God, you will no longer feel the need to strive for righteousness. You will feel empowered by His Spirit to make a difference in the world for the better. This week as you meditate on Ephesians 3:20, write this prayer and make it a declaration for your life: "Lord, I lay my life at Your feet and trust that You are working all things out for the good of all who love and serve You. I pray for eyes to see the world through Your vision and a heart that is aligned with that which You desire here on earth. Use me as a living vessel to show others Your love."

TWO

When **TWOS** grow in spiritual awareness toward their personal mountaintop, they are genuinely interested in the health and well-being of others. They do things out of the goodness of their heart without hoping for anything in return. They are caring and giving. They willingly share their resources, time, and energy with others.

Awareness for Twos: When you find your identity in God, you will no longer feel the need to strive for attention, believing it will fill a void. You can grasp God's power at work within you and shower people around you with unconditional love and support. This week as you meditate on Ephesians 3:20, write the following prayer and make it a declaration for your life: "Lord, I come before You asking You to fill me with endless love and compassion. Help me to love others from a place of humility and thanksgiving. Use me to share Your love and nurture to all I come into contact with."

THREE

When **THREES** grow in spiritual awareness toward their personal mountaintop, they see the world and its endless possibilities. They see potential in every person and mobilize others to use the gifts and talents placed within them. They bring positive advancement to the world through their many achievements.

Awareness for Threes: When you find your identity in God, you will no longer feel the need to strive for affirmation, believing it will position you for success. You can see how God uses the many talents within you to advance His kingdom. This week as you meditate on Ephesians 3:20, write the following prayer and make it a declaration for your life: "Lord show me Your magnificent ways. Open my eyes to Your wonders. Fill me with hope as I go into the world and use the gifts You have placed within. Help me to be an encouragement to others."

FOUR

When **FOURS** grow in spiritual awareness toward their personal mountaintop, they see everyone and everything as sacred and special. They are incredibly attuned to the beauty that lies within every aspect and creation here on earth. They long for others to experience life in the same way.

Awareness for Fours: When you can grasp the magnificence of this world and the important role you play in it, you will understand your true value. This week as you meditate on Ephesians 3:20, write the following prayer and make it a declaration for your life: "Lord, You are marvelous, and Your creation is breathtaking. Help me to grasp Your infinite love as I witness the beauty all around me. Teach me to share with others Your wisdom and love."

FIVE

When **FIVES** grow in spiritual awareness toward their personal mountaintop, they use their keen observations to bring clarity and simplicity to difficult or confusing situations. They have a deep discernment and are full of wisdom. When they share their knowledge with the world, they often bring new ideas and approaches that have not yet been explored.

Awareness for Fives: You are brilliant and important to the kingdom of God. This week as you meditate on Ephesians 3:20, write the following prayer and make it a declaration for your life: "God of the universe, fill me with Your knowledge and wisdom. Teach me your ways and help me to see You in every situation. Allow me to share with others the many fascinating concepts I have learned through studying the Word of God."

SIX

When **SIXES** grow in spiritual awareness toward their personal mountaintop, they find themselves safe in the shelter of the Most High. They are confident in their abilities because they are anchored in the Lord. They have a solid faith and a trustworthy spirit that draws others to them as they enjoy providing support and guidance for all.

Awareness for Sixes: When you are in a partnership with the Lord of lords and you can live confidently secure in Him. This week as you meditate on Ephesians 3:20, write the following prayer and make it a declaration for your life: "Lord, as I anchor my life to You and walk out my days according to Your word, give me strength and courage. I pray for knowledge as I take on new challenges, as I desire to work alongside people. Use me to show others how You are loving and safe."

SEVEN

When **SEVENS** grow in spiritual awareness toward their personal mountaintop, they are catalysts for joy, and they dream about the endless possibilities. They love to learn about new ideas, explore new information, and gather interesting facts. Their enthusiasm is contagious to those around them.

Awareness for Sevens: When you find your identity in God, you will no longer feel the need to fear limitations and boundaries, because you view them as healthy guidelines for you to live safely. This week as you meditate on Ephesians 3:20, write the following prayer and make it a declaration for your life: "Lord, I worship You and praise You. You are worthy of all of the glory. I pray for insight and understanding as I explore Your beautiful creation. Fill me with new ideas and bring people into my life who will walk alongside me as I accomplish what You have put in my heart."

EIGHT

When **EIGHTS** grow in spiritual awareness toward their personal mountaintop, they are full of passion and purpose. They desire to empower the powerless and mobilize others to take on injustices. They are fun and inspiring and can create movements for positive change in the world.

Awareness for Eights: When you find your identity in God, you no longer feel the need to lead with control. You embrace the passion Christ has put inside you and use it to make an impact on the world. This week as you meditate on Ephesians 3:20, write the following prayer and make it a declaration for your life: "Lord, thank You for giving me strength and wisdom. Help me to use it for your glory. Allow me to sense Your movement for justice and join You in making a difference in the world."

NINE

When **NINES** grow in spiritual awareness toward their personal mountaintop, they have clarity about what they desire to pursue. They move forward in this endeavor, focused on the contribution they believe they will be making to the world. Since they do not function with a hidden agenda, they allow others to feel safe to engage and join them as they make an impact on society.

Awareness for Nines: When you find your identity in God, you will no longer feel invaluable. You are excited about the possibilities that lie ahead and energized about playing an important part for change. This week as you meditate on Ephesians 3:20, write the following prayer and make it a declaration for your life: "Lord, go before me and guide me. Give me ears to hear what it is You are saying to me. Give me the confidence to walk in the calling You have for me so that I might make a difference for Your Kingdom here on earth."

APPLICATION

As you reflect on your Enneagram number this week, how are you growing in spiritual awareness?

_____

_____

_____

What positive traits did you discover about yourself after reading your Enneagram number this week?

_____

_____

_____

In what ways are you able to recognize the beautiful spiritual awareness of those in your life after reading the other Enneagram reflections?

_____

_____

_____

What have you been able to do through God, far more than you could have done on your own? How are you hearing God speak to you about your mountaintop?

_____

_____

_____

♥ MEDITATION

Go to page 336 and try the Reflection Meditation exercise.

My prayer this week:

_____

_____

_____

_____

_____

_____

_____

_____

_____

WEEK 32

"

GUIDE ME IN YOUR TRUTH AND TEACH
ME, FOR YOU ARE GOD MY SAVIOR,
AND MY HOPE IS IN YOU ALL DAY LONG.

PSALM 25:5

DIVINE ATTRIBUTES
TEACHER OF TRUTH

WHEN YOU EMBRACE YOUR ATTRIBUTES
AND SHOW THEM OFF TO THE WORLD,
YOU ALSO SHOW CHRIST TO THE WORLD.

If you are feeling insignificant today or insecure in your abilities, look toward your heavenly Guide, the God of all creation. You, like all of us, have been given divine attributes uniquely crafted from the Maker of heaven and earth. Your beautifully designed qualities could include your joy, goodness, creativity, generosity, or even your spirit of peace. Because you reflect Christ, when you embrace your attributes and show them off to the world, you also show Christ to the world. After all, each Enneagram number reflects an aspect of God's character, since you were created directly from His image. One way to display your unique nature is to grab on to your Savior's truth. Continue embracing the spiritual discipline of studying the Scriptures and keeping His desire deep inside your soul. Just as feeding your body healthy nutrition fuels your energy, feeding your soul with the truth of His Word fuels your faith in the Lord. For Jesus declared himself the Bread of Life. Stay hungry and grounded in His wisdom. Ask for guidance from your Teacher and fill your spirit full of His continual hope.

——— ONE ———

The characteristic of God reflected by **ONES** is goodness. They seek truth through the Word of God, and they can let go of control and display character and integrity. This exemplifies rightness, which draws others to Christ.

Awareness for Ones: This week as you meditate on Psalm 25:5, ask God to guide you in truth as you put your hope in Him continuously. Write down the following scripture and be hopeful in the reminder that your goodness comes from the Lord: "Surely your goodness and love will follow me all the days of my life, and I will dwell in the house of the LORD forever" (Psalm 23:6).

——— TWO ———

The characteristic of God reflected by **TWOS** is nurture. They seek truth through the Word of God and show compassion to the world through their divine attribute of love. They express care and concern to those around them from a place of humility.

Awareness for Twos: This week as you meditate on Psalm 25:5, ask God to guide you in truth as you put your hope in Him continuously. Write down the following scripture and be hopeful in the reminder that your love and nature come from the Lord: "Above all, love each other deeply, because love covers over a multitude of sins" (1 Peter 4:8).

——— THREE ———

The characteristic of God reflected by **THREES** is hope. They seek truth through the Word of God and can let go of the fear of incompetence and show the world who Christ is through their divine attribute of radiance. They believe that life is worth living to the fullest.

Awareness for Threes: This week as you meditate on Psalm 25:5, ask God to guide you in truth as you put your hope in Him continuously. Write down the following scripture to remind yourself that your hope comes from the Lord: "May your unfailing love be with us, LORD, even as we put our hope in you" (Psalm 33:22).

FOUR

The characteristic of God reflected by **FOURS** is creativity. They seek truth through the Word of God and can offer gratitude to the world and show who Christ is through their divine attribute of emotional depth. They display an authentic and sincere perspective to the world.

Awareness for Fours: This week as you meditate on Psalm 25:5, ask God to guide you in truth as you put your hope in Him continuously. Write down the following scripture and be hopeful in the reminder that your creativity comes from the Lord: "It is he who made the earth by his power, who established the world by his wisdom, and by his understanding stretched out the heavens" (Jeremiah 10:12, ESV).

FIVE

The characteristic of God reflected by **FIVES** is truth. They seek knowledge through the Word of God and can let go of cynicism and show the world who Christ is through their divine attribute of wisdom. They gather facts and grow in deep understanding about a variety of topics.

Awareness for Fives: This week as you meditate on Psalm 25:5, ask God to guide you in truth as you put your hope in Him continuously. Write down the following scripture and be hopeful in the reminder that your wisdom comes from the Lord: "If any of you lacks wisdom, you should ask God, who gives generously to all without finding fault, and it will be given to you" (James 1:25).

SIX

The characteristic of God reflected by **SIXES** is faithfulness. They seek truth through the Word of God and can let go of doubt and show the world who Christ is through their divine attribute of courage. They do what is right, even in the face of fear.

Awareness for Sixes: This week as you meditate on Psalm 25:5, ask God to guide you in truth as you put your hope in Him continuously. Write down the following scripture and be hopeful in the reminder that your courage comes from the Lord: "I thank Christ Jesus our Lord, who has given me strength, that he considered me trustworthy, appointing me to his service" (1 Timothy 1:12).

Notes

SEVEN

The characteristic of God reflected by **SEVENS** is abundance. They seek truth through the Word of God, and they are able to let go of impulsivity and show the world who Christ is through their divine attribute of joy. They express happiness and excitement.

Awareness for Sevens: This week as you meditate on Psalm 25:5, ask God to guide you in truth as you put your hope in Him continuously. Write down the following scripture and be hopeful in the reminder that your joy comes from the Lord: "I have told you this so that my joy may be in you and that your joy may be complete" (John 15:11).

EIGHT

The characteristic of God reflected by **EIGHTS** is strength. They seek truth through the Word of God, and they are able to let go of excessiveness and show the world who Christ is through their divine attribute of protection. They fight for the underdog and care for those in need.

Awareness for Eights: This week as you meditate on Psalm 25:5, ask God to guide you in truth as you put your hope in Him continuously. Write down the following scripture and be hopeful as you are reminded your protection comes from the Lord: "But the Lord is faithful, and he will strengthen you and protect you from the evil one" (2 Thessalonians 3:3).

NINE

The characteristic of God reflected by **NINES** is oneness. They seek truth through the Word of God; they can let go of appeasing people and show the world who Christ is through their divine attribute of harmony. They bring a calmness wherever they go. This display of peace draws others to Christ.

Awareness for Nines: This week as you meditate on Psalm 25:5, ask God to guide you in truth as you put your hope in Him continuously. Write down the following scripture and be hopeful as you are reminded that your peace comes from the Lord: "And the peace of God, which transcends all understanding, will guard your hearts and your minds in Christ Jesus" (Philippians 4:7).

APPLICATION

As you reflect on your Enneagram number this week, what did you discover about your divine attribute?

_____

_____

_____

How do you feel you display your number's characteristic of God to the world?

_____

_____

_____

After reading the Enneagram reflections, in what ways can you support those you care for in a new way now that you understand their divine attributes?

_____

_____

_____

How can you put your hope in God continually? How are you hearing God speak to you about the ways you reflect Him to the world?

_____

_____

_____

MEDITATION

Go to page 342 and try the Contemplation exercise.

My prayer this week:

_____

_____

_____

_____

_____

_____

_____

_____

_____

_____

WEEK 33

"

USE YOUR FREEDOM TO SERVE ONE ANOTHER
IN LOVE; THAT'S HOW FREEDOM GROWS.
FOR EVERYTHING WE KNOW ABOUT GOD'S
WORD IS SUMMED UP IN A SINGLE SENTENCE:
LOVE OTHERS AS YOU LOVE YOURSELF.
THAT'S AN ACT OF TRUE FREEDOM. IF YOU BITE
AND RAVAGE EACH OTHER, WATCH OUT— IN
NO TIME AT ALL YOU WILL BE ANNIHILATING
EACH OTHER, AND WHERE WILL YOUR
PRECIOUS FREEDOM BE THEN?

GALATIANS 5:14-15 (MSG)

RELATIONSHIPS
FREEDOM GROWS

WHEN YOUR ACTIONS MATCH WHAT GOD CREATED YOU TO DO, YOUR HEART WILL FIND TRUE FREEDOM.

The idea of people "ravaging" or "annihilating" each other certainly is disturbing. Thankfully, you can counteract this feeling if it arises by focusing instead on loving others as you love yourself, by responding with selflessness and rejecting an egocentric view of the world—one in which you see yourself at the center of everything. Repeatedly, the Bible commands us to love and serve others before ourselves. The truth is, when you serve, you are the one being blessed, as your heart feels amazingly full and your spirit is brought back to life. This is simply because God created you to help others. An inwardly focused view is binding and repressing. You experience the free life when you are deliberately thinking beyond yourself and pouring time, effort, empathy, and kindness into your relationships. When your actions match what God created you to do, your heart will find true freedom and an ability to love and be loved.

ONE

When **ONES** can accept their loved ones as they are without trying to fix them, they will feel a deep connection and true enjoyment in their relationships. There is true freedom when they can accept other people's points of view and different perspectives.

Awareness for Ones: When you realize you are capable of loving, serving, and understanding people, no matter their circumstances and differences, you will find joy in your relationships. This week as you meditate on Galatians 5:14-15, journal about areas of your life where you need to release judgment and instead extend love and acceptance.

TWO

When **TWOS** are in secure relationships, they can love unconditionally and give sacrificially. As they disclose their needs, wants, and desires with those close to them, they can relax and feel deeply connected to them. This allows their relationships to grow in comfort and depth.

Awareness for Twos: You can embrace yourself when you realize you are capable of being loved and understood by others. When you truthfully express your needs, you are also willing to serve people well with compassion. This week as you meditate on Galatians 5:14-15, journal about how you can release the desire to appear flawless and where you need to extend grace for yourself.

THREE

When **THREES** share their honest feelings and emotions in their relationships, they will find a freedom in their soul they truly desire. They will no longer find it necessary to wear a mask of disguise to create an image they deem worthy of affirmation. Unveiling their true self allows them to share their lives and serve others in a transparent and authentic way.

Awareness for Threes: When you realize you are worth loving, not because of your achievements and accolades but because you are God's amazing creation, you are able to open up to people close to you. You will then be comfortable sharing your true thoughts and motivations. This week as you meditate on Galatians 5:14-15, journal about the areas in your life where you need to be honest with your emotions instead of trying to hide them.

FOUR

When **FOURS** let down their walls of protection and trust that their loved ones will accept them without casting judgment, their relationships will richly improve. They will feel secure and free while being able to serve and cherish others without constantly comparing their own flaws and weaknesses with everyone else.

Awareness for Fours: When you realize you do not have to live a life ashamed because you are not like everyone else, you can embrace the fact you are different. You can accept yourself and others with love and compassion. This week as you meditate on Galatians 5:14-15, journal about the areas of your life where you have felt shamed and judged. Then, release all of those moments over to God.

FIVE

When **FIVES** let their loved ones into their lives by sharing their passions and ideas, they find true joy and comfort. They realize they can open up in their relationships enjoying life with others, and this brings freedom and contentment to their lives.

Awareness for Fives: When you invite people into your life in a way that leaves them feeling valued and seen, you can understand the importance of community and deep relationships. This week as you meditate on Galatians 5:14-15, journal about the areas and situations going on in your life that you need to share with others instead of keeping them closed off and private.

SIX

When **SIXES** can cast aside their suspicions and embrace the relationships in their lives, they thrive in community. Because they are dependable companions, they seek only loyal friends they can rely on and trust.

Awareness for Sixes: When you can trust that the people around you mean what they say and say what they mean, you can respect and commit to those friendships. This week as you meditate on Galatians 5:14-15, journal about times in your life when you have trusted others and they have then become true and close friends.

Notes

SEVEN

When **SEVENS** slow down and focus on the relationships in their lives, they find connection with others and internal contentment. They learn to stay present in the moment and value friendships. They seek out people who are loving, caring, and willing to be adventurous with them, enjoying their same zest for life.

Awareness for Sevens: When you value people and give them your full attention, you gain the benefit of community and the richness of authentic relationships. This week as you meditate on Galatians 5:14–15, journal about ways you can stay emotionally present in your relationships.

EIGHT

When **EIGHTS** allow others to be exactly who they are without trying to project their own ideas, agendas, or plans onto them, they find deep, meaningful connections in their relationships. As they learn the importance of letting others express their own thoughts, feelings, and opinions, they find beauty in letting people around them shine and succeed.

Awareness for Eights: When you embrace other people's ideas and opinions, you release the burden of feeling as if you need to be in control of the conversation and situation, because you laid down your power and took up love. This week as you meditate on Galatians 5:14–15, journal about the aspects in your relationships that you need to stop trying to control.

NINE

When **NINES** value their own thoughts and opinions in their relationships, they bring a sense of calm and hope into every conversation. They no longer feel the need to shrink back to keep the peace, but instead they stay fully present and engaged in conversation. This brings everyone together.

Awareness for Nines: When you value your self-worth, you openly share your thoughts and ideas, confidently knowing you are fully accepted. This week as you meditate on Galatians 5:14–15, journal about the areas in your life where you need to speak up and use your voice more.

APPLICATION

In what ways can you connect deeper in your current relationships?

_____

_____

_____

How has reading your Enneagram reflection challenged you to embrace your loved ones in a new and meaningful way?

_____

_____

_____

After reading the Enneagram reflections, in what ways can you better understand how others in your life handle your relationship with them?

_____

_____

_____

How are you loving and serving others? How are you hearing God speak to you about your current relationships?

_____

_____

_____

MEDITATION

Go to page 332 and try the Box Breathing exercise.

My prayer this week:

_____

_____

_____

_____

_____

_____

_____

_____

_____

_____

WEEK 34

"

BUT THE WISDOM FROM ABOVE IS
FIRST PURE, THEN PEACEABLE, GENTLE,
OPEN TO REASON, FULL OF MERCY
AND GOOD FRUITS, IMPARTIAL AND SINCERE.
AND A HARVEST OF RIGHTEOUSNESS
IS SOWN IN PEACE BY THOSE
WHO MAKE PEACE.

JAMES 3:17–18 (ESV)

PEACE
WISDOM FROM ABOVE

DEPEND ON GOD'S MERCY,
GENTLENESS, SINCERITY,
AND DAILY PEACE.

What brings you peace daily? Before you answer that, take a moment and briefly think about scenarios that cause you feelings of angst or stress. In a world in which we have faced a pandemic, it is common to experience fear, anxiety, and exasperation, and sometimes it feels as if you are living in a tempest of chaos. However, when you feel that way, reach for scripture full of wisdom from your heavenly Father. Whether you are tempted to withdraw, escape, self-protect, or bulldoze your way through challenges, when you are tethered to God's Word, you can easily exchange your self-reliance with a reliance on God. Depend on His mercy, gentleness, sincerity, and daily peace. Then take all His good fruits and become a peace ambassador, confidently spreading peace around you. Notice all the great reasons to be open to God's reasoning.

━━━━━━━━━ ONE ━━━━━━━━━

ONES process information through yielding. They yield to social norms, which are the unwritten guidelines they expect all of us to follow. They align themselves with people of integrity, character, and strong values, in an effort to feel at peace and secure in the world.

Awareness for Ones: This week as you meditate on James 3:17–18, seek first God's wisdom in all your situations. Take account of how you have processed information in the past. Write down the ways in which aligning your life with Scripture has allowed you to feel secure in your decision-making skills.

━━━━━━━━━ TWO ━━━━━━━━━

TWOS process information by acting in agreement with others. They find peace and security by forming their opinions while first watching what others are doing to learn what's acceptable. They are relationship-oriented and agreeable as a way to stay safe and feel secure.

Awareness for Twos: This week as you meditate on James 3:17–18, allow yourself to realize the blessing you are to others by being gentle and full of mercy. Journal your thoughts about how being peaceful has had a positive impact on those around you.

━━━━━━━━━ THREE ━━━━━━━━━

THREES process information by determining the most efficient and successful ways to accomplish their goals. They are assertive with others and go after what they desire by being task-oriented, since they want to make a major impact on the world. They find peace when they can craft a creative plan and execute it with excellence.

Awareness for Threes: This week as you meditate on James 3:17–18, allow yourself to see the importance of seeking the wisdom of God. Write down the ways your impartial and sincere approach has helped you produce good fruit through your relationships and achievements.

FOUR

FOURS process information by withdrawing and moving away from others as a way of self-protection. They are afraid to be too emotional for fear of being considered dramatic and irrational. What brings them peace is being given space to quietly process their thoughts before they can verbally express them.

Awareness for Fours: This week as you meditate on James 3:17–18, embrace the wisdom of God. Allowing yourself to process your feelings and thoughts before reacting allows you to respond in a calm and kind way. When you think about responding peacefully, write down the words that resonate with you.

FIVE

FIVES process information by being reserved and calm. They tend to find peace and security when they retreat into their private space. Since they are not reactionary, they take time to figure out wise solutions to difficult situations. They tend to hold back their emotions until they have had a chance to sit with their thoughts, since they prefer to understand how they feel and think.

Awareness for Fives: This week as you meditate on James 3:17–18, embrace your God-given gifts that allow you to bring peace to all situations as you seek wisdom from your heavenly Father. This week ask God to reveal the ways you have shown those around you mercy and grace through your even-tempered responses.

SIX

SIXES process information by verbally discussing with others. This gives them a feeling of peace and security as they bounce ideas and troubleshoot with those they trust. They prefer to collaborate with others, rather than tackling tasks or figuring out situations on their own.

Awareness for Sixes: This week as you meditate on James 3:17–18, praise God for his infinite wisdom and loving mercy in giving you the ability to be a great team player. Write down the times you have been open to reason while welcoming other ideas and opinions.

Notes

SEVEN

SEVENS process information through enterprising since they are innovative in creating a unique path for their lives. What brings them peace is being able to follow their passions without limitations. This assertiveness allows them to take calculated risks by trying new things and being adventurous.

Awareness for Sevens: This week as you meditate on James 3:17–18, allow yourself to embrace the idea of Godly wisdom bringing peace in all circumstances in your life. You like to ask the questions "Why not?" and "How will this impact the world around me?" Write down the ways you can show others true sincerity and impartiality.

EIGHT

EIGHTS process information through ambition. They go after what they want with passion and purpose. What brings them peace and security is the ability to visualize the big picture and then delegate and execute the plan of action to accomplish it and move it forward.

Awareness for Eights: This week as you meditate on James 3:17–18, ask yourself how you can lean into God's wisdom and establish more peaceful communication with others. Write down how you can communicate with others through mercy and grace.

NINE

NINES process information by being self-contained. They prefer to rely on their own abilities, thoughts, and ideas. They find peace and security when their environments and relationships are harmonious. This allows them to withdraw in a healthy way and process information without being reactionary.

Awareness for Nines: This week as you meditate on James 3:17–18, recognize the importance of your intentions, being pure and sincere in situations and relationships. Write down the ways you find peace when you are comfortable sharing how you truly feel with those close to you.

APPLICATION

What did you learn about the way you process information this week?

_____

_____

_____

How does the way in which you respond and process information shape the way you experience peace?

_____

_____

_____

After reading the Enneagram reflections, in what ways have you become aware of how others respond and process information?

_____

_____

_____

How are you embracing James 3:17–18 and becoming a peace ambassador?

_____

_____

_____

MEDITATION

Go to page 334 and try the Concentration Meditation exercise.

My prayer this week:

_____

_____

_____

_____

_____

_____

_____

_____

_____

WEEK 35

"

"I WILL REMEMBER THE DEEDS OF THE LORD;
YES, I WILL REMEMBER YOUR MIRACLES
OF LONG AGO. I WILL CONSIDER ALL YOUR
WORKS AND MEDITATE ON ALL YOUR MIGHTY
DEEDS." YOUR WAYS, GOD, ARE HOLY.
WHAT GOD IS AS GREAT AS OUR GOD?

PSALM 77:11-13

THE YOUNGER YOU
REMEMBER LONG AGO

GOD KNOWS EACH TONE OF YOUR VOICE AND BEAT OF YOUR HEART'S DESIRES.

You long to do what matters and aspire to matter to others. You long to build healthy relationships and build a legacy of purpose. Yet, sometimes, shame about your past and patterns of behavior you adopted at a very young age distract you. To counteract these tendencies, meditate in the presence of the Almighty, for His miracles and mercies are new each morning. When you long for acceptance, perfection, or someone's attention, recall your one true relationship that's never transactional. Your Father in heaven is the conductor of your orchestra. He knows each tone of your voice and beat of your heart's desires—and in Him, there's never a false note. He will not ask you to count your mistakes or list your shortcomings. Rather He expects you to just rest in His grace, His miracles, and His mighty ways. You never have to act in a way to earn His Love or work toward His acceptance. This week meditate on all His truths about you and remain inspired by the sound of His beautiful symphony of scriptures: "The Lord your God is with you, the Mighty Warrior who saves. He will take great delight in you; in his love he will no longer rebuke you, but will rejoice over you with singing" (Zephaniah 3:17).

ONE

From a very young age, **ONES** felt they must be responsible and serious. They worked hard and tried to protect themselves; therefore, their character and integrity are never brought into question. As children, they received praise and acceptance for being on their best behavior, keeping things neat and clean, getting good grades, and staying out of trouble. They began to believe that through this type of good behavior, they would receive love.

Awareness for Ones: The kingdom of God is holy and great, and you do not have to "earn" your heavenly Father's love and grace. This week take time to meditate on Psalm 77:11–13 and the goodness of God, knowing there is no other god as good as yours. Write down the ways He has shown you his grace, regardless of your actions.

TWO

From a very young age, **TWOS** believed they must earn love and affection. They felt they had to work hard to be what others needed them to be in hopes of being liked, valued, and wanted. As children, they helped out around the house and took the initiative whenever they noticed something needed to be done. They thought that sacrificing their own wants, desires, and needs would eventually be rewarded with acceptance.

Awareness for Twos: You are accepted through the grace of God because He loves you just for being exactly how He created you. This week take time to meditate on Psalm 77:11–13 and the goodness of God, knowing there is no other god as good as yours. Write down all the ways you can share with God and others your honest thoughts, feelings, and opinions without the fear of rejection.

THREE

From a very young age, **THREES** often played the role of the family hero. They felt it was not okay to express hurt, sadness, or their true emotions, but rather they acted strong by always trying to save the day. As children, they recognized what the people closest to them valued and then performed to their high expectations. They often disassociated with their own hopes, dreams, and desires out of the belief that their feelings were unacceptable. For Threes to feel love and acceptance, they think they need to conform to how others think they should act.

Awareness for Threes: You are welcome just as you are through the grace of God because He loves you. There is no need to deny your feelings, thoughts, or hopes, because the God of miracles is on your side. This week take time to meditate on Psalm 77:11–13 and be reminded of the many ways He has paved new paths for you to walk. Make a list of your hopes and dreams and place them before the throne.

FOUR

FOURS sense they are different from their family members. As children they always struggled with the feeling of being misunderstood. Often, they weren't accepted by their peers because they wouldn't conform to social norms. However, because being true to themselves always matters more to them than pleasing others, they embrace their creativity and differences and find comfort with being themselves.

Awareness for Fours: When you accept Christ as your Lord and Savior, you are welcomed into the kingdom with open arms and are loved for simply being you, along with all your creativity and differences. You can't earn your way there or work harder to get God to love you any more than He already does. This week take time to meditate on Psalm 77:11–13 and the goodness of God. Write down all the ways He has walked with you through your highs and your lows and describe what you have learned along the way.

FIVE

FIVES are often afraid of being overwhelmed by the demands placed on them by their family members. When they were children, they tried to take care of their own needs, asking little from those around them. They kept to themselves and welcomed quiet and privacy. They would often suppress their emotional needs and try to fill the void with their vivid imagination or personal hobbies.

Awareness for Fives: The kingdom of God is different in that you don't have to earn your way there. When you accept Christ as your Lord and Savior, you and all your needs are welcomed into the kingdom. This is the miracle of salvation. This week as you meditate on Psalm 77:11–13, praise God for knowing exactly who you are and what you need. Write down the cares and concerns you have, for He is never bothered by your desires and wants you to lift them up to Him.

SIX

SIXES have a desire to feel supported but at the same time not overwhelmed and controlled. As children, they would often test authority and those around them to see if they truly were trustworthy. They would ask themselves, "Will they really do what they say they are going to do? Do these people really have my back?" They often appear outwardly cooperative yet inwardly rebellious.

Awareness for Sixes: When you reflect on what God has done to rescue you, all you can do is fall at His feet and worship Him. This week take time to meditate on Psalm 77:11–13 and be reminded of His many deeds and that you can trust His Word. He will never falter or fluctuate. Pray He will renew your mind and give you a deeper sense of knowing you are found in Him and Him alone. You are safe in the arms of your Savior.

SEVEN

SEVENS learned to self-soothe early on in their lives. They used creative play and imagination to calm their anxieties and need for emotional support. As children, they would do whatever it took to keep people happy because—after all—everyone likes fun and happy people. They look for adventure and stimulation to feel alive and free.

Awareness for Sevens: The miracle of salvation is you are loved and cared for by your heavenly Father by simply accepting Him as your Lord and Savior. You don't have to earn your way or prove you are worth loving or be fun or happy to be accepted by Him. You are simply received through the grace of God. This week as you take time to meditate on Psalm 77:11–13, be reminded of the many miracles you have witnessed in your own life. Write down all the ways your heavenly Father has shown you how He has been at work in your life, orchestrating all things for your good.

EIGHT

EIGHTS learned early on that being strong meant being in control. As children, they were adventurous and assertive. They liked to be in charge, so they knew how things were going to go and didn't have to be surprised. They didn't like to rely on others or have restrictions put on them. They preferred never to be vulnerable in any way, because having control gave them a sense of security.

Awareness for Eights: The kingdom of God is different in that you don't have to push your way in. When you grasp His infinite love for you, you see your longing for control doesn't compare to how much He cares for you. This week take time to meditate on Psalm 77:11–13 and the many ways God has proven He is on your side. Write down all the ways He has shown you He is trustworthy and has your back.

NINE

NINES learned early on that it is easier to go along with everyone in order to get along. As children, they would try to keep the peace by doing what others wanted to do and very rarely asserted their opinions or desires. They felt being low-maintenance and undemanding was the best way to "keep the peace," and believed that retreating and having few needs was how they could receive love.

Awareness for Nines: When you accept Christ as your Lord and Savior, you are welcomed into the Kingdom with open arms and don't have to confirm His acceptance. When you reflect on what God has done to rescue you, all you can do is fall at His feet and worship Him. This week take time to meditate on Psalm 77:11–13 and be reminded of His love for you. Write down all the ways He has renewed your mind and given you a deeper sense of knowing you are found in Him and Him alone. There is room for you.

APPLICATION

As you reflect on your Enneagram number this week, how can you relate to the childhood patterns of your type?

_____

_____

How can you connect your childhood patterns of behavior with your current situation?

_____

_____

_____

In what ways can you display compassion to those close to you after reading about their childhood patterns of behavior?

_____

_____

_____

How have you seen God work miracles in your life? How are you hearing God speak to you as you seek spiritual transformation through awareness in your life?

_____

_____

_____

MEDITATION

Go to page 336 and try the Reflection Meditation exercise.

My prayer this week:

_____

_____

_____

_____

_____

_____

_____

_____

_____

_____

WEEK 36

"

I KNOW WHAT IT IS TO BE IN NEED,
AND I KNOW WHAT IT IS TO HAVE PLENTY.
I HAVE LEARNED THE SECRET OF BEING
CONTENT IN ANY AND EVERY SITUATION,
WHETHER WELL FED OR HUNGRY,
WHETHER LIVING IN PLENTY OR IN WANT.
I CAN DO ALL THIS THROUGH HIM WHO
GIVES ME STRENGTH.

PHILIPPIANS 4:12-13

SPIRITUALLY CONNECTED
SECRET SHARING

GOD KNOWS EACH TONE OF YOUR VOICE AND BEAT OF YOUR HEART'S DESIRES.

We all want to be the best version of ourselves daily. No matter if you are in a season of plenty or a season of drought, nobody desires to live at their worst or live a life of mediocrity. You, like the rest of us, yearn to be joyful while living a meaningful and purposeful life, chock-full of love, acceptance, confidence, hope, and faith. Truth be known, God has the answer to the secret of you living a life full of these spiritual riches that are well beyond the material or monetary possession. His promise is also one of strength that will grant you the peace of mind for which you've been searching. He does not simply promise you can do little, or some, or the average amount. He promises that you can do *all* things. This secret of being able to capture your dreams, conquer your fears, or continue your successes is actually not a secret at all—Christ wants everyone to know you can do *anything* through His strength.

—————— **ONE** ——————

When **ONES** are spiritually connected to Christ, they grow in wisdom. They are full of hope, accepting of others, and find joy in life. They are playful as they celebrate the goodness of God's creation. They no longer react emotionally or get caught up in judgment, because they realize their desire for life to be perfect is not their responsibility to control.

Awareness for Ones: Growth for you is allowing yourself to enjoy life whether you have plenty or just enough. This week as you meditate on Philippians 4:12–13, ask yourself, "Am I embracing joy in my life?" Write down several ways you can experience joy in your life by letting go of your rigid list of expectations and allowing yourself to be playful and fun.

—————— **TWO** ——————

When **TWOS** are spiritually connected to Christ, they embrace grace in their lives. They are self-loving, caring, generous, humble, and free as they accept Christ's love as enough. They no longer look to others to meet their needs because they have found their own inner strength and personal value.

Awareness for Twos: As you embrace God's grace in your life, you can love yourself and be confident in your many gifts and talents. This week as you meditate on Philippians 4:12–13, ask yourself, "Do I know the secret in being content?" Journal about the ways in which you recognize when you feel contentment and at peace in your life.

—————— **THREE** ——————

When **THREES** are connected to Christ, they can invest in their own spiritual maturity. They realize the importance of anchoring themselves to the word of God and the role that spiritual depth has in their life. They are confident, empowering visionaries who no longer try to make themselves valuable or loveable because they are secure in who they are in Christ.

Awareness for Threes: As you seek depth in your relationship with Christ, you will find the hope in which you have been searching. This week as you meditate on Philippians 4:12–13, find a quiet place to contemplate the word of God. Write down the ways He has shown you His faithfulness through opening doors for you and paving paths for your success.

FOUR

When **FOURS** are spiritually connected to Christ, they find balance in their lives. They embrace their own inner beauty, gifts, and talents and are willing to share them with the world. They no longer live their lives in the fantasy of their minds but instead embrace reality and accept life as it is.

Awareness for Fours: As you find balance in your life and seek to accomplish realistic goals, you will find there's nothing missing within you. This week as you meditate on Philippians 4:12–13, thank God for being with you when you are lacking or when you have plenty. Write down the names of several people who have helped anchor you in your spiritual journey as you have sought to find your place in this world.

FIVE

When **FIVES** are spiritually connected to Christ, they are acutely aware of God's ability to do far more than anyone has ever written, spoken, or even imagined. They are committed, clear-headed, compassionate, and able to move into action, trusting God is going before them and preparing the way.

Awareness for Fives: As you embrace God and His sovereignty, you can accept the things you cannot change, knowing Christ is ultimately in control. This week as you meditate on Philippians 4:12–13, allow yourself to reflect on times in your life when you have been in need. Write down the ways in which God provided for you whether through a job, a relationship, or supernatural means.

SIX

When **SIXES** are spiritually connected to Christ, they grow in their faith. They are secure, levelheaded, and courageous. They no longer look toward authority figures to give them guidance and direction because they have grown in confidence in their relationship with Christ.

Awareness for Sixes: As you grow in faith, you no longer operate out of fear and worry because your trust is placed in God. This week as you meditate on Philippians 4:12–13, try to see how you can do all things because He has given you the strength. Write down the fears that have kept you from pursuing what you feel called to do. Then find scriptures that combat those fears and start praying them over your life.

SEVEN

When **SEVENS** are spiritually connected to Christ, they desire to be in a relationship with Him and obey His commands and honor His word. They are cooperative, authentic, appreciative, and grateful, knowing God is enough whether they have little or much. They no longer operate in pleasure-seeking behaviors because they understand true joy is found in feeling all the emotions life provokes.

Awareness for Sevens: Honoring God's Word through your actions has given you a sense of security and peace. This week as you meditate on Philippians 4:12–13, allow yourself to see that obeying God is what gives you the strength to pursue your calling. Write down the many ways God has sustained you throughout your life even when you felt as if you couldn't take the next step on your own.

EIGHT

When **EIGHTS** are spiritually connected to Christ, they can embrace mercy for themselves and extend it to others. They are fierce protectors of the weak, courageous, forgiving, and action-oriented. They no longer position themselves as the "know it all," but instead embrace other opinions and help people execute their innovative ideas.

Awareness for Eights: Embracing mercy for yourself is life-changing. You can then extend compassion to those around you without feeling the need to control your environment. This week as you meditate on Philippians 4:12–13, reflect on the many ways God has been there for you. Write down how you have found renewed strength in Christ as you have learned to lean into His provisions for your life.

NINE

When **NINES** are spiritually connected to Christ, they can love unconditionally. They prioritize what needs to be done and are consistent in following through. They no longer fear what others think of them, but instead are fully present in their own lives, comfortable using their voices and willing to take risks.

Awareness for Nines: As you tether yourself to Christ, you experience wholeness in your life. You live your life to the fullest no matter if you have a lot or a little. This week as you meditate on Philippians 4:12–13, praise God for showing you He is always by your side. Write down the ways He has proven to you He is enough as His strength is what propels you forward.

APPLICATION

As you reflect on your Enneagram number this week, which part of being spiritually connected most resonates with you?

_____

_____

_____

In what ways have you discovered how you have been displaying your healthy characteristics?

_____

_____

After reading the other Enneagram reflections, in what ways can you identify with those closest to you when it comes to being spiritually connected?

_____

_____

How have you seen God work in your life during seasons of plenty and seasons of drought? How are you hearing God speak to you about the ways in which you are able to do all things through His strength?

_____

_____

_____

MEDITATION

Go to page 342 and try the Contemplation Meditation exercise.

My prayer this week:

_____

_____

_____

_____

_____

_____

_____

_____

WEEK 37

"

FOR THIS VERY REASON, MAKE EVERY EFFORT TO SUPPLEMENT YOUR FAITH WITH VIRTUE, AND VIRTUE WITH KNOWLEDGE, AND KNOWLEDGE WITH SELF-CONTROL, AND SELF-CONTROL WITH STEADFASTNESS, AND STEADFASTNESS WITH GODLINESS, AND GODLINESS WITH BROTHERLY AFFECTION, AND BROTHERLY AFFECTION WITH LOVE. FOR IF THESE QUALITIES ARE YOURS AND ARE INCREASING, THEY KEEP YOU FROM BEING INEFFECTIVE OR UNFRUITFUL IN THE KNOWLEDGE OF OUR LORD JESUS CHRIST.

2 PETER 1:5-8 (ESV)

PURPOSE
FRUITFUL IN KNOWLEDGE

AS YOUR VIRTUES INCREASE ONE BY ONE, AND YOUR FAITH EXPANDS MOMENT BY MOMENT,

One infinite joy when you follow the God of all creation is realizing He is the quintessential illustrator of your story and the gift-giver of your vast array of talents. Through His wisdom, grace, favor, and strength, you can chase after your purpose-filled life with limitless and immeasurable possibilities. No matter your heart's desire, chase after His calling, stacking all of these qualities listed in this scripture. Place one on top of the other like building blocks for your heart to be anchored on His foundation of strength. First, lay down your faith and stack virtue on top. Then place knowledge on top followed by self-control, steadfastness, godliness, brotherly affection, and finally LOVE as your pinnacle. As your virtues increase one by one, and your faith expands moment by moment, each moral value eventually builds an effective and fruitful life leading to your knowledge of your Lord. This is a life pursued with purpose.

ONE

As **ONES** pursue their purpose, they can lean into their many gifts and talents, such as creating processes and bringing about structure. They care deeply about quality control and are detail-oriented. They are ethical and responsible people who have a great desire to make an impact on the world.

Awareness for Ones: As you pursue your purpose here on earth, be mindful of the importance of brotherly kindness. Kindness and love will help you make the biggest difference for Christ. This week as you reflect on 2 Peter 1:5–8, write down ways you can love your brothers and sisters in Christ more authentically.

TWO

As **TWOS** pursue their purpose, they can embrace their many gifts and talents, such as seeing the positive attributes in people and happily supporting others. They find true joy and contentment being of service to others. They enjoy having fun and lifting the moods of those around them. Creating positive experiences and connecting people is one of the most fulfilling ways in which they find their true purpose and identity here on earth.

Awareness for Twos: For a fruitful and prosperous life, embrace your ability to love and be loved. Through the knowledge you gain by studying the Word of God, you will be able to live a life full of laughter and connection. This week as you reflect on 2 Peter 1:5–8, find ways you can show godly love and kindness to your neighbors.

THREE

As **THREES** pursue their purpose, they seize the many gifts and talents that help them accomplish their goals. They have a unique ability to shape their message so that it is appealing to their audience. They are extremely competitive and goal-oriented. Listing tasks allows them to see their progress and help them to meet expectations. They enjoy inspiring others and helping people achieve success in their own lives.

Awareness for Threes: As you go into the world hoping to make a difference, hold tightly to God's virtue. Build your character on the Word of God and watch the fruitfulness that comes from it. This week as you reflect on 2 Peter 1:5–8, write down a few sentences about the difference of living your life for yourself and living your life as unto the Lord.

FOUR

As **FOURS** pursue their purpose, they can embrace their depth of emotional connection due to their healthy awareness of the human state of others. They use their intuition as a tool to help them understand others better. They express their creativity in many ways as they seek to find truth and knowledge through exploration and curiosity.

Awareness for Fours: As you explore the many elements of your creativity, embrace perseverance in one specific area of your life, knowing it will bear good fruit. This week as you reflect on 2 Peter 1:5–8, write a few sentences about how doing the right thing even when it has been difficult has proven to bear fruit in your life.

FIVE

As **FIVES** pursue their purpose, they can see the value in their quick thinking and intellectual minds. They are incredibly self-sufficient and independent; however, when they grasp the importance of brotherly kindness and their need for others, they begin to see the fruit that kindness and connection produces.

Awareness for Fives: As you humbly embrace faith in God, you can see it is not only knowledge but also lovingkindness that is important for the world to observe who Christ is. Brotherly kindness is more than an act of service; it is a way of living. As you reflect on 2 Peter 1:5–8, take notice of the many ways your life can be fruitful when you are gathering knowledge through the Word of God.

SIX

As **SIXES** pursue their purpose, they embrace the virtue of Christ. They are insightful and attuned to what will produce the best results in their lives. They gather knowledge in the hopes of making the best-educated decision to try to avoid any possible problems. They are loyal and committed to those they respect and admire. Their hope is in a life full of fruit-bearing relationships and accomplishments.

Awareness for Sixes: As you focus your attention on godliness, you desire for your life to represent loyalty, kindness and compassion. Share your faith with others as you continue to grow in virtue. As you reflect on 2 Peter 1:5–8, be encouraged as you recognize the healthy fruit that has been produced through your life.

Notes

SEVEN

As **SEVENS** pursue their purpose, they become steadfast in their pursuit of their vision for a better life. They are fast-paced, innovative thinkers who desire to work together with others to accomplish their goals. As they seek knowledge through the Word of God, they use their imagination and creative planning to produce lasting fruit for the kingdom of God.

Awareness for Sevens: As you stay steadfast and connected to the Word of God, you can mobilize others and make a huge impact that will be life-changing for all involved. As you reflect on 2 Peter 1:5–8, be reminded of the importance Scripture plays in your life. Write down the ways you have learned to be steadfast from reading the Word of God.

EIGHT

As **EIGHTS** pursue their purpose, they embrace the strength and confidence within themselves. They can tackle tough situations and are not afraid of conflict. As they activate self-control in their lives, they are humble and kind. This allows them to mentor, lead, and empower those in whom they see great potential.

Awareness for Eights: As you boldly pursue the big ideas you envision—while using lovingkindness as your guide in your relationships—you will find everlasting fruit. As you reflect on 2 Peter 1:5–8, write down the ways you have found enrichment by activating the Word of God in your life.

NINE

As **NINES** pursue their purpose, they value their ability to see different people's points of view. Their gift of helping to align others brings unity and peace into their situations and relationships. They see every person as equal, and they champion others' ideas and goals. They exemplify brotherly affection and love, and this allows them to be used as kingdom builders for the Lord.

Awareness for Nines: You are gracious and kind, which draws people into your presence. Allow God to use your many gifts and talents to show the world who He is through your support and care of others. As you reflect on 2 Peter 1:5–8, write down the ways you have seen fruitfulness in your life when it comes to the ways you have shown mutual love to all people.

APPLICATION

How do you relate to the way you pursue your purpose?

_____

_____

_____

After reading about your number, how do think your gifts and talents shape the way you chase after your purpose?

_____

_____

_____

In what ways can you see how other Enneagram numbers pursue their passions and purpose differently than you do?

_____

_____

_____

Write down the virtues that fill your heart and anchor you to God's foundation. How are you hearing God speak to you about your life purpose?

_____

_____

_____

MEDITATION

Go to page 332 and try the Box Breathing exercise.

My prayer this week:

_____

_____

_____

_____

_____

_____

_____

_____

_____

_____

_____

_____

WEEK 38

"

DON'T FRET OR WORRY. INSTEAD OF
WORRYING, PRAY. LET PETITIONS
AND PRAISES SHAPE YOUR WORRIES
INTO PRAYERS, LETTING GOD KNOW YOUR
CONCERNS. BEFORE YOU KNOW IT, A SENSE
OF GOD'S WHOLENESS, EVERYTHING
COMING TOGETHER FOR GOOD, WILL COME
AND SETTLE YOU DOWN. IT'S WONDERFUL
WHAT HAPPENS WHEN CHRIST DISPLACES
WORRY AT THE CENTER OF YOUR LIFE.

PHILIPPIANS 4:6 (MSG)

SURRENDER
RUNNING THE RACE

CHRIST CAN DISPLACE YOUR WORRY—LITERALLY, HE WILL TAKE ITS PLACE.

Worry is a normal and natural emotion and looks different for all people. You, like everyone, can stumble into seasons of chronic worry. At the heart of worry is fear, and it can be debilitating. Interestingly, fear isn't all bad. It's a natural response to help you avoid dangerous situations. A certain amount of "healthy" fear is positive. However, the facts are that 85 percent of what you fear never happens, and most of the remaining 15 percent is out of your control. That means you spend an inordinate amount of time worrying, and it can drain the life out of you. Understanding what is happening within yourself when worry arises will help you take it to God instead of getting overwhelmed. God didn't create you to live in an unhealthy state of panic. Whether your fear is real or justified, stop, take a deep breath, and pray. Christ can displace your worry—literally, He will take its place. Yes, and Amen! This week, work toward stepping aside, laying your concerns at the foot of the cross, and speaking of them directly to God. Then, feel the peace that calms your spirit as you grab ahold of His wholeness!

ONE

Because **ONES** are in the instinctual triad, as mentioned in Week 6, when worry arises, Ones become edgy and begin to demand perfection, trying to take control of their feelings. If the situation becomes too big, they may find themselves depressed or withdrawn.

Awareness for Ones: Pay attention to how your body is responding to worry or anxious thoughts. The Lord desires for you to invite Him into the situation. He does not view your struggle with worry as a failure, nor is He taken by surprise by your current situation. This week as you reflect on Philippians 4:6, write down your concerns and bring them before the Lord, knowing He will settle you.

TWO

Because **TWOS** are in the heart triad, as mentioned in Week 6, when worry arises, Twos become irritable, defensive, and even demanding. They are trying to figure out how to calm the worried feeling inside by taking control and making things happen their way. If the situation becomes too big, they may find themselves looking for someone to blame.

Awareness for Twos: You are keenly aware of how your body responds to worry. Inviting God into your circumstance leaves you feeling vulnerable and exposed. However, this is exactly what you need to do. This week as you reflect on Philippians 4:6, write down the perceptions that worry causes you to believe about yourself and your situation. Take your list and surrender it to God, asking Him to fill you with peace.

THREE

Because **THREES** are in the heart triad, as mentioned in Week 6, when worry arises, their emotions are not easily accessible. Threes unconsciously suppress their emotions, for fear of being overtaken by them. Consequently, they are unable to achieve at the level they desire. Instead, they would rather devise a plan to quiet the worry that is surrounding them. If the situation becomes too big, they may find themselves withdrawing by binge watching TV, playing video games, overeating, or getting lost in a novel.

Awareness for Threes: Worry often causes you to work harder and achieve more. When you recognize this pattern, allow yourself to slow down and process what it is you're worried about. God desires you to bring your worry and concern to Him so He can help you carry it. This week as you reflect on Philippians 4:6, make a list of what you are trying to accomplish and place it before God. Ask Him to enter into your circumstances and help you to surrender yourself to Christ, knowing He will fill you with a sense of peace.

FOUR

Because **FOURS** are in the heart triad, as mentioned in Week 6, when worry arises, they become clingy and hypersensitive. They need others to validate their feelings; therefore, Fours draw others into the vortex of their emotions. Fours are trying to calm their feelings of worry by sharing them with others, in hopes others will help them find clarity. If the situation becomes too big, Fours may find themselves sliding down a slippery slope of emotions toward depression.

Awareness for Fours: You process life through past experiences. Therefore, when situations arise that feel like something you have experienced before, you immediately try to make sense of it by dwelling on those past circumstances. This causes your body to respond with heightened emotions. Worry seems to sit just below the surface of every situation. This week as you reflect on Philippians 4:6, try to identify where you feel worry resting in your body. Take in a deep breath, and as you slowly exhale, ask God to carry away this burden of worry.

FIVE

Because **FIVES** are in the head triad, as mentioned in Week 6, when worry arises, they become calm and collected. Fives are excellent under pressure. They try to keep their worry at bay by figuring out how to fix the situation. If the situation becomes too big, however, they may find themselves feeling scattered and distracted.

Awareness for Fives: You have a unique ability to compartmentalize your emotions and feelings, which helps you function effectively in times of stress. However, in the quiet of your own private space, you will allow yourself to process the feelings and worry that exist. This week as you reflect on Philippians 4:6, write down the ways you have tried to calm your feelings of worry on your own. Ask God to fill you with His peace as you surrender your worry to Him.

SIX

Because **SIXES** are in the head triad, as mentioned in Week 6, when worry arises, it can overshadow them. Sixes already have a lot of anxiety and fear. Therefore, something minor can increase their worry, which feels suffocating. Sixes try to figure out how to calm the anxious feeling by keeping themselves busy. If the situation becomes too big, they may find themselves becoming increasingly irritable and even arrogant.

Awareness for Sixes: Hypervigilance has caused you to live in a constant state of worry. Allowing God to displace worry at the center of your life will give you a sense of peace and freedom you never thought possible. This week as you reflect on Philippians 4:6, allow yourself to lift all your concerns and worries to the Lord in prayer. Write down the areas in your life you need freedom from worry.

SEVEN

Because **SEVENS** are in the head triad, as mentioned in Week 6, when worry arises, they go into overdrive and become perfectionistic and critical. Sevens often don't recognize worry or anxiety within themselves because they work very hard at keeping those feelings at bay. If the situation becomes too big, they may find themselves becoming hypercritical of others and looking for ways to escape.

Awareness for Sevens: Allowing yourself to actually feel worried, scared, or even fearful is counterintuitive to who you are. This week as you reflect on Philippians 4:6, allow yourself to explore the idea of worry lingering just below the surface. How have you tried to quiet the whispers of worry in your life? Write down what you fear and turn this list into a prayer of surrender to Christ.

EIGHT

Because **EIGHTS** are in the instinctual triad, as mentioned in Week 6, when worry arises, they become assertive. Because Eights don't like to feel out of control, they isolate themselves and try to solve the problem. Eights try to figure out how to calm the worried feeling by looking at the big picture and making a plan of action. If the situation becomes too big, they may find themselves detaching from others and retreating into themselves, fearful of disappointment or betrayal.

Awareness for Eights: Admitting you are worried feels very vulnerable and exposing. Understanding that Christ desires to take your worry and displace it with peace can be very freeing for you. This week as you reflect on Philippians 4:6, allow yourself to surrender all the areas you are trying to grip tightly in order to control. Write down the feelings that emerge as you release your worry to God. Praise Him in the midst of knowing He will bring you comfort and peace.

NINE

Because **NINES** are in the instinctual triad, as mentioned in Week 6, when worry arises, they retreat and withdraw, hoping to find peace. Nines don't like when their environment is not harmonious, as worry makes everything feel unpredictable. They try to figure out how to calm the worried feeling by processing it alone. If the situation becomes too big, they may find themselves becoming testy and defensive, with racing thoughts and increasing anxiety.

Awareness for Nines: You desperately want peace and harmony and truly do not like to be in conflict with yourself or others. Therefore, carrying worry and concern feels too heavy on your heart. God desires to walk with you and carry your worry as you lean on Him. This week as you reflect on Philippians 4:6, write down the worries you have been carrying by yourself. Lift them to God knowing He will take your concerns and replace them with His peace.

APPLICATION

As you reflect on your Enneagram number this week, how do you resonate with the way you deal with worry?

_____

_____

_____

How are you able to recognize the way worry plays out in your life?

_____

_____

_____

In what ways can you allow those around you dealing with worry to express themselves with a deeper understanding?

_____

_____

_____

How can you petition your worries in your prayers? How are you hearing God speak to you about your surrender?

_____

_____

_____

MEDITATION

Go to page 334 and try the Concentration Meditation exercise.

My prayer this week:

_____

_____

_____

_____

_____

_____

_____

_____

WEEK 39

"

SEE TO IT, BROTHERS AND SISTERS
THAT NONE OF YOU HAS A SINFUL, UNBELIEVING
HEART THAT TURNS AWAY FROM THE LIVING
GOD. BUT ENCOURAGE ONE ANOTHER DAILY,
AS LONG AS IT IS CALLED "TODAY," SO THAT
NONE OF YOU MAY BE HARDENED BY SIN'S
DECEITFULNESS. WE HAVE COME TO SHARE IN
CHRIST, IF INDEED WE HOLD OUR ORIGINAL
CONVICTION FIRMLY TO THE VERY END.

HEBREWS 3:12-14

SPIRITUAL WELL-BEING
ENCOURAGE ACCOUNTABILITY

*"DON'T BE AFRAID, FOR I AM
WITH YOU. DON'T BE DISCOURAGED,
FOR I AM YOUR GOD."*

How would you describe your current "heart health"? Are you harboring resentment, shame, anxiety, or jealousy? Have you allowed certain influences to take precedence above the words and promises of God? In the Enneagram system, each number has a three-tier level of health. The range is between healthy, average, and unhealthy. When you are in the healthy-to-average range, you are able to see yourself as Christ sees you, feel peace within yourself, and accept the parts from the past that once kept you in bondage. When you begin to slip into the unhealthy side of your personality, you lose sight of God, forget you are found in Him, and tend to chase after things or people to meet your needs. The truth is, like every single person on earth, you will experience "unhealthy" seasons when you fail and falter. To counteract this, stay connected in community with fellow believers, because they, along with you, serve a God who resurrects, redeems, and restores souls back to life. "Don't be afraid, for I am with you. Don't be discouraged, for I am your God. I will strengthen you and help you. I will hold you up with my victorious right hand" (Isaiah 41:10, NLT).

ONE

ONES descend into an unhealthy state when they become laser-focused on something they want to change about themselves, justify their actions to save their self-image, or act out their repressed desires while continuing to publicly condemn them. When Ones are open to awareness and can discern these unhealthy patterns, they choose to let go of self-judgment and become sensible and objective.

Awareness for Ones: It is important for you to have someone you respect and with whom you can be honest. The benefit of allowing someone to speak truth to you when you are heading down a path that leads you to judgment and isolation is a sign of spiritual growth. This week as you meditate on Hebrews 3:12–14, take inventory of your life. Write down the areas where you are feeling conviction from the Holy Spirit. Thank God for placing a friend in your life who will walk alongside of you and love you even in times of trouble.

TWO

TWOS descend into an unhealthy state when they rationalize their behavior while calling other people "selfish." When they feel they deserve love and affection, they become martyrs and fall to pieces; others must step in and care for them. However, when they recognize these patterns rising, they understand the detriment of living this way and instead choose to extend unconditional love toward themselves, living a life full of joy and peace.

Awareness for Twos: You need a friend to come alongside to hold you accountable as you desire to grow spiritually. This week as you meditate on Hebrews 3:12–14, take some time to reflect on the passage. Are you able to take wise counsel from a friend? Journal about how it felt to allow a friend into your most intimate thoughts.

THREE

THREES descend into an unhealthy self when they say things to impress others to get off the hook or they concoct stories to keep their agendas hidden. They react out of emotions, and they seek revenge on those who have rejected them. When threes recognize these patterns and use them as a warning sign, they are reminded of the love Christ has for them. They no longer must hide or strive, and they become self-accepting while attuned to the needs of others.

Awareness for Threes: Having someone who you trust and is truthful will help anchor you as you seek to live a life of integrity. It is important for your spiritual growth to have a friend come alongside and hold you accountable. This week as you meditate on Hebrews 3:12–14, write down the areas in your life you would like to have Godly transformation.

FOUR

FOURS descend into an unhealthy state when they push away people who don't support their views. Fours also resent others for not saving them. When they are at the lowest point, they might even begin to act out in self-destructive ways. However, when they begin to view themselves as significant, they embrace their sensitive side and trust those close to them to empathize with their vulnerability.

Awareness for Fours: Believing that those who are close to you care for you deeply allows you to express your thoughts, fears, and concerns. Having someone come alongside and hold you accountable prevents you from getting caught up in old negative patterns of thinking. This week as you meditate on Hebrews 3:12–14, take some time to reflect on the passage and write down how God can transform you from the inside out.

FIVE

FIVES descend into an unhealthy state when they retreat by cutting off connections from the outside world. They often consume themselves with vivid dreams and are unable to stop their mind from racing. When they are at the lowest version of themselves, they might try to escape life however possible. However, as they recognize these patterns and choose to confidently engage life, they find they are clear-minded and compassionate.

Awareness for Fives: As you embrace the importance of having someone come alongside and hold you spiritually accountable, you will find your life enriched. This week as you meditate on Hebrews 3:12–14, embrace the wise counsel God has placed in your life. Write down the spiritual transformation you have experienced through listening to this wise counsel.

SIX

SIXES descend into an unhealthy state when they feel panicky, helpless, or depressed. Because of their reactive behavior to a situation, they can become paranoid or punish themselves through self-hatred. However, as they find liberation through their relationship with Christ, they trust their inner guidance and become secure and courageous.

Awareness for Sixes: As you learn to rely on yourself while having stability, you trust others to speak into your life and hold you spiritually accountable. This week as you meditate on Hebrews 3:12–14, ask God to reveal the areas you have kept hidden as a way to feel safe. Write down the name of a trusted friend with whom you can share your fears and trepidations.

SEVEN

SEVENS descend into an unhealthy state when they become highly impulsive and irresponsible. They also become reckless by medicating through intense stimulation, excessive spending, overeating, and seeking out constant activity in order to avoid pain of any kind. However, as they let go of the belief that they must fill a void within, they experience contentment through Christ and become deeply grateful and appreciative of all they have.

Awareness for Sevens: Allowing someone to speak truth in your life and hold you spiritually accountable will help you grow in maturity and depth. This week as you meditate on Hebrews 3:12–14, take some time to reflect on the passage allowing God to expose the areas in your life in which you are living in excess. Write down ways you can prune the excess and live by setting more boundaries.

EIGHT

EIGHTS descend into an unhealthy state when they become distrusting of others and are determined to protect themselves at any cost—or when they no longer respect boundaries and assert themselves in inappropriate ways. Eights tend to destroy relationships in their lives to prevent others from having the upper hand. However, as they let go of their need for control while trusting God is taking care of them, they become generous, forgiving, and magnanimous.

Awareness for Eights: Recognizing the importance of trusted friends and faithful companions to speak truth and hold you accountable is one of the best gifts you can give yourself. This week as you meditate on Hebrews 3:12–14, take inventory of relationships and how they impact your decision-making. Write down the times you have given God control over your life and in turn have watched your relationships with Him and others flourish.

NINE

When **NINES** are unwilling to deal with their problems, they often become depressed. They have descended into an unhealthy self when they become nitpicky, passive aggressive, or disassociated from reality. However, as they find inner stability and learn to trust that their self-worth is found in Christ, they live a more present and peaceful existence.

Awareness for Nines: As you value yourself and allow others to be close to you, you find great comfort and serenity knowing they are championing your spiritual growth through mutual accountability. This week as you meditate on Hebrews 3:12–14, ask God to reveal which people around you will give you wise counsel. Write down when you have had clear discernment in your relationships that displayed Godly fruit.

APPLICATION

Can you identify where you currently stand on the three-tier level of health?

_____

_____

_____

How do you relate to your Enneagram number when experiencing "unhealthy" seasons?

_____

_____

_____

In what ways have you affected those around you when experiencing both your healthy and unhealthy sides?

_____

_____

_____

Can you remember a time when you were held accountable in a healthy fashion by someone God clearly put in your life?

_____

_____

_____

MEDITATION

Go to page 336 and try the Reflection Meditation exercise.

My prayer this week:

_____

_____

_____

_____

_____

_____

_____

_____

_____

_____

_____

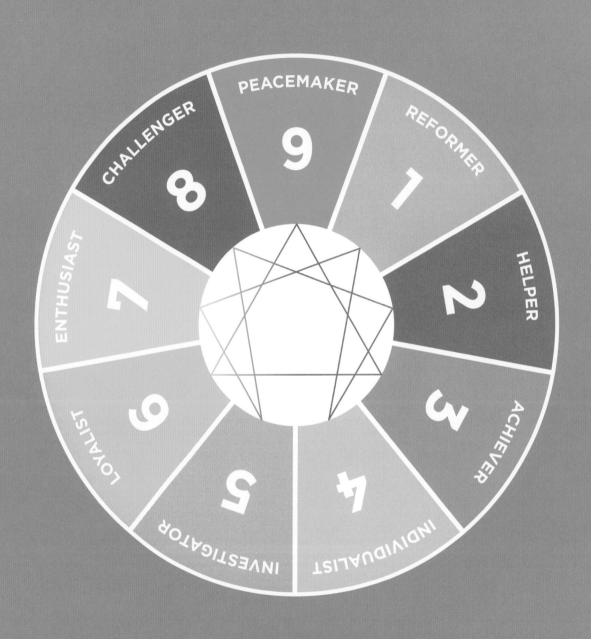

QUARTER FOUR

YOUR PERSONAL GROWTH

Infusing yourself with biblical truth as well as Enneagram knowledge encourages self-reflection and awareness. This new insight helps propel you while you work toward personal growth.

WEEK 40

"

DO NOT BE ANXIOUS ABOUT ANYTHING,
BUT IN EVERYTHING BY PRAYER
AND SUPPLICATION WITH THANKSGIVING
LET YOUR REQUESTS BE MADE KNOWN
TO GOD. AND THE PEACE OF GOD,
WHICH SURPASSES ALL UNDERSTANDING,
WILL GUARD YOUR HEARTS AND
YOUR MINDS IN CHRIST JESUS.

PHILIPPIANS 4:6–7 (ESV)

YOUR CORE DESIRE
PRAY FIRST

HE WILL MEET YOUR EVERY NEED.

You, like all of us, have a core desire—patterns you have developed to feel safe and secure through your life—of which you might not even be aware. When these desires aren't met, it causes you deep anxiety. Your basic desire, which is different for each Enneagram number, is pulling at your heart and influencing your decisions to combat your fears and worries. Notwithstanding, as you move toward self-awareness, and personal and spiritual growth, you can shift your time spent worrying into time spent finding peace in God's Word. You begin to realize you have a Father listening and ready to carry your heavy burdens when they are too much for you to bear. He answers to many names; Peacemaker, Defender, Miracle Worker, Creator, a Sun and Shield, the Giver of grace and glory. Therefore, getting into the rhythm of paying attention to your core desires and shaping your concerns into prayers settles your spirit, as He will meet your every need. Each time you start to clench your fists or wring your hands in worry, reposition your posture by lifting and opening up your palms, surrendering your every care and concern to your Jehovah-Shalom, the God of your Peace.

ONE

ONES' core desire to maintain integrity and balance often leads to worry. At times, they can get caught up in trying to do all the right things so they are seen as good. They can find themselves dealing with feelings of worthlessness and depression when they feel unable to meet their own high expectations.

Awareness for Ones: When you become critical and judgmental of yourself and others, surrender these thoughts to the Lord in prayer. Allowing Him to carry your cares keeps you centered and able to accomplish the tasks at hand, knowing everything will come together for good. This week as you meditate on Philippians 4:6–7, allow God to reveal the areas in your life where worry is causing you to make decisions that keep you from your calling. Write down the ways you have witnessed how lifting your worry to God has allowed you to find peace in your spirit even amid uncertainty.

TWO

TWOS' core desire to feel loved and wanted leads to anxiety within relationships. When Twos get caught up in the overwhelming worry that they are not enough, they might chase after feelings of "belonging" and "love" to the point that their personal anxiety becomes all consuming.

Awareness for Twos: Allow God to care for the desires of your heart, since this will release your tight grip of worry. Trust that He is working all things out for good. Settling down your spirit and knowing He has your back is a huge relief. This week as you meditate on Philippians 4:6–7, allow God to reveal the areas in your life where worry causes you to make decisions that keep you from your healthy relationships. Write down the areas in your life where you are seeking Christ to displace the worry you feel.

THREE

THREES' core desire to be loved and accepted without having to perform can lead to worry. The thought of removing their mask of performance can be incredibly overwhelming, causing Threes to feel crushed under the weight of vulnerability.

Awareness for Threes: When you are willing to invite God into your struggles, He is able to carry the weight of your worry. As a result, you find peace in knowing everything will come together for good, and your spirit will feel settled. This week as you meditate on Philippians 4:6–7, allow God to reveal the areas of your worry that cause you to make decisions that keep you from your authentic self and your calling. Write down the concerns that are overwhelming your mind and lift them up in prayer, praying for Christ to calm your spirit.

FOUR

FOURS' core desire to be seen as unique and accepted as their true selves feels like an overwhelming task. They get caught up worrying that they will never be enough or that there is nothing special about them.

Awareness for Fours: When you bring your worry and concerns to God, He will show you just how special you really are. He will lead you in His direction and open your eyes to see yourself through His lens. The more you allow God into your circumstances, the more you will find peace in the knowledge that you are a child of God. This week as you meditate on Philippians 4:6–7, write down how God has calmed your worry and revealed the gifts and talents He has placed within you as you pursue your calling.

FIVE

FIVES' core desire to be capable and competent can become overwhelming. They can get sidetracked trying to ensure they have all the resources they need to take care of themselves and those they love. They tend to worry about the future and are fearful they will run out of assets, time, or even money.

Awareness for Fives: Surrender to God by inviting Him into your worry. This may feel scary at first. However, once you realize He can meet your every need, you will feel more confident in knowing everything will come together and your spirit will settle. This week as you meditate on Philippians 4:6–7, allow God to reveal the many ways He has provided for you, as this reminder will calm your worries. Write down how His provision in the past has given you confidence in knowing everything will work out for the good.

SIX

Because **SIXES**' desire for guidance and support is crucial to their well-being, they can often fall into a cycle of constant worrying. They begin to question everyone and everything while searching for what and whom they can trust.

Awareness for Sixes: As you bring your concerns to the Lord in prayer, ask Him to cover you with His peace that passes all understanding. There is a beauty in God's protection that will settle your spirit. This week as you meditate on Philippians 4:6–7, allow God to reveal the ways He has protected you, as this reminder will calm your worries. Write down what you are worrying about right now and lift it to God, knowing His desire is to care for you.

Notes

SEVEN

SEVENS' core desire to have their needs met in the moment can lead to feelings of disappointment and frustration. Trying to constantly keep themselves in a state of satisfaction can lead to anxiety. Also, if they feel they are lacking or missing out on something, they can easily spiral into a frenzy of worry.

Awareness for Sevens: When you learn to turn your worry into prayer and praise, God will do something special within you. He will remove your overwhelming feelings, replacing them with peace and contentment. This week as you meditate on Philippians 4:6–7, allow God to reveal the areas in your life where you feel discontent. He desires for you to live worry free because your trust is found in Him. Write down the ways in which you have found contentment in the past, while reminding yourself that being content is always possible when you trust in God's peace.

EIGHT

EIGHTS' desire to protect themselves keeps them on guard. Allowing anyone to see their vulnerability makes them feel fearful and concerned. Because they work hard at always being prepared and being in control, worry tends to make them raise their defenses.

Awareness for Eights: When you recognize this is happening, release your cares and concerns to God. Inviting the Lord into your vulnerable places and asking Him to lift your burden of worry allows Him to calm your spirit in the way only He can. God is in full control and will bring peace into your situations and work on your behalf. This week as you meditate on Philippians 4:6–7, allow God to reveal the areas of worry that cause you to put up your guard. Write down why you have a hard time being vulnerable about your concerns and ask Christ to help you trust Him as He will carry your worry and protect you.

NINE

NINES' core desire to have inner peace and stability is of utmost importance. Therefore, when their world seems to be spinning out of control, worry takes hold of their thoughts. They may find themselves retreating and withdrawing from people and situations in the hope of insulating themselves and keeping their environment peaceful.

Awareness for Nines: When you notice yourself shutting down, ask God to lift your weight of worry. Ask Him to help you see the situation with fresh eyes. When God is in the middle of your mess, He brings a sense of peace and well-being to your soul. This week as you meditate on Philippians 4:6–7, allow God to reveal His peace to you and calm any issues of worry. Write down the ways in which you shut out worry by withdrawing and ask God to help you bring worry to Him instead.

APPLICATION

In what ways do you resonate with the core desire of
your Enneagram number?

_____

_____

_____

How can you work on releasing the worry with which
you struggle?

_____

_____

_____

In what way can you identify with someone close to you
in how they struggle with worry, now that you have read
all of the Enneagram reflections?

_____

_____

_____

Through your prayers, how has God turned a past worry
into something positive? How are you hearing God
speak to you about your core desire?

_____

_____

_____

MEDITATION

Go to page 342 and
try the Contemplation
Meditation exercise.

My prayer this week:

_____

_____

_____

_____

_____

_____

_____

_____

_____

_____

WEEK 41

I PRAISE YOU, FOR I AM FEARFULLY
AND WONDERFULLY MADE. WONDERFUL
ARE YOUR WORKS; MY SOUL
KNOWS IT VERY WELL.

PSALM 139:14 (ESV)

WINGS
WONDERFULLY MADE

YOU WERE CREATED ON PURPOSE AND THERE IS A PURPOSE FOR YOUR LIFE.

One of the beauties of the Enneagram coupled with spiritual growth is discovering you are a complex human being with both strengths and weaknesses. As you become more familiar with your Enneagram personality, you will begin to see how you also use the numbers to the right and left of your primary number, known as your wings. You will use different aspects of each of your wings throughout your life as they round out your personality and give you a better understanding of how you process and react to information and relationships. Because you are fearfully and magnificently made and full of His splendor, understanding you have been beautifully created by your Creator can help you accept the way you are designed. Truth be known, your heart was remarkably and wholly made and so were your mind, body, and soul for this very time and this very moment. Truth: God has chosen you. Truth: God planned you. Truth: You were created on purpose and there is a purpose for your life. Sure, like every human being, you make mistakes. However, your life is not a mistake. Allow His truth to drown out the noise when the Deceiver tries to define who you are and whose you are. Unpack the wonderful works the Lord has woven together to uniquely create you. Your soul knows this well.

ONE

ONES whose dominant wing is a Nine are more introverted, objective, detached, and relaxed. They tend to be very discerning and have a strong desire to fix things with a more hands-off and caring approach. Ones whose dominant wing is a Two tend to be warmer, action-oriented, controlling, and helpful. They are fueled with empathy and compassion and are willing to do the hard work to see life change happen for either the people or the projects they care about.

Awareness for Ones: Having a deeper understanding of how both of your wings can help you navigate life can bring you a sense of relief. As you embrace the many parts of who you are, remember your abilities have a far greater reach when you harness them for the good. As you meditate on Psalm 139:14, write down some of the ways you can see how God has used your unique makeup to bring about change in your relationships, work environments, and in your life as a whole.

TWO

TWOS whose dominant wing is a One are more reasonable, objective, quiet, and judgmental. They take on less pretentious jobs and desire to be Good Samaritans and caretakers. Twos whose dominant wing is a Three tend to be charming, outgoing, ambitious, and competitive. They are driven by a desire for personal connection and tend to focus on their own qualities instead of serving others.

Awareness for Twos: As you embrace the many parts of who you are, allow yourself to see the good qualities in both of your wings. This week as you meditate on Psalm 139:14, write down some of the ways you can identify how you have used both of your wings in different circumstances. Thank God for creating you just as you are.

THREE

THREES whose dominant wing is a Two are more encouraging, social, warm, and attention seeking. They desire to be close to people and enjoy the public life even at the expense of their own inner stability. Threes whose dominant wing is a Four tend to be introspective, work-oriented, sensitive, and creative. They are career focused and driven by a need to be well regarded and viewed as successful.

Awareness for Threes: Understanding how both of your wings greatly impact the way in which you pursue life can bring a deeper sense of awareness to your actions. Both of your wings have many great qualities. As you meditate on Psalm 139:14, write down the situations in which you have used your dominant wing and how your specific attributes are a beautiful reflection of Christ in you.

FOUR

FOURS whose dominant wing is a Three are more extroverted, ambitious, image conscious, and upbeat. They work toward self-improvement and are goal-oriented. They desire to appear both accomplished and distinctive. Fours whose dominant wing is a Five tend to be intellectual, introverted, observant, and withdrawn. They are attuned to the way others perceive them, concerned with culture and social acceptance. They can be competitive and express their opinions more openly.

Awareness for Fours: As you embrace the unique qualities that exist within you, celebrate them in the knowledge that you are a wonderful creation of the Lord of lords. As you meditate on Psalm 139:14 this week, write down some of the ways you can embrace the many attributes displayed using both your wings.

FIVE

FIVES whose dominant wing is a Four are more creative, empathetic, sensitive, and self-absorbed. They are drawn to the arts and are whimsical and innovative. They seek to create something that is "their own." Fives whose dominant wing is a Six tend to be extroverted, loyal, skeptical, and cautious. They are often drawn toward technology and science, hoping to make significant advances in those fields through new discoveries.

Awareness for Fives: The beautiful mind of a Five is a gift to be treasured. No matter which wing is dominant, the depth of creativity found in you suggests a God who is full of imagination and playfulness. As you meditate on Psalm 139:14, thank God for creating you just as you are. This week write down some of the ideas you have kept in your head and heart that you have been afraid to share with others for fear of being misunderstood or dismissed.

SIX

SIXES whose dominant wing is a Five are more introverted, focused, withdrawn, and intellectual. They are laser focused and often are drawn to careers that have well-established rules and systems. Sixes whose dominant wing is a Seven are more extroverted, sociable, playful, and impulsive. They are less serious. However, their focus of attention is often on the safety and security of their loved ones.

Awareness for Sixes: As you embrace the many parts of who you are, remember you are fearfully and wonderfully made. Your friendliness and loyalty draw others to you, which positions you to be a great witness for Christ. As you meditate on Psalm 139:14, thank God for creating you just as you are. This week write down some of the ways you see how God has used your unique makeup for His purpose and plan.

SEVEN

SEVENS whose dominant wing is a Six are more loyal, playful, relationship-oriented, and anxious. They have a positive outlook on life and are full of enthusiasm and joy. Their quick and curious minds allow them to accomplish many tasks in a short amount of time. Sevens whose dominant wing is an Eight are more adventurous, assertive, creative, and tough-minded. They tend to be extremely driven and desire material possessions and positions of leadership. They are strategic thinkers and use their resources to get what they want.

Awareness for Sevens: Embrace the many facets of your personality and see them as a beautiful complement to the wonderful way God made you. Your high energy is contagious and your passion for life ignites others to join you in pursuit of God's purpose. As you meditate on Psalm 139:14, write down some of the ways you have seen your dominant wing displayed through a project you have accomplished.

EIGHT

EIGHTS whose dominant wing is a Seven are more extroverted, energetic, materialistic, and resourceful. They can attract others to help them accomplish ideas they have envisioned. They are entrepreneurial and seek independence from others. Eights whose dominant wing is a Nine tend to be mild-mannered, receptive, quiet leaders, and people-oriented. They are quietly determined and less aggressive. Having the ability to lead others with calmness and clarity positions them to be more protective and family-oriented.

Awareness for Eights: God has made you exactly how you are in order to accomplish many things here on earth for His glory. Being strong, assertive, and independent allows you to lead with confidence, coupled with Christian character and integrity. The impact you make for God's kingdom is unimaginable. This week as you meditate on Psalm 139:14, write down some of the ways you have seen God use your strong leadership skills for His purpose and plan.

NINE

NINES whose dominant wing is a One are more compliant, idealistic, emotionally controlled, and orderly. They are highly relational and excellent negotiators. They express both strength and gentleness as they engage with others. Nines whose dominant wing is an Eight are more outgoing, assertive, imaginative, and at times pacifying. They are friendly people who are gifted at nonverbal communication. They are confident in their ideals and purpose.

Awareness for Nines: Allow yourself to see the marvelous work God did when He created you. You are kind and caring while uniquely gifted to show the world who Christ is through your many strengths. As you meditate on Psalm 139:14, write down some of the ways you can see how God has used your unique makeup.

APPLICATION

In what ways do your wings play a part in how you function in your life?

_____

_____

_____

Do you see yourself leaning more toward one wing than the other? Why or why not?

_____

_____

_____

_____

In what ways have you been enlightened after reading about those close to you through their Enneagram reflections?

_____

_____

_____

_____

In what ways do you see how God has created you uniquely and wonderfully? How have your wings helped you use your gifts and talents to fulfill your purpose?

_____

_____

_____

_____

♡ **MEDITATION**

Go to page 332 and try the Box Breathing exercise.

My prayer this week:

_____

_____

_____

_____

_____

_____

_____

_____

_____

_____

_____

WEEK 42

"

I WILL BLESS THE LORD AT ALL TIMES;
HIS PRAISE SHALL CONTINUALLY
BE IN MY MOUTH. MY SOUL MAKES ITS
BOAST IN THE LORD; LET THE HUMBLE
HEAR OF IT AND BE GLAD. OH, MAGNIFY
THE LORD WITH ME, AND LET US
EXALT HIS NAME TOGETHER. I SOUGHT
THE LORD, AND HE HEARD ME, AND
DELIVERED ME FROM ALL MY FEARS.
THEY LOOKED TO HIM AND WERE RADIANT,
AND THEIR FACES WERE NOT ASHAMED.

PSALM 34:1–5 (NKJV)

EMOTIONAL STRUGGLE
RADIANT REFLECTION

YOU ARE NOT DEFINED BY YOUR STRUGGLES, FOR JESUS TOOK YOUR SIN, YOUR ANGER, YOUR ANXIETY, AND SHAME ALL TO THE CROSS.

Each of us processes the emotions of shame, anger, or anxiety differently, according to our Enneagram triad: the head, heart, or gut. The common thread to these emotions is rooted in fear. Those in the gut triad struggle with anger. Those in the heart triad struggle with shame. And those in the head triad struggle with anxiety. You are not defined by your struggles, for Jesus took your sin, your anger, your anxiety, and shame all to the cross. Like all of us, at some point you have been triggered by fear, which perhaps you are enduring at this very moment. This scripture encourages all of us to exalt Jesus' name. Thankfully, we can quiet our fears by seeking the Lord, who is our Deliverer. His blood covers all suffering and turmoil, and He promises that those who look to Him will be radiant and shall never be ashamed. The Hebrew word for ashamed is *bosh,* meaning "to fall into disgrace" or "come into shame." God says you should never plummet into a state of disgrace. Seek Him, praise Him, and magnify Him, for He is listening to your every word, your every fear, and your every need.

ONE

As mentioned before, **ONES** are in the gut triad. Their emotional struggle is with anger. They are fearful that others will see them as angry, so they repress it, which in turn causes bitterness and resentment. But anger is not a wrong or bad emotion. It is acting on anger that causes sin. Anger is an emotion that is a warning sign for you to ask yourself, "What am I feeling and why am I reacting in this way?"

Awareness for Ones: Allow yourself to feel angry and process what you are angry about, instead of shoving it aside and letting it turn into bitterness. This week as you meditate on Psalm 34, ask the Lord this question, "Am I unwilling to show people my true anger-causing feelings because I am afraid they will perceive me as bad?" Write about a time you sought the Lord and He helped you release your anger. How did it feel to release your anger to God instead of focusing on looking good and right in the eyes of others?

TWO

As mentioned before, **TWOS** are in the heart triad. Their emotional struggle is with shame. They try to be good in every way, hoping to keep their feelings of shame at bay. They are fearful that others will see them as unwilling to help or as acting neglectful in some way. They believe their self-worth is directly connected to how other people view them and their kindness.

Awareness for Twos: Shame rises up and keeps you in constant pursuit of pleasing others, while also making you feel taken advantage of and then lonely. Learning to let go of the fear of what others think of you and embrace who you are in Christ is the key to your emotional freedom. This week as you meditate on Psalm 34, ask the Lord, "Am I allowing the fear of what others think about me to dictate how I live?" Journal about a time you recognized you were operating in a people-pleasing way but were able to find peace by asking God to deliver you from this pattern.

THREE

As mentioned before, **THREES** are in the heart triad. Their emotional struggle is with shame. They are fearful that others will see them as worthless and stagnant. Shame rises, telling them, "You had better be an achiever or else you have no value." This fear causes them to constantly chase after success and statues.

Awareness for Threes: When you feel fearful of not being seen as valuable unless you are successful, remember it is shame within you being triggered. Shame tries to keep your authentic self hidden, for fear of not measuring up. This week as you meditate on Psalm 34, ask the Lord, "Am I allowing the fear of not being viewed as successful to control my thoughts and actions?" Write down an activity or idea you would like to pursue. How has the fear of failure kept you from trying it?

FOUR

As mentioned before, **FOURS** are in the heart triad. Their emotional struggle is with shame. They avoid feelings of shame by taking on the victim role and overdramatizing their feelings of hurt and disappointment. Their fear of rejection causes them to constantly put up walls trying to insulate themselves from pain.

Awareness for Fours: When you feel yourself putting up walls around you in hopes of protecting yourself, ask yourself what is causing you to feel the need to pull away or attack. This week as you meditate on Psalm 34, ask the Lord, "Am I allowing the fear of rejection to keep me from close personal relationships?" Write a list of words or phrases that cause you to feel shame in your life. Find Scripture verses and write them on index cards to combat those words or phrases that trigger shame and fear.

FIVE

As mentioned before, **FIVES** are in the head triad. Their emotional struggle is with anxiety. They are fearful that the people closest to them, or any outside support from others, cannot be trusted or are not available. This fear causes them to retreat inward and to gather any resources they may need for personal survival.

Awareness for Fives: Don't let anxiety have the last word in your life. You are brilliant and gifted. Even if the world seems overwhelming and demanding, you have what it takes to become a thriving member of society. This week as you meditate on Psalm 34, ask the Lord, "Am I allowing fear to overtake me from truly living my life?" Write a list of what you pray for when you seek safety and security in the world.

SIX

As mentioned before, **SIXES** are in the head triad. Their emotional struggle is with anxiety. They are fearful of making the wrong decisions and being left without support. This fear causes them to test the people and establishments in their lives to see if they are trustworthy.

Awareness for Sixes: Fear often has a grip on your thoughts, which causes your anxiety to be the driving force behind your inability to make quick decisions. This week as you meditate on Psalm 34, ask the Lord, "Am I allowing the fear of making a mistake or being without support prevent me from truly living my life?" Write down the ways you have learned to surrender your anxiety and worry to the Lord, knowing He will care for you.

SEVEN

As mentioned before, **SEVENS** are in the head triad. Their emotional struggle is with anxiety. They are fearful of being trapped in emotional pain and not having anyone they can lean on for support. This fear causes them to be in constant motion. They try to make sure they have everything they need, while keeping their emotions at bay.

Awareness for Sevens: Quieting your mind and asking God to take every thought captive is the first step toward emotional awareness. Trusting you will not be stuck in sad, dark, or fearful emotions for extended periods of time will also allow you to explore how you are really feeling about situations and relationships in your life. This week as you meditate on Psalm 34, ask the Lord, "Am I allowing the fear of abandonment and negative feelings to keep me from truly living in the present?" Write down your feelings that surface as you process this question.

EIGHT

As mentioned before, **EIGHTS** are in the gut triad. Their emotional struggle is with anger. They are not always aware of how fear plays a role in their lives. Their fear of being without control or being made to look insignificant or small will trigger anger within them. They use anger as fuel, a process that allows them to make tough choices and push their agenda forward.

Awareness for Eights: The fear of being exposed in any way leaves you feeling vulnerable and angry. You will take control of the situation however possible, hoping to regain a position of authority. This week as you meditate on Psalm 34, ask the Lord, "Am I allowing the fear of losing control or my autonomy to dictate how I am living?" Write down the areas in your life in which you are easily triggered by anger. Ask God to humble your spirit and give you a sense of peace.

NINE

As mentioned before, **NINES** are in the gut triad. Their emotional struggle is with anger. Although they don't like to acknowledge anger, it often bubbles just below the surface of their being. They fear this emotion because it causes division. Anger feels scary to them; therefore, they often make themselves smaller in situations until they can no longer repress their anger, and then they explode with emotion.

Awareness for Nines: Anger is an emotion that often suggests boundaries of some sort have been violated. As you process your reaction to the anger you feel, can you identify ways you have felt taken advantage of? This week as you meditate on Psalm 34, ask the Lord, "Am I allowing the fear of losing connection with others dictate how I am living?" Write down how the fear of expressing your true thoughts and feelings has caused anger to build up in your life. Ask the Lord to give you peace, as you no longer allow fear to control you.

APPLICATION

What emotional triad did you discover you are in and how do you see it playing out in your daily life?

_____

_____

_____

How does your emotional triad shape your personality?

_____

_____

_____

By reading the Enneagram reflections for the other emotional triads, how can you understand those around you better?

_____

_____

_____

How can you release your fear to God? How are you hearing God speak to you when it comes to your anger, shame, and anxiety?

_____

_____

MEDITATION

Go to page 334 and try the Concentration Meditation exercise.

My prayer this week:

_____

_____

_____

_____

_____

_____

_____

_____

_____

WEEK 43

"

FOR THIS REASON, SINCE THE DAY WE
HEARD ABOUT YOU, WE HAVE NOT STOPPED
PRAYING FOR YOU. WE CONTINUALLY ASK
GOD TO FILL YOU WITH THE KNOWLEDGE
OF HIS WILL THROUGH ALL THE WISDOM AND
UNDERSTANDING THAT THE SPIRIT GIVES,
SO THAT YOU MAY LIVE A LIFE WORTHY OF
THE LORD AND PLEASE HIM IN EVERY WAY:
BEARING FRUIT IN EVERY GOOD WORK,
GROWING IN THE KNOWLEDGE OF GOD, BEING
STRENGTHENED WITH ALL POWER ACCORDING
TO HIS GLORIOUS MIGHT SO THAT YOU MAY
HAVE GREAT ENDURANCE AND PATIENCE.

COLOSSIANS 1:9–11

HEALTHY CHARACTERISTICS

RADIATE GOOD FRUIT

APPRECIATE YOUR EVERY GOOD WORK AS YOU RADIATE GOOD FRUIT.

Through this past year of doing the hard work of striving toward personal and spiritual growth, you have come a LONG way! There is such beauty in growing in your heavenly Father's knowledge, leaning on His strength, powered by His glorious might. Your light shines brightly for all to clearly see. His spirit spills out from your thoughtful actions, behavior, and words. You can break patterns and replace them with the truth of who God says you are. You no longer need to listen to the Enemy of deceit talk about your past, and your present is no longer defined by your unhealthy behavioral cycles that at one time stumped your growth. While each Enneagram number has an arrow leading you toward where you go in stress, as you become more self-aware and grounded in who you are in Christ, you will begin to act out the healthy characteristics of your Enneagram "stress" number. And, your deeper dive into God's Word inspires you to continue building a deeper relationship with you Creator. Appreciate your every good work as you radiate good fruit. Glean wisdom from scriptures, be confident and comfortable expressing your vulnerability, empathy, grace, authenticity, and kindness to yourself and others. Whether your strengths are as a defender of truth, a giver of grace, a visionary, a peacemaker, a nurturer, or a purpose-driven individual, know you are worthy! Believe in yourself with humility to fiercely run the race of endurance with great patience, peace, and love all for His glory.

——— ONE ———

Personal growth for **ONES** allows them to move toward spiritual depth and understanding. When they can harness the positive traits of the Enneagram Four, even though it is their "stress" number, they can become more self-accepting and self-nurturing. While letting go of the tension they have carried throughout much of their lives, they are more relaxed and patient with themselves and others. Being open-minded allows them to embrace the beauty of creativity.

Awareness for Ones: Growing in knowledge of the Word of God and living a life of integrity allows you to live with a deep inner peace and contentment in your life. This week as you meditate on Colossians 1:9–11, write the words from this scripture that resonate with you. Take fifteen minutes and allow yourself to rest in the presence of God while reflecting on the words you picked.

——— TWO ———

Personal growth for **TWOS** allows them to see the value of a deep personal relationship with the Lord. When they can embrace the healthy traits of the Enneagram Eight, even though it is their "stress" number, they can feel empowered by their own strength. They can love others with balance and self-awareness, no longer losing their identity while trying to gain connection. Love is no longer the reward they seek, because they have a deeper understanding of the purity of love.

Awareness for Twos: Seeking to live a life worthy of God allows you to find rest in the fact that you are loved by Him in this moment, the same way you have always been loved by Him and always will be. This week as you meditate on Colossians 1:9–11, breathe in the beautiful words written in this scripture. Write down how embracing who you are in Christ has allowed you to love others without strings attached.

——— THREE ———

Personal growth for **THREES** allows them to embrace God's knowledge and will for their lives. When they can learn to use the healthy traits of the Enneagram Nine, even though it is their "stress" number, they can live authentic and genuine lives. Humility and honesty allow them to find peace and contentment. When they remove the mask of others' expectations and of the desire for social acceptance, they will truly find freedom. Instead of chasing achievement, they find their value in who Christ says they are.

Awareness for Threes: Your desire to live a life of purpose, combined with your knowledge of the Word of God, brings a new depth to your soul. This week as you meditate on Colossians 1:9–11, make a list of what they asked of God in this scripture. Pray those specific words over your life and believe for great endurance and patience along your life's journey.

FOUR

Personal growth for **FOURS** allows them to become spiritually awakened and thus receive the pure love of Christ. When they can learn to use the healthy traits of the Enneagram Two, even though it is their "stress" number, they can embrace their genuine self. Once they are aware of their many qualities, such as determination, resilience, and strength, they no longer look at life as a burden they must endure, but as a beautiful gift to be treasured.

Awareness for Fours: When you realize you don't need to be rescued, because you have found peace within yourself, you are able to live each day seeing and experiencing God's creation with love and acceptance. This week as you meditate on Colossians 1:9–11, write down the areas in your life you have witnessed your transformation by embracing the wisdom of God.

FIVE

Personal growth for **FIVES** allows them to embrace the wisdom and knowledge of the Word of God. When they can learn to use the healthy traits of the Enneagram Seven, even though it is their "stress" number, they are able to be fully present in experiences instead of observing the experience from a distance. They are fully engaged with reality and able to trust their inner knowing, because it is grounded in the Lord. They live each day fully present.

Awareness for Fives: You trust God to be your source as He gives you the ability to have a quiet mind. Seeking His wisdom allows you to grow spiritually and emotionally, giving you great vision and clarity. This week as you meditate on Colossians 1:9–11, thank God for His strength and power. Write down what it feels like to be present in your body as you engage in a new experience.

SIX

Personal growth for **SIXES** allows them to trust in God's will and perfect plan for their life. When they can use the healthy traits of the Enneagram Three, even though it is their "stress" number, they can let go of fear and grab hold of courage. They are confident in their abilities because they are secure in who they are in Christ. They no longer seek outside support, because the Word of God makes them feel steady and safe. They stand firm, leaning on inner strength, knowing Christ has made them perfect in His image.

Awareness for Sixes: You stand firm in your faith because you have witnessed God move on your behalf. Seeking wisdom and knowledge through the Word of God has given you a solid foundation for you to build upon. This week as you meditate on Colossians 1:9–11, reflect on the ways you need God's strength in your life. Write a note to yourself about what it has been like to put your trust in Christ, knowing He is directing your path.

SEVEN

Personal growth for **SEVENS** allows them to engage in transformational work on their spiritual journey of finding true freedom in Christ. When they are able to use the healthy traits of the Enneagram One, even though it is their "stress" number, they can let go of the constant need for stimulation and find a deep inner peace in being still. Embracing self-discipline allows for completion of projects and the ability to be fully present in the moments of their lives.

Awareness for Sevens: Living a life filled with joy and peace found by grounding yourself in the Word of God allows you to stop chasing external fulfillment and start truly living. You no longer try to fulfill your earthly desires, because you understand how fleeting they really are. This week as you meditate on Colossians 3:9-11, ask God to fill you with His wisdom and knowledge. Write a prayer that reflects how you feel as you read the scripture above.

EIGHT

Personal growth for **EIGHTS** allows them to fully surrender to the Lord, since they know they have a higher purpose found in Him. When they can use the healthy traits of the Enneagram Five, even though it is their "stress" number, they can let go of their need to control, by realizing what they truly seek is respect. They find inner peace and strength, which will allow them to be vulnerable with others and relaxed.

Awareness for Eights: As you grow spiritually and emotionally, your focus is no longer on your personal survival. Instead you are focused on the positive impact your life and purpose can make on the world. This week as you meditate on Colossians 3:9-11, write down how God has shown you His divine purpose for your life through the wisdom and knowledge you have found in the Word of God.

NINE

Personal growth for **NINES** allows them to fully embrace the grace of God and the strength and power found in His Word. When they can use the healthy trait of the Enneagram Six, even though it is their "stress" number, they awaken to their lives and see the beauty within themselves. They live life alert and excited, ready to engage in the purpose and plan that Christ has for them. Feeling whole and complete in who they are in Christ allows them to feel confident and self-assured.

Awareness for Nines: You have a quiet strength and an even temper, which when coupled with the power of God, displays His wisdom and knowledge. You can use your many gifts to bring healing to this world. This week as you meditate on Colossians 3:9-11, reflect on the good fruit you have produced because of choosing to live your life surrendered to God's will. Write down the emotions you feel when you bring peace into situations.

APPLICATION

What new awareness do you have about yourself after reading your Enneagram number?

_____

_____

_____

In what ways have you seen yourself use the healthy attributes of your "stress" number?

_____

_____

_____

Which of the other Enneagram numbers in growth do you find most complement your number?

_____

_____

_____

How has the healthy fruit you display in your life shown the world your love and devotion for Christ?

_____

_____

_____

MEDITATION

Go to page 336 and try the Reflection Meditation exercise.

My prayer this week:

_____

_____

_____

_____

_____

_____

_____

WEEK 44

"

THIS IS GOD'S MESSAGE, THE GOD WHO
MADE THE EARTH, MADE IT LIVABLE
AND LASTING, KNOWN EVERYWHERE
AS GOD: "CALL TO ME AND I WILL ANSWER
YOU. I'LL TELL YOU MARVELOUS AND
WONDROUS THINGS THAT YOU COULD
NEVER FIGURE OUT ON YOUR OWN.

JEREMIAH 33:2–3 (MSG)

HEARING GOD
YOUR LISTENING SKILLS

YOUR VOICE IS SWEETER THAN NECTAR AND THE CRY OF YOUR HEART IS LOUDER THAN THUNDER.

Hypothetically speaking, let's say when you wake up tomorrow morning, you realize you've completely lost your voice. You try calling out, but you are silent. Are there words you should have said but did not? Are there words you should not have said but did? Are there calls to God you should have uttered but ignored because you were feeling afraid, defeated, disconnected, or insignificant? Your voice matters to God. Don't be silent or silenced. The scripture says, "This is God's Message," meaning He is talking directly to YOU. If you expect answers, you must communicate the desires of your heart. When you call out your sins in repentance, He forgives and forgets as it is buried deep within the ocean's floor. When you call out for acknowledgment, He speaks with grace and peace. When you call out in desperation, He provides words of comfort and wisdom, for the Holy Spirit reveals all thoughts you could not decipher on your own. To God, the sound of your voice is sweeter than nectar and the cry of your heart is louder than thunder. Speak to your Father, "Ask in my name, according to my will, and he'll most certainly give it to you. Your joy will be a river overflowing its banks!" (John 16:24, MSG).

ONE

ONES long for perfection in their specific areas of focus. They tirelessly work toward this, hoping situations will come together seamlessly so they can feel the deep sense of peace and satisfaction they have been longing for. As Ones embrace the gospel message, they realize what they are seeking can be found through developing a deep and lasting relationship with Christ.

Awareness for Ones: Hearing God speak requires you to identify the difference between your inner critic and God's truth. Learning to honor your limitations and allowing yourself rest positions you to hear His voice more clearly. Not punishing yourself for feeling the full range of your emotions enables you to seek God and all His wonder. This week as you meditate on Jeremiah 33:2-3, allow the words to bring childlike wonder to your imagination. Write down the many questions you have for the Lord and take some time to allow His Spirit to bring you peace.

TWO

TWOS long for deep relational connections. They often struggle with creating boundaries in their lives out of a fear that doing so will cause others to turn away from them. As they continue to develop their relationship with Christ, they begin to see the ways in which they have used flattery to get what they desire. However, they no longer feel the need for validation because they can go directly to the one true source—Jesus Christ.

Awareness for Twos: Hearing God speak requires you to be humble and honest with yourself and others about your true thoughts, feelings, and emotions. Placing boundaries in your life helps you to respect your time and establish a healthy routine in which you can continue to cultivate a relationship with your heavenly Father. This week as you meditate on Jeremiah 33:2-3, ask Him to show you marvelous and wondrous things about your everyday life. Write down the thoughts that come to your mind and praise Him for new perspectives.

THREE

THREES long for others to see the value within them aside from their success and achievements. They very rarely, if ever, feel like they can authentically be themselves and still be accepted and loved. Knowing they serve a God who will answer when they call allows them to trust He loves them unconditionally.

Awareness for Threes: Hearing God speak requires you to give yourself permission to rest. Your constant forward motion can inhibit your ability to hear His voice; therefore, practicing meditation and deep breathing will help you to slow down and listen. This week as you meditate on Jeremiah 33:2-3, spend time being still in His presence. Write down a few hopes you have and watch as He reveals His marvelous ways.

FOUR

FOURS long to be understood and embraced. They have a unique view of the world. Knowing they serve a God who holds mysteries and wonders in the palm of His hand excites them. They feel a deep connection to spiritual ideas. Therefore, trusting that God is beckoning them to ask Him to reveal these mysteries makes them feel known by the Creator. Believing they can go to God and ask Him for renewed creativity and wisdom beyond their years is exhilarating.

Awareness for Fours: Hearing God requires you to acknowledge the feelings you are experiencing and discerning what is true about them. Establish healthy routines in which you schedule time for spiritual development as well as finding a creative outlet. This week as you meditate on Jeremiah 33:2–3, write down how you have been inspired by this week's reflection.

FIVE

FIVES long to seek silence and solitude as a way of protecting themselves from an overwhelming world. As they continue to develop a deep and rich relationship with God, they find it safe to express themselves more openly with others. They love to investigate, learn, and grow. Therefore, giving themselves permission to go to God with their questions makes them feel loved and accepted.

Awareness for Fives: Hearing God requires you to be present in your body and mind. Allowing yourself to experience your emotions will release the healing your heart desperately needs. As you turn your focus of attention toward what brings you peace, the chatter in your mind will quiet down. This week as you meditate on Jeremiah 33:2–3, take a walk as you process what He is depositing in your mind.

SIX

SIXES long for loyal and trusted relationships. They spend a lot of time processing the "what if's" and often miss out on activities, events, and even connection with others. As they continue to develop a relationship with Christ and feel they can trust His Word, their anxiety levels lower. Knowing they serve a God who invites them to ask questions and promises to show them many marvelous and wonderful things brings them a sense of peace.

Awareness for Sixes: Hearing God requires you to cultivate quiet time. Notice how your body responds when you feel safe. Every once in a while, allow yourself to relax your rigid routine and embrace a new experience whether it be trying a new food, exercise routine, or book. This week as you meditate on Jeremiah 33:2–3, engage in an activity that requires movement. Ask God to reveal something new and unexpected to you about yourself.

SEVEN

SEVENS long to find joy and excitement in all of their experiences and relationships. Their minds are always busy trying to make connections between all the information they are processing in their environments. As they practice cultivating quiet time with the Lord, they can find peace within themselves. They love serving a God who allows them to experience life full of wonder and amazement.

Awareness for Sevens: Having a sense of peace and an understanding within yourself enables you to discern the voice of God in your life. Learning to be patient with yourself as you develop new skills and talents positions you to accomplish whatever it is God places on your heart. Practice meditation that focuses on the beautiful simplicity of life. This week as you meditate on Jeremiah 33:2-3, journal the feelings you are experiencing.

EIGHT

EIGHTS long to know they are honored and valued. They often appear strong, confident, and assertive. However, they project this demeanor because they fear this is the only way they will be respected. As they grow in the knowledge of Christ, they begin to realize He is the maker of both heaven and earth. They turn toward God, humbly honoring Him and the power in which He exhibits. When they understand God has infinitely more wisdom and knowledge than they do, they submit to His ultimate authority.

Awareness for Eights: Hearing God requires you to not only schedule quiet time alone with Him but also to make sure this time is used in a productive way, such as scripture meditation, scripture journaling, or a specific Bible study. Allowing yourself to be intimate and vulnerable with a few close people will soften your heart and position you to receive God's Word more easily. This week as you meditate on Jeremiah 33:2-3, journal the areas in which you would like Him to reveal His power.

NINE

NINES long for others to see them as valuable and worthwhile. They have wonderful ideas, although they often second-guess themselves and their abilities. As they fully embrace who they are in Christ, they go to God and ask Him to give them strength as they seek to express themselves.

Awareness for Nines: Work toward establishing the gifts and talents within you so you can use them to advance the kingdom of God. Value your voice as you establish healthy boundaries. This allows you to discern what is of God and what is someone's expectations being placed on you. Practice calling on God and sharing with Him your thoughts, feelings, and ideas. This week as you meditate on Jeremiah 33:2-3, journal what God is revealing about His plan and purpose for your life.

APPLICATION

As you reflect on your Enneagram number this week, how do you relate to the longing you desire?

_____

_____

_____

How can you allow yourself space this week to be still and reflect on what you are longing to hear or know about yourself as you process this week's Enneagram reflection?

_____

_____

_____

After reading each Enneagram reflection this week and seeing what others are longing for, in what ways can you have more empathy and compassion for those in your life?

_____

_____

_____

What do you need at this moment that you can ask God to provide? How are you hearing God speak to you in a way you couldn't figure out on your own?

_____

_____

_____

MEDITATION

Go to page 342 and try the Contemplation Meditation exercise.

My prayer this week:

_____

_____

_____

_____

_____

_____

_____

_____

_____

_____

_____

WEEK 45

THE ONE WHO BLESSES OTHERS
IS ABUNDANTLY BLESSED; THOSE WHO
HELP OTHERS ARE HELPED.

PROVERBS 11:25 (MSG)

FRIENDSHIPS
A HELPING HEART

WHEN YOU FOCUS ON OTHERS FIRST, YOU WILL NOTICE HOW YOU FLOURISH AND THRIVE.

Outside of immediate family, your community of dear friends can be your biggest blessing. Friends who walk with you in times of crisis, celebrate with you in times of triumph, and encourage you when you stumble can breathe life into your soul. But if you want to maintain a healthy inner circle of confidants, avoid transactional relationships. Love cannot be bartered and rather should be given freely and without condition. It is amazing to see life transformation when you reach across the table from another person and love them well. Each Enneagram type has a different longing in their heart when they engage with others. Accordingly, instead of focusing on what you can get from the people around you, concentrate on becoming the best friend *you* can be to those you love. Engage with them in their preferred language. Spend time asking yourself questions like, "Today, how can I help make this world better for the people in my life?" and "How can I bless those around me without becoming burdensome?" Uplift others as you foster and strengthen your friendships. When someone has success in life, be the first to celebrate. When a friend gets excited, get excited for them. When a friend is feeling vulnerable or overwhelmed, empathize by leaning in and listening. When you focus on others first, you will notice how you— along with all your healthy relationships—flourish and thrive.

ONE

ONES want to know that other people think they are good and respectable. They wish others understood how loud their inner critic sounds in their head. They hope others see them as valuable in relationships.

Awareness for Ones: Seeing what others desire within their relationships helps you to have compassion and understanding. You are a good friend who is trustworthy and respectable, so as you work toward understanding others, your relationships will grow wide and deep. This week as you meditate on Proverbs 11:25, think about a relationship that is life-giving to you. What do you think is the reason you feel so fulfilled by this relationship?

TWO

TWOS want to know that they are wanted, needed, and loved. They like to be included in upbeat and positive experiences, activities, and conversations. They are passionate and expressive people who enjoy the company of those who feel the same way about the given situation or experience.

Awareness for Twos: It is worth taking the time to understand what you need. It is also beneficial for you to understand what others need from you, and this is where transformation happens in your relationships. Helping others feel loved and supported goes a long way. This week as you meditate on Proverbs 11:25, think about the people God has placed in your life. Ask yourself, "Do they love me well? Have I expressed my needs to them?" and "Am I loving others in the way they want to be loved?"

THREE

THREES want to know they are loved for simply being themselves. They do not enjoy sharing deep personal feelings. Rather, they like to engage in competitive activities. They keep a very full schedule, so making time for relationships usually needs to be planned.

Awareness for Threes: You do not like to fail in any area of your life including relationships. Understanding what other people want and need can help you care for them well. This week as you meditate on Proverbs 11:25, write down a few ways you can care for those in your life in a more genuine way.

FOUR

FOURS want to know they will be embraced just as they are. They enjoy connecting with others in deep, meaningful, and purposeful ways. They openly express their thoughts, feelings, and emotions within their relationships and are NOT looking for others to cheer them up and fix them.

Awareness for Fours: Understanding that not all people feel as deeply as you do will help you care for others without feeling frustrated or dismissed. Listening and watching how others in your life receive love and affection will help you care for them the way they need. This week as you meditate on Proverbs 11:25, think about the people you care for and ask yourself, "Am I paying attention to their needs, wants, and desires?" Write down a few ways you can be more intentional in your relationships.

FIVE

FIVES want to know their needs are not a problem. They do not enjoy drama or talking about their emotions. They like to understand what is expected of them and they also like to know the plan ahead of time.

Awareness for Fives: You enjoy your alone time and tend to have just a few people you are close to. Allowing others to express themselves and their needs within your relationships will help you grow in emotional connection. This week as you meditate on Proverbs 11:25, reflect on your relationships. Do you feel understood? Write down what you wish others knew about you and then share this with someone close to you.

SIX

SIXES want to know they are safe. They look for those they believe have strong character and integrity in relationships. They like to ask a lot of questions. Before they can give answers, they need others to be patient with them as they research and process information.

Awareness for Sixes: Your anxiety at times can get the best of you, keeping you from deep, meaningful relationships. Allow yourself to see what others are hoping for in a relationship, and with understanding and compassion, love them in this way. This week as you meditate on Proverbs 11:25, can you see the benefits in loving and caring for others? Write down the name of a friend you are going to intentionally care for in a new way.

Notes

SEVEN

SEVENS want to know they will be taken care of, but not in the sense of having a "caretaker." Rather, Sevens want to know they matter in relationships and that they can trust others. They desire mutual respect and appreciation.

Awareness for Sevens: Allow yourself to notice the needs others have in your relationships. Instead of focusing on your wants and desires, turn your attention toward what would be mutually beneficial for all. This week as you meditate on Proverbs 11:25, think about the people God has placed in your life. Are you paying attention to what they need? Write down a few ways you can become more attuned to the needs of others.

EIGHT

EIGHTS want to know they will not be disrespected, made to feel stupid, or exposed in some way. Trust is very important to them. They also want to feel supported as they pursue their dreams.

Awareness for Eights: Having people in your life who are supportive and caring is important to you. Equally, though, they need to know you understand their heart's desire and will champion them in their pursuit of happiness. This week as you meditate on Proverbs 11:25, how can you help others without telling them what to do? Write down a few phrases that help you care for others just as they are.

NINE

NINES want to know there is room for them in this world. They are sensitive to conflict and criticism. They want all people to be regarded as valuable and special.

Awareness for Nines: Your tender heart and gentle spirit allow you to be attuned to the needs of others. You have the unique ability to see all sides of a situation and have empathy and compassion for all. This week as you meditate on Proverbs 11:25, ask God to help you share your needs with a friend, knowing that not only will you be blessed, they will be too.

APPLICATION

How do you resonate with what your heart longs for in relationships?

_____

_____

_____

How often do you share your needs in your current relationships?

_____

_____

_____

_____

In what ways can you help those you are in relationship with feel loved and valued after reading their Enneagram reflections?

_____

_____

_____

How do you feel you are blessing others? How are you hearing God speak to you about your friendships?

_____

_____

_____

_____

MEDITATION

Go to page 332 and try the Box Breathing exercise.

My prayer this week:

_____

_____

_____

_____

_____

_____

_____

_____

_____

_____

_____

_____

_____

WEEK 46

"

MY DEAR BROTHERS AND SISTERS,
TAKE NOTE OF THIS: EVERYONE SHOULD
BE QUICK TO LISTEN, SLOW TO SPEAK,
AND SLOW TO BECOME ANGRY, BECAUSE
HUMAN ANGER DOES NOT PRODUCE
THE RIGHTEOUSNESS THAT GOD DESIRES.
THEREFORE, GET RID OF ALL MORAL FILTH
AND THE EVIL THAT IS SO PREVALENT
AND HUMBLY ACCEPT THE WORD
PLANTED IN YOU, WHICH CAN SAVE YOU.

JAMES 1:19-21

DEFENSE MECHANISMS
THE WORD PLANTED

CALM YOUR NATURAL REFLEXES AND BREAK
DOWN THE BARRIERS THAT EMOTIONALLY
KEEP YOU FROM FEELING AT PEACE.

How often do you feel yourself putting up your guard or pushing others away?
How often do you find yourself speaking before listening? This week try to listen
more and react less. Even though each Enneagram number has a coping-strategy
defense mechanism they unconsciously use when they feel uncomfortable
in difficult situations, you should strive to intentionally respond with grace
whenever you feel yourself building a wall of defense. Your spirit will be more
peaceful because your responses will be much calmer, especially when dealing
with difficult people and difficult situations. When you are meditating on the
Word of God and staying attuned to your patterns of frustration, you will be in
the right heart space. Of course, human anger is a natural part of life, but God
yearns for you to curb your outbursts. This message from James teaches you to
calm your natural reflexes and break down the barriers that emotionally keep you
from feeling at peace, even if you think those barriers are protecting you from
pain, disappointment, guilt, shame, or conflict. Though your defense strategy
appears to keep you safe, keep in mind you serve the biggest Defender of all—the
Creator of the universe.

ONE

ONES use reaction formation as an unconscious coping strategy. They try to reduce or eliminate anxiety caused by their own thoughts, feelings, or behaviors they consider unacceptable by responding in a manner that is the exact opposite of how they really feel. This coping strategy helps them deal with their own unresolved sadness, anxiety, anger, and shame.

Awareness for Ones: When you become more aware of how you use your defense mechanism of reaction formation and learn to share your feelings of frustration and anger, this no longer causes bitterness and resentment to build inside you. For instance, you may think you could have done something better than someone else, but instead of correcting the situation, you praise that person for it. This week as you meditate on James 1:19–21 examine yourself and your response to people. How has anger caused you to react in ways you are less than proud of?

TWO

TWOS use repression as an unconscious coping strategy by trying to hide their true selves from themselves and others. They often try to comfort others who are dealing with similar issues as a way of comforting themselves. This allows them to continue to ignore their true feelings and needs. In other words, they focus on other people's needs instead of acknowledging their own.

Awareness for Twos: When you can express your true needs and emotions in all of your situations, you will find repression actually keeps you from the freedom you have longed for—for example, being honest with someone about how you are feeling in the moment, rather than trying to hide those emotions like you usually do. This week as you meditate on James 1:19–21, humbly accept God's Word planted in your life. Write down what you have been trying to process on your own and confide this situation in a trusted friend.

THREE

THREES use identification. They assume false identities as an unconscious coping strategy when they feel insecure. In these moments, they morph into other people's behaviors by copying others' characteristics and beliefs. They can even go as far as adopting their ideas, hobbies, and interests as their own.

Awareness for Threes: You are likely not consciously aware of this pattern, as it can be very hard to untangle this web and discover your true self. It takes patience and self-awareness to recognize behaviors, thought patterns, and beliefs you have adapted that are not truly yours—for example, if you have a boss who is a NASCAR fanatic and you suddenly become just as big of a fan in order to gain favor. This week as you meditate on James 1:19–21 write down the patterns that are keeping you from being your best in Christ.

FOUR

FOURS use introjection as an unconscious coping strategy by taking criticism personally and internalizing the feelings of shame and inadequacy. They focus on the negative and begin to believe they caused the problem, disregarding any positive feedback.

Awareness for Four: When you notice yourself becoming negative and internalizing everything that is being said to you as if it is all your fault, you need to be reminded of how special you are to God. For example, when a friend compliments your hairstyle, you might internally process this and ask yourself, "Has my hair been looking bad lately? What did my hair look like yesterday? Should I do something different with my hairstyle?" This week as you meditate on James 1:19–21, notice the importance of having the word of God planted in you. Write this scripture, Psalm 139:14: "I praise you because I am fearfully and wonderfully made; your works are wonderful, I know that full well."

FIVE

FIVES use isolation as an unconscious coping strategy by withdrawing and retreating. They believe this will help them avoid becoming overwhelmed or empty. But when they retreat into their own thoughts, they cut themselves off from their true feelings and emotions.

Awareness for Fives: When you recognize yourself isolating, try staying present in the moment and processing your feelings and thoughts. For example, when you're with a crowd of people and you begin to feel overwhelmed by the conversation, activity, or stimulation, try not to drift away from the crowd and disappear. This week, as you meditate on James 1:19–21, recognize the situations that trigger righteousness within you. Write down how you can respond in a way different from retreating or isolating.

SIX

SIXES use projection as an unconscious coping strategy by falsely accusing others. They tend to misplace their anger, inappropriate thoughts, and behaviors on other people. They believe they are creating safety and security using this defense mechanism. However, it often leads to insecurities and heightened anxiety.

Awareness for Sixes: When you recognize you are projecting your own fabricated thoughts and feelings onto others, ask yourself what is the deeper issue that is really bothering you. For example, think about when you accuse someone of thinking or feeling the way you think or feel, even though they have never expressed themselves, nor is it true. This week as you meditate on James 1:19–21, write out this scripture and ask God to reveal where you lash out in anger toward others.

Notes

SEVEN

SEVENS use rationalization as an unconscious coping strategy by avoiding their true motivations, intentions, or consequences. They explain away unacceptable thoughts, feelings, and behaviors. They do this by using positive reframing, which involves deferring personal responsibility and ignoring pain, sadness, guilt, and anxiety.

Awareness for Sevens: When you notice yourself reframing difficult situations or feelings, ask yourself what you are trying to avoid. For example, do you reframe feelings of sadness or loss by dismissing the seriousness of the situation by saying, "Perhaps it is for the best"? This week as you meditate on James 1:19–21, be reminded of the importance of being quick to listen and slow to respond. Write down all the feelings you are trying to avoid.

EIGHT

EIGHTS use denial as an unconscious coping strategy by negating anything that makes them feel anxious, by acting as if it never happened. They deny it in several ways. First, they might deny the reality of the unpleasant information. Or, they might acknowledge the information but deny the severity of it. Or, they could acknowledge the information and the severity of it but deny their involvement in it altogether.

Awareness for Eights: You likely have not realized how you have used your defense mechanism of denial. As you become aware of how you use this pattern of behavior for self-protection, you may see how anger and even a flippant response has caused hurt within your relationships. This week as you meditate on James 1:19–21, ask God to give you wisdom in how to respond to situations. Write about a time you used your defense mechanism of denial out of anger.

NINE

NINES use narcotization as an unconscious coping strategy by numbing themselves to avoid situations too painful, overwhelming, difficult, or uncomfortable to handle. They will also avoid their circumstances by performing routines that are rhythmic, habitual, and familiar, which require little of their attention and energy. The reason for this is that it brings them comfort and creates a calming in their environment.

Awareness for Nines: When you notice yourself falling into familiar and mundane routines, ask yourself if you are trying to avoid a difficult situation—such as doing the dishes or busywork instead of addressing a hard topic of conversation with a loved one. Be reminded God is the true comforter, and when you bring your concerns to Him, it will bring you peace. This week as you meditate on James 1:19–21, write down another scripture you have used to calm your anxiety.

APPLICATION

What did you discover about your defense mechanism this week?

_____

_____

_____

How has your defense mechanism kept you safe through the years?

_____

_____

_____

In what way can you identify how those close to you use their defense mechanism, after reading their Enneagram reflections?

_____

_____

_____

How can you currently work toward being "quick to listen, slow to speak, and slow to become angry"? How are you hearing God speak to you when it comes to your defense mechanism?

_____

_____

_____

MEDITATION

Go to page 334 and try the Concentration Meditation exercise.

My prayer this week:

_____

_____

_____

_____

_____

_____

_____

_____

_____

WEEK 47

"

SO HERE'S WHAT I WANT YOU TO DO, GOD HELPING
YOU: TAKE YOUR EVERYDAY, ORDINARY LIFE—
YOUR SLEEPING, EATING, GOING-TO-WORK, AND
WALKING-AROUND LIFE— AND PLACE IT BEFORE
GOD AS AN OFFERING. EMBRACING WHAT GOD DOES
FOR YOU IS THE BEST THING YOU CAN DO FOR HIM.
DON'T BECOME SO WELL-ADJUSTED TO YOUR CULTURE
THAT YOU FIT INTO IT WITHOUT EVEN THINKING.
INSTEAD, FIX YOUR ATTENTION ON GOD. YOU'LL BE
CHANGED FROM THE INSIDE OUT. READILY RECOGNIZE
WHAT HE WANTS FROM YOU, AND QUICKLY RESPOND
TO IT. UNLIKE THE CULTURE AROUND YOU, ALWAYS
DRAGGING YOU DOWN TO ITS LEVEL OF IMMATURITY,
GOD BRINGS THE BEST OUT OF YOU, DEVELOPS
WELL-FORMED MATURITY IN YOU.

ROMANS 12:1-2 (MSG)

CYCLE OF BEHAVIOR
COUNTER CULTURE

GOD CREATED YOU TO HAVE A FUN-LOVING
SIDE, EMPATHETIC TOWARD OTHERS,
AND POSSESS A KIND SPIRIT.

As with all Enneagram numbers, you develop patterns of behavior in your daily life that become second nature to who you are. Because you are so accustomed to these patterns formed in early childhood, you often excuse them by saying, "This is just who I am." But God did not create you to be a machine that robotically follows certain patterns or habits. He created you to have a fun-loving side, to be empathetic toward others, and to possess a noble strength and a kind spirit. And He wants to renew all these aspects in you every day. Society might try to tear you down or put immense pressure on you to measure up to a particular standard, but God wants more for you. You are striving toward spiritual and personal growth, hence whenever you feel tempted to act a certain way or maintain a specific persona, listen to the voice of the Holy Spirit, fix your attention on God, and allow Him to transform and renew you from the inside out.

—————— ONE ——————

ONES are uncomfortable admitting—to themselves or anyone—patterns of behavior they have developed. However, due to their perfectionist tendencies, they tend to look as if they have everything in order and under control.

Awareness for Ones: To combat your inner critic who is always whispering such lies as, "You will never measure up," or "You are not as good as they think you are," you must use the Word of God as your weapon. Memorize scriptures that speak the truth about who you are. Practice letting things go and instead play a game, watch a show, or perhaps take a walk. This week as you meditate on Romans 12:1–2, surrender your daily activities to Christ. Write down one task you are going to intentionally put off while doing something you enjoy.

—————— TWO ——————

TWOS are relationship-oriented and look toward others to find acceptance and approval. Therefore, it may be uncomfortable for them to look at their life objectively to become aware of any unsettling patterns of behavior. Often, they have a difficult time taking responsibility for the role they play in situations. However, their desire for a connection with God inspires them to explore their true motivations and intentions.

Awareness for Twos: When you realize all that God has planned for your life, you are able to see the patterns that are keeping you trapped in a cycle of self-denial. Journaling your thoughts and deep feelings helps you to process them in a healthy way. Allow yourself to have personal alone time without feeling guilt or shame. This week as you meditate on Romans 12:1–2, write down the name of a trusted friend who speaks spiritual truth into your life. Make it a point to spend time with this friend monthly.

—————— THREE ——————

It is uncomfortable for **THREES** to admit to themselves or anyone else their developed patterns of behavior, because it is difficult for them to identify personal attributes other than those which revolve around ambition and achievement. They subconsciously spin situations to protect their image.

Awareness for Threes: Once you see the patterns that are keeping you trapped in a cycle of chasing affirmation, you can choose to ask Christ to help you change these patterns. Establish a routine in which you spend time reading your Bible. Turning your focus toward relationships and being intentional to pray for others will create a longing for connection. Surrounding yourself with people who are of strong moral character and sound judgment will greatly influence your life decisions. This week as you meditate on Romans 12:1–2, surrender your life to Christ, allowing the words to bring conviction to your heart.

FOUR

Although **FOURS** are very attuned to their feelings, they cycle through the same emotions day after day. They can easily get caught up in a victim mentality or believing others are better than they are.

Awareness for Fours: Because you are now able to see the patterns that are keeping you trapped in the cycle of feeling as if you do not measure up, you can fight them with the Word of God. Spend time daily listening to worship music that brings peace to your soul. At least monthly allow yourself to express your love for Christ through a creative outlet. Commit to reading a proverb a day for the next month and watch your hunger and knowledge of Christ grow. This week as you meditate on Romans 12:1-2, pray your heart would be tender toward yourself and others.

FIVE

It is uncomfortable for **FIVES** to admit to themselves or anyone else their behavioral pattern of needing privacy or wanting to withdraw from conversations or social situations. Even when they become aware of these patterns, they want to protect themselves from having to listen to other people's input.

Awareness for Fives: When you allow the Word of God to bring conviction to your heart, you become aware of self-righteousness. Making it a point to get involved in a Bible study with a small group of people will help you grow in spiritual maturity. Being purposeful to emotionally connect with loved ones will help you feel loved and known in return. A couple times a month, do something someone else wants to do while having a good attitude about it. This week as you meditate on Romans 12:1-2, pray your eyes would be open to see what God is revealing to you.

SIX

One natural pattern for **SIXES** is problem solving, a tendency that urges them to poke and prod at aspects of their own lives so they can get rid of whatever is keeping them in bondage. They accept the challenge of taking a deeper look at themselves, hoping to discover the patterns of why they do the things they do.

Awareness for Sixes: This is a positive pattern because, as it says in Romans 12:1-2, you are encouraged to place your everyday, ordinary life before God. His hope is that you will learn to trust Him as He continues to reveal mysteries about you. Study the Word of God daily and write affirmations about who He says you are. Make it a point to take walks as often as possible and spend time noticing the creation that exists around you. This week, allow yourself to rest and enjoy the life you live without feeling guilty.

SEVEN

It is difficult for **SEVENS** to be still long enough to process their emotions and thoughts. They have such a visceral reaction to emotional pain that staying in something uncomfortable makes them feel as though they will be overwhelmed by it and unable to find joy again. Therefore, they try to escape through a pattern of busyness.

Awareness for Sevens: When you surrender your fears to the Lord, He gives you peace as you grow in spiritual awareness. His hope is that you would be able to see the patterns that are keeping you trapped in a cycle of busyness. Intentionally set times on your calendar to read the Word and reflect through journaling. Spend time with a group of friends that are life-giving and spiritually sound. Allow yourself to process your emotions in short segments until completion, knowing Christ will be with you every step of the way. This week as you meditate on Romans 12:1–2, pray He would help you to be still as you allow Him to speak to your heart.

EIGHT

Because of their desire to protect themselves, **EIGHTS** are uncomfortable admitting to themselves or anyone else what their developed patterns of behavior are. They don't want to look weak, unprepared, or out of control.

Awareness for Eights: Your obedience and surrender to Christ bring out the best in you as you grow and mature. His hope is that you would be able to see the patterns that are keeping you trapped in a cycle of dominance. Try allowing someone else to make small decisions, and not overriding them. Study verses about how God is powerful and mighty. Occasionally, do something nice for a friend without letting them know it was you. This week as you meditate on Romans 12:1–2, be encouraged as you see His faithfulness and protection.

NINE

It is difficult for **NINES** to determine their patterns of behavior because they tend to take on the patterns of the people around them. Seeing themselves as their own person with their own ideas, dreams, hopes, and abilities is key for them to recognize this cycle of behavior.

Awareness for Nines: Place your everyday, ordinary life before God. His hope is that you would be able to see the patterns that are keeping you trapped in a cycle of pleasing and realize He has more for you. Make a list of the activities you enjoy doing and be intentional to do them throughout your week. Engage in a Bible study that is on a topic you are interested in. Make it a point to get outside and explore nature regularly. This week as you meditate on Romans 12:1–2, take inventory of the many ways He has been caring for you.

APPLICATION

What patterns of behavior can you identify that you have used since childhood?

_____

_____

_____

How have your patterns of behavior kept you from getting what you want out of life?

_____

_____

_____

_____

In what ways has it been helpful to read about the different Enneagram numbers through the reflections?

_____

_____

_____

In your current season, what is God revealing to you about your patterns? How are you hearing God speak to you when it comes to your behavior?

_____

_____

_____

MEDITATION

Go to page 336 and try the Reflection Meditation exercise.

My prayer this week:

_____

_____

_____

_____

_____

_____

_____

_____

_____

WEEK 48

FINALLY, ALL OF YOU,
HAVE UNITY OF MIND, SYMPATHY,
BROTHERLY LOVE, A TENDER HEART,
AND A HUMBLE MIND.

1 PETER 3:8 (ESV)

COMPATIBILITY
UNITY OF MIND

GOD DIDN'T CREATE YOU TO
BE LIKE EVERYONE ELSE.

In our culture today, does it seem like people just throw jabs and insults like spears to inflict as much pain as possible? Just look at the comments section on any social media platform. You also see this unfold on reality TV and in the political arena where mudslinging is a common sport. Unfortunately, you might also witness this damaging practice in your own relationships, family circles, and community, as people often get on an emotional high that lifts them up when they put others down. Nevertheless, you can maintain a posture of empathy, even with others who do not necessarily see the world the same way you do. God didn't create you to be like everyone else, nor did He intend for you to fight with others because of your differences. He reminds us in Ephesians 6 that our struggle isn't against flesh, as people are not our problem. Our war is against the schemes of the Enemy. All of us are humans, created by God, which in and of itself unifies us. God says a unified world is the world He desires for you. Be a witness this week as you exemplify sympathy and sensitivity while adopting a tender heart toward others—regardless of their points of view. As you treat others as you wish to be treated and recognize the parts of relationships you desire most, based on your own Enneagram personality, you will discover a God-given peace that comes with unity.

——— ONE ———

ONES often wish that others would take responsibility for their actions and apologize when they have wronged someone. Ones also want to be affirmed for doing a good job and need others to understand they are sensitive to criticism. Furthermore, Ones appreciate when others encourage them to let loose and have a little fun.

Awareness for Ones: As you learn to grow in patience through embracing who Christ is and how He was the only perfect person who ever lived here on earth, you will find it easier to accept the things about yourself and others that are not perfect. Living in unity requires you to extend empathy and compassion toward all other Enneagram numbers and their individual journeys. When you learn to accept yourself without judgment and perfectionism, you no longer get angry and disappointed with others when they are not living up to your unattainable standards. This week as you meditate on 1 Peter 3:8, write down ways you can show others brotherly love, regardless of their imperfect performance.

——— TWO ———

TWOS need others to be gentle with them and their emotions. Twos also need others to take an interest in what is going on in their lives and even do something spontaneous for them that expresses, "You are special."

Awareness for Twos: You need to have space to express your needs. The more you understand them, the more you are willing to look at all the other Enneagram numbers and their different perspectives. When you find freedom from living under others demanding expectations, you no longer place expectations on people. Unity is when you grow in empathy and compassion toward yourself, which will extend into all your relationships. This week as you meditate on 1 Peter 3:8, write down how you can continue to display your tender heart to people in all parts of their journey.

——— THREE ———

THREES need others to be kind when giving honest feedback and to value them for just simply being themselves. They also need the environment to remain as peaceful as possible.

Awareness for Threes: Your emotions are not something to run from; rather, they are something to embrace for life-change to take place. The more you understand what your personal needs are, the more you'll be willing to look at all the other Enneagram numbers and their different perspectives. Unity is when you put your hope in the Lord and no longer strive for others' validation, instead embracing yourself and all people with empathy. This week as you meditate on 1 Peter 3:8, write down the ways God is teaching you compassion.

FOUR

FOURS need others to speak kindly about them. Fours also hope others will allow them to look at life through a different perspective, without criticizing them for expressing their emotions.

Awareness for Fours: You need to accept yourself just as you are. Remember, there is nothing missing within you, and you need to love yourself the way Christ loves you. The less you wallow in self-pity, the easier it is to celebrate your many life blessings and the beautiful qualities displayed in all the other Enneagram numbers. Unity is found when you no longer compare yourself to others, but rather see yourself as worthy and gifted while showing compassion for all people. This week as you meditate on 1 Peter 3:8, write down the ways you have built unity in your relationships by showing sympathy and love.

FIVE

FIVES need others to be independent, straightforward, and trustworthy. They also appreciate it when others understand how social gatherings often leave them feeling overwhelmed and awkward.

Awareness for Fives: You need space to recharge and process emotions, while allowing yourself to set boundaries to avoid feeling drained or depleted. However, this time alone should be limited and used to re-energize yourself for you to embrace life to the fullest while appreciating the diversity of all other Enneagram numbers. Unity is recognizing there are numerous ways to see situations and embracing others' points of view with empathy and compassion. This week as you meditate on 1 Peter 3:8, write down the ways God has given you new perspectives on people as you have humbly sought His wisdom.

SIX

SIXES need others to be clear and direct. They need to be listened to and not judged when their anxiety rises.

Awareness for Sixes: You need to develop relationships with trustworthy and reliable people and a support system to reassure you everything is going to be okay. You also need to trust God in the process. The more you understand the ways of Jesus and His desire for all people to be loved and accepted equally, the more you can embrace the importance of inclusiveness for all other Enneagram numbers. Unity is not about a hierarchy to keep you safe, but about extending empathy and compassion in all your relationships, building trust and security. This week as you meditate on 1 Peter 3:8, write down the ways you have experienced a unity of mind with people from different backgrounds.

Notes

SEVEN

SEVENS need others to give them encouragement and accept them the way they are. They need others to share conversations and laughter with them.

Awareness for Sevens: You need space to be creative, to slow down, and to be in the moment, while realizing that boundaries allow you to live freely. You express empathy and compassion for others when you don't judge them for not being as free-spirited and spontaneous as you. This open-mindedness allows for unity between you and all the other Enneagram numbers. This week as you meditate on 1 Peter 3:8, write down the ways you have shown brotherly love to others by allowing them to be authentically themselves and living life at their own pace.

EIGHT

EIGHTS need others to stand up for them, to not sugarcoat the truth, and to acknowledge the more tender side of Eight's personality.

Awareness for Eights: You need to develop relationships with those you trust by being vulnerable as you allow those close to you to see your softer side. You also need to trust that God is your ultimate protector. You can show your strength while also being disarming and vulnerable without having a posture of pretentiousness. When you can express your own vulnerability, you are then able to show kindness to all other Enneagram numbers. Unity is when you stand up against the injustices of the world and extend empathy and compassion for all mankind. This week as you meditate on 1 Peter 3:8, write down the times you have shown sympathy for the lonely and downtrodden.

NINE

NINES need others to really listen to them and not discredit their ideas. They also need others to affirm them and speak in a kind manner if conflict arises.

Awareness for Nines: You need community with others who value and inspire you. You also need to spend time with yourself, discovering what you like. Your appreciation for all humanity allows you to embrace all the other Enneagram numbers. Unity is what your heart longs for, which motivates you to easily extend compassion and empathy for all people. This week as you meditate on 1 Peter 3:8, write down the ways you have shown the tenderness of Christ to those who otherwise would be overlooked.

APPLICATION

What are a few more "needs" you would add to the list for your Enneagram number?

_____

_____

_____

How can you express what you need in a healthy way in your relationships moving forward?

_____

_____

_____

In what ways can you become more aware of what those close to you need in a relationship with you after reading the Enneagram reflections?

_____

_____

_____

How are you displaying compassion and empathy in your relationships? How are you hearing God speak to you about your compatibility?

_____

_____

_____

MEDITATION

Go to page 342 and try the Contemplation Meditation exercise.

My prayer this week:

_____

_____

_____

_____

_____

_____

_____

_____

WEEK 49

"

"DON'T WORRY OR SURRENDER TO YOUR
FEAR. FOR YOU'VE BELIEVED IN GOD,
NOW TRUST AND BELIEVE IN ME ALSO.
MY FATHER'S HOUSE HAS MANY DWELLING
PLACES. IF IT WERE OTHERWISE, I WOULD
TELL YOU PLAINLY, BECAUSE I GO TO PREPARE
A PLACE FOR YOU TO REST. AND WHEN
EVERYTHING IS READY, I WILL COME BACK
AND TAKE YOU TO MYSELF SO THAT
YOU WILL BE WHERE I AM.

JOHN 14:1-3 (TPT)

CHILDHOOD MESSAGE
PERFECTLY PREPARED FOR YOU

JESUS IS INVITING YOU INTO A SPECIAL PLACE WHERE ALL YOUR NEEDS WILL BE MET AND YOUR TRUE IDENTITY, SECURED.

Do you ever feel yourself longing for a time or place where you no longer must encounter trouble, heartache, or disappointment? Doesn't a place where you can rest—away from the grip of fear or worry—sound wonderful? This type of peaceful rest is exactly what Jesus promises in John 14. Holding on to this promise can help you overcome any negative messages that tend to cycle repeatedly through your mind. Unfortunately, many of these messages carried over from childhood, whether or not they were true. In fact, each Enneagram number believes a certain message about itself that it—subconsciously or not—heard as a child. Allowing God to replace that message with one of love and purpose may not be easy, but it's a vital step in our spiritual growth. Your childhood home could have been one full of wonder, beauty, and safety, but it also might have been marked by fear, abuse, pressure, poverty, or anger. Regardless of how healthy or unhealthy your upbringing was, you should remember that any harmful messages you received as a child or young adult do not define you. If you are currently harboring any pain, confusion, or emotional scars, lift them up to the One who is building your perfect heavenly home. Jesus is inviting you into a special place where all your needs will be met and your true identity, secured. Let your soul find rest in His message of unfailing love and His promise to never leave you or forsake you.

ONE

For **ONES**, the message "It's not okay to make mistakes" has shaped them from an early age. As a result, they have navigated life trying to be "good." Their loud inner critic is constantly whispering—and sometimes screaming—as a way of pointing out all the places where they are failing. However, God's message to them is one of love and acceptance.

Awareness for Ones: His thoughts toward you are kind and loving. Psalms 103:8 shares with you how He truly feels: "The Lord is compassionate and gracious, slow to anger, abounding in love." God not only restores what has been lost but also has prepared a place for you to be with Him in eternity. This week as you meditate on John 14:1–3, take some time to reflect on the ways God loves you. Write down the words your heart needs to hear.

TWO

For **TWOS**, the message "It's not okay to have your own needs" has shaped them from an early age. Growing up they felt as though either there was not enough room for their needs or their needs were being dismissed in some way. They learned to get love and acceptance by always trying to be what other people wanted, while often denying their own needs.

Awareness for Twos: God has always seen your needs and cared for you with endless love and compassion. John 14:27 reminds you of how important you are to Him: "Peace I leave with you; my peace I give to you. Not as the world gives do I give to you. Let not your hearts be troubled, neither let them be afraid." This week as you meditate on John 14:1–3, write down how it makes you feel that your heavenly Father is preparing a place for you.

THREE

For **THREES**, the message "It's not okay to have your own feelings or identity" has shaped them from an early age. They learned they needed to take on the role of what was socially acceptable in their environments to be loved and accepted. They have navigated life trying to prove their worth through achievements, giving little—if any—room to their emotions.

Awareness for Threes: God has created you just as you are, and your many gifts and talents are to be used for the glory of God, not for the adoration of man. Understanding just how important you are to God allows you to stop chasing success and embrace a life filled with human connection. Ephesians 2:8 is a reminder of the price that has already been paid: "For by grace you have been saved through faith. And this is not your own doing; it is the gift of God" (esv). This week as you meditate on John 14:1–3, write down ways you can find rest, no longer striving for acceptance.

FOUR

For **FOURS**, the message "It's not okay to be too practical or happy" has shaped them from an early age. They have always had big emotions and often heard, "Stop being so overdramatic," or, "You're making such a big deal out of a small issue." They have navigated life trying to find love and acceptance by being authentic and unique.

Awareness for Fours: You are a magnificent creation of the Lord. You are full of creativity and depth. All your emotions are acceptable because they have been crafted by the Creator of the universe. Psalm 104:24 is full of expression: "O Lord, how manifold are your works! In wisdom have you made them all; the earth is full of your creatures" (ESV). Find comfort in knowing God delights in your ability to sense and see the world in all its awe and wonder. This week as you meditate on John 14:1–3, write yourself a note reflecting on God's love for you.

FIVE

For **FIVES**, the message "It's not okay to be content in this world" has shaped them from an early age. They have always felt the world is not a place they could find comfort and security. This has caused them to navigate life trying to have as few needs as possible, all the while making sure they can provide for themselves.

Awareness for Fives: God has created you and crafted you with a purpose and plan in mind. It is liberating to know your heavenly Father is preparing a place where you no longer struggle with feeling as if your world is crashing down around you. 2 Corinthians 9:8 (ESV) can bring you comfort, "And God is able to make all grace abound to you, so that having all sufficiency in all things at all times, you may abound in every good work." This week as you meditate on John 14:1–3, let go of the fear you have been carrying and embrace the rest God desires you to find.

SIX

For **SIXES**, the message "It's not okay to trust your own instincts" has shaped them from an early age. They have felt like their thoughts, ideas, and decisions have always been second-guessed or corrected by a person in authority. Because of this, they have navigated life trying to find safety and security in their relationships and environments.

Awareness for Sixes: Knowing you serve a God that you can trust and cares deeply for you brings comfort to your soul. At times, your anxiety can get the best of you and cause you to hold off from making decisions. 1 Peter 5:7 (ESV) shares with you another option: "Casting all your anxieties on him, because he cares for you." This week as you meditate on John 14:1–3, write down what you imagine the place being prepared for you is like.

SEVEN

For **SEVENS**, the message "It's not okay to depend on anyone for anything" has shaped them from an early age. Either they heard this message directly or it was implied, which has caused them to live with the fear of abandonment and rejection. They have navigated life trying to meet their own needs and take care of themselves.

Awareness for Sevens: God loves you and will always care for you. You no longer have to live fearful of being abandoned, because He will always be with you, no matter what you face in life. Psalm 28:7 (NLT) states that He is your protector and fills you with joy when you put your trust in Him: "The LORD is my strength and shield. I trust him with all my heart. He helps me, and my heart is filled with joy. I burst out in songs of thanksgiving." This week as you meditate on John 14:1–3, write down how you can depend on God.

EIGHT

For **EIGHTS**, the message "It's not okay to be vulnerable or to trust anyone" has shaped them from an early age. They learned to be strong and assertive, taking charge to ensure they are not taken advantage of. They have navigated life trying to protect themselves and those they care about.

Awareness for Eights: Trusting God allows you to finally find rest. You have been strong and resilient throughout your life, and knowing your heavenly Father is preparing a place where you no longer feel the weight of responsibility to keep yourself and everyone safe is freeing. Psalm 121:7–8 is a reminder for you: "The LORD will keep you from all harm—he will watch over your life; the LORD will watch over your coming and going both now and forevermore." This week as you meditate on John 14:1–3, write about the peace you feel knowing God is watching over your life.

NINE

For **NINES**, the message "It's not okay for you to assert yourself" has shaped them from an early age. They learned to go with the flow and not question authority. Instead they did what was expected to keep the peace.

Awareness for Nines: You are an important piece to God's masterful plan. He gifted you with a gentle spirit and kind disposition. He longs to hear your voice. Matthew 7:7 grants you permission to come to Him: "Ask and it will be given to you; seek and you will find; knock and the door will be opened to you." He cares deeply about what is in your heart. This week as you meditate on John 14:1–3, find comfort in knowing your heavenly Father is preparing a place for you to be with Him forever. Write down some of the questions you have about life and find rest in knowing Christ desires to answer them in His time.

APPLICATION

In what ways do you resonate with your childhood message?

_____

_____

_____

How has this message shaped your life?

_____

_____

_____

In what ways are you able to understand those close to you better after reading the Enneagram reflections?

_____

_____

_____

What does it mean to you that the Lord has, "prepared a place for you to rest"? How are you hearing God speak to you when it comes to your childhood message?

_____

_____

_____

MEDITATION

Go to page 332 and try the Box Breathing exercise.

My prayer this week:

_____

_____

_____

_____

_____

_____

_____

_____

_____

_____

_____

_____

WEEK 50

"

IF ANY OF YOU LACKS WISDOM, YOU SHOULD
ASK GOD, WHO GIVES GENEROUSLY
TO ALL WITHOUT FINDING FAULT, AND IT
WILL BE GIVEN TO YOU.

JAMES 1:5

PROGRESSION
GOD GIVES GENEROUSLY

GOD WILL GRANT YOU THE CLEAR UNDERSTANDING YOU NEED WITHOUT POINTING OUT YOUR IMPERFECTIONS.

Are you currently trying to solve a problem, resolve an issue, search for truth, or understand yourself better? Are you searching for wisdom beyond your own understanding? Each Enneagram number approaches self-growth differently, based on a unique learning style. But no matter your number, gaining knowledge is always free and invaluable. All you need to do to receive wisdom is ask the God of the universe. There is no special formula or secret religious recipe, and you do not have to earn your way toward this virtue. Because you have a relationship with God, He will grant you the clear understanding you need without pointing out your imperfections. He loves when you communicate with Him, as you are His child and He never tires of hearing your voice. This week as you seek wisdom, know that God will freely give you His insight and intellect through His unswerving grace. Practice the discipline of asking God for wisdom as part of your daily prayer.

ONE

ONES are always looking for ways to grow in wisdom and become better people. Their journey is filled with seeking out truth and a better way of doing things.

Awareness for Ones: As you seek wisdom in Christ, you will become more self-accepting, optimistic, and lighthearted. You will be able to view life in a new way. You need to understand it is not about perfecting yourself and your surroundings, but rather about embracing a relationship with the King of kings. This week as you meditate on James 1:5, ask God to fill you with wisdom and help you embrace the beauty of who you are. Write down some of the ways God is granting you wisdom beyond your own understanding.

TWO

TWOS grow in wisdom and discernment as they humbly surrender to Christ. They gain the courage to set healthy boundaries, no longer putting the needs of others above their own.

Awareness for Twos: God wants to fill you with wisdom and help you see yourself as valuable and worthy of love. As you grow in your faith journey, ask God for wisdom in all areas of your life. He will help you become more aware of who you are and why you do what you do. Owning your emotions and allowing them to be expressed will help you understand yourself better. This week as you meditate on James 1:5, write down some of the ways God is granting you wisdom beyond your own understanding.

THREE

THREES grow in wisdom when they put their hope in Christ and trust His divine plan. They no longer seek their identity and security through their leadership and the need to get things done. Their focus shifts from projects to tasks to building truthful, genuine, and lasting relationships.

Awareness for Threes: Because you are moving too fast, sometimes you forget you have access to wisdom by simply asking. When you are focused on the quickest way from point A to point B, you tend to make rash decisions, hoping they are right. For you, spiritual growth is going to require slowing down and praying for wisdom in all situations. Then, you will find you are more compliant and understanding. Slowing down allows you to be more aware of your true feelings, giving you space for emotions to surface. As you seek God's wisdom, you will also be more committed to others and grounded in who you are. Gone are the days of putting a facade to please others. This week as you process James 1:5, allow God to show you the areas you lack wisdom. Pray specifically over those areas, asking God to grow you in wisdom and knowledge.

FOUR

FOURS grow in wisdom when they embrace the truth that they are already complete in Christ. They no longer deal with their emotional swings, but instead find contentment and peace when they can appreciate their own gifts and celebrate the gifts of others.

Awareness for Fours: As you journey toward spiritual growth, you will find you are much more grounded and disciplined when you ask God for wisdom in all situations. You can make decisions based on facts not just feels. You become more productive and able to do what is right instead of being swept up in emotions. This week as you meditate on James 1:5, ask God for wisdom and discernment. Take some time and write down what is stirring in your heart as you read this week's scripture.

FIVE

FIVES grow in wisdom when they seek alone time with Christ, rather than seeking isolation for survival purposes. Their desire is for a deeper connection with the heart and presence of God. This allows them to be generous with their talents, time, and resources.

Awareness for Fives: As you journey toward spiritual growth, ask God to fill you with spiritual wisdom. Ask Him to open your eyes to see life the way He sees it. As you draw close to your heavenly Father, you will grow in confidence. You can trust your instincts and make wise decisions. This week as you meditate on James 1:5, ask God for wisdom beyond your years. Allow Him to draw you closer, teaching you His ways. Write down some of the ways God is granting you wisdom beyond your own understanding.

SIX

SIXES grow in wisdom when they put their trust in the faithfulness and strength of God. They embrace the inner peace found in Christ and let go of their insecurities and anxiousness. They can step up, take charge, become more independent, and no longer seek outside support.

Awareness for Sixes: On this spiritual journey toward growth, ask God to fill you with wisdom and understanding. He says all you must do is ask and He will give it to you. As you grow in your relationship with Christ, you are becoming relaxed because your trust is in Him. When you seek spiritual wisdom, it brings a sense of peace to you. You can live less anxiously and more in the present. This week as you meditate on James 1:5, ask God to continue to fill you with spiritual wisdom. Write down several ways you are seeing life through a different lens because of the wisdom He is imparting to you.

SEVEN

SEVENS grow in wisdom when they trust that Christ is with them always during the enjoyable times along with the unpleasant moments in their life. Believing that God is enough prevents them from trying to fill themselves up with fleeting experiences; instead they embrace the quiet moments in their mind and find God's joy in the simplicities of life.

Awareness for Sevens: As you journey toward spiritual growth, you will see often how less is more. It is important for you to slow down and seek God's wisdom every day, because you are inclined to want to do it all and have it all. Asking God for wisdom will slow you down and challenge you to ask yourself, "Is this the best decision for me and my situation at this time?" This week as you meditate on James 1:5, ask God to fill you with wisdom and discernment. Write down what decisions you must make, no matter how small or large, and ask God to guide you as you try to figure out what is best.

EIGHT

EIGHTS find wisdom when they trust in God's strength and power, allowing them to shift to collaboration and agreement. They no longer fight opposition and rather become tender and merciful, embracing their quiet strength.

Awareness for Eights: As you journey toward spiritual growth, ask God to shower you with His wisdom. He will help you slow down and understand the importance of trusting in Him along the way. You will grow in empathy and compassion for others. You will no longer feel you are orchestrating the plan. You will be able to see that God is working all things out for your good according to His riches and glory. This allows you to be present in moments of your life and to trust God is in control. Wisdom is given freely to those who ask. This week as you meditate on James 1:5, ask for wisdom. Allow God to show you what is ahead and seek Him in all you do.

NINE

NINES find wisdom when they lean on their God-given discernment, even in conflict. When they embrace dissension and use it as a tool for growth instead of shutting down and retreating, they find deep and meaningful connections with others.

Awareness for Nines: As you move toward spiritual growth, ask God for wisdom to see yourself in a whole new light. The more you use your voice and are willing to show up in conversations or decision-making, the more at peace you will become. This week as you meditate on James 1:5, ask God to give you wisdom. Ask Him to show you the areas in your life you have shied away from your fear of not being heard or seen. Write down a few ways you can use your voice this week.

APPLICATION

Can you identify the areas in your life where you desire to see growth?

_____

_____

_____

How can you begin to change the situations and obstacles that are getting in the way of your growth?

_____

_____

_____

In what way can you have more empathy and compassion for others as you read about how each Enneagram type struggles to grow and seek wisdom?

_____

_____

_____

In what specific areas of your life can you ask God to grant you wisdom beyond your understanding?

_____

_____

_____

♥ MEDITATION

Go to page 334 and try the Concentration Meditation exercise.

My prayer this week:

_____

_____

_____

_____

_____

_____

_____

_____

_____

_____

WEEK 51

"

YOU KNOW ME INSIDE AND OUT,
YOU KNOW EVERY BONE IN MY BODY;
YOU KNOW EXACTLY HOW I WAS MADE,
BIT BY BIT, HOW I WAS SCULPTED
FROM NOTHING INTO SOMETHING.
LIKE AN OPEN BOOK, YOU WATCHED
ME GROW FROM CONCEPTION TO BIRTH;
ALL THE STAGES OF MY LIFE WERE
SPREAD OUT BEFORE YOU, THE DAYS
OF MY LIFE ALL PREPARED BEFORE
I'D EVEN LIVED ONE DAY.

PSALM 139:15-16 (MSG)

SELF-IMAGE
BEAUTIFULLY SCULPTED

EMBRACE YOUR EVER-CHANGING SEASONS AND CHAMPION YOUR FLUCTUATING STAGES OF LIFE.

Your self-image can be based on either God's unshakable truth or the Enemy's deceitful strategy. Take comfort in recognizing that God has hand-sculpted your external and internal beauty and calls you breathtaking: uniquely, beautifully, and marvelously carved in His image. He knows and loves your every feature. He knows your every thought, your every intention, and your every detail, and He still always chooses you as His beloved child. He has formed your every fiber and crafted you from conception. Embrace your ever-changing seasons and champion your fluctuating stages of life, believing He has planned and prepared every flourishing step of your growth. This week, no matter what complications you are facing or how you are feeling about yourself, remember this truth of how you were designed specifically by your Creator. He fashioned you on purpose, with a purpose, for a purpose: "You are precious and honored in My sight, and because I love you" (Isaiah 43:4).

ONE

When **ONES** have a healthy self-image, they see themselves as reasonable and objective.

Awareness for Ones: Imagine God sees you as even so much more because He knows every intricate part of your being. As you meditate on this scripture, allow yourself to understand just how special and beautiful you are. When you lose sight of who you are, your inner critic can be incredibly cruel and convince you to believe lies about yourself. Therefore, it is so important to consistently remind yourself that you have been created perfectly in the image of God. This week as you meditate on Psalm 139:15–16, write down the ways the Enemy attacks your thought process. Combat any lies you are telling yourself by using the Word of God, which speaks truth about who you really are. You are breathtaking.

TWO

When **TWOS** have a healthy self-image, they believe themselves to be caring and loving people, known for being hospitable, adventurous, and entertaining.

Awareness for Twos: God did a beautiful job creating you. When you lose sight of who you are or get caught up trying to get others to love you, remember you are already enough. God has His hand on you from conception. He has watched you grow into the person you are today, and He knows what the future holds for you. This week as you meditate on Psalm 139:15–16, write down the ways the Enemy attacks your thought process. Combat any lies you are telling yourself about who you are by using the Word of God. Find rest in seeing the beauty of your self and His wonderful craftsmanship. You are marvelous and breathtaking.

THREE

When **THREES** have a healthy self-image, they see themselves as successful, admirable, and productive. However, due to their desire to always present the best image possible, they sometimes have a difficult time believing God created them perfectly in His image.

Awareness for Threes: You feel you must always be "on" and become who people need you to be in the moment. As you read this week's scripture, understand God has created a marvelous masterpiece in you. You have been shaped bit-by-bit and bone-by-bone for a calling and a purpose that God has laid out before you. Allowing yourself to embrace the truth that God knows you inside and out, yet still wants a relationship with you, should bring you comfort. He longs for you to see yourself as a beautiful masterpiece. This week as you meditate on Psalm 139:15–16, write down the ways the Enemy attacks your thought process. Combat any lies you are telling yourself about who you are using the Word of God, which speaks truth about who you really are. You are loveable just as you are.

FOUR

When **FOURS** have a healthy self-image, they see themselves as unique, sensitive, and authentic.

Awareness for Fours: You can appreciate the masterpiece that Christ has made in you, yet you sometimes struggle with feeling there is something still missing within you. Take your time understanding that you are whole and completely created in the image of God and allow these words to penetrate your heart. He sculpted you, you are a masterpiece, you are marvelously made, and what a wonderful creation you are! God delights in you. This week as you meditate on Psalm 139:15–16, write down the ways the Enemy attacks your thought process. Combat any lies you are telling yourself by using the Word of God, which speaks truth about who you really are. God has watched you from conception, knowing every part of you and preparing each step you take. You are His perfect masterpiece.

FIVE

When **FIVES** have a healthy self-image, they see themselves as insightful, curious, and self-reliant.

Awareness for Fives: You know you have what you need to accomplish the tasks at hand. You feel confident in your own abilities, and you typically like yourself. You can look in the mirror and see God's handiwork and feel confident in what you see within yourself. However, at times, you may feel you need to gather knowledge and resources to ensure your self-worth. But, at the depth of who you are, you know you are a marvelous work of art created by a loving God. This week as you meditate on Psalm 139:15–16, write down the ways the Enemy attacks your thought process. Combat any lies you are telling yourself by using the Word of God, which speaks truth about who you really are. You are brilliant.

SIX

When **SIXES** have a healthy self-image, they see themselves as loyal, trustworthy, and responsible.

Awareness for Sixes: Although you sometimes question your own abilities and your self-worth, when you are connected to Christ, you remember you are His masterpiece. As you walk out your faith, you are learning to trust He has knit you in your mother's womb, knowing the plans He has for you to accomplish. This week as you meditate on Psalm 139:15–16, write down the ways the Enemy attacks your thought process. Combat any lies you are telling yourself by using the Word of God, which speaks truth about who you really are. You are a valuable masterpiece.

SEVEN

When **SEVENS** have a healthy self-image, they see themselves as optimistic, enthusiastic, and free-spirited.

Awareness for Sevens: At times, you fear being left to fend for yourself. This can spiral you into a place of feeling worthless. You tend to keep yourself busy to keep these emotions at bay. However, if you can truly grasp just how precious and marvelous you are, you will begin to trust that God is always looking out for you and you will never be alone. God has been with you since the moment of conception, and He has seen your life laid out before Him. This week as you meditate on Psalm 139:15–16, write down the ways the Enemy attacks your thought process. Combat any lies you are telling yourself by using the Word of God, which speaks truth about who you really are. You are a vibrant creation that God looks upon and is well pleased.

EIGHT

When **EIGHTS** have a healthy self-image, they see themselves as strong, assertive, and honest. They typically like what they see when they look in the mirror and can appreciate God's handiwork.

Awareness for Eights: At times you can lose sight of the Creator because of your fast-paced mind. Because you are constantly moving everything forward and getting stuff done, you often lose the ability to recognize that God has been at work helping you the whole time. He has had your life in His hands, and He has been behind you for all your many successes and by your side during your failures. This week as you meditate on Psalm 139:15–16, write down the ways the Enemy attacks your thought process. Combat any lies you are telling yourself by using the Word of God, which speaks truth about who you really are. You are beautifully made and full of strength.

NINE

When **NINES** have a healthy self-image, they see themselves as peaceful, relaxed, and content. They find comfort in knowing they serve a God who has knit them together in their mother's womb and continues to care for them all the days of their life.

Awareness for Nines: When you find yourself feeling unseen or feel your voice doesn't matter, remember you have a purpose and a calling. You have been carefully crafted to be exactly who you are. This week as you meditate on Psalm 139:15–16, write down the ways the Enemy attacks your thought process. Combat any lies you are telling yourself by using the Word of God, which speaks truth about who you really are. You matter, your voice is valuable, and you are important to your Creator.

APPLICATION

As you reflect on your Enneagram number this week, do you feel better understood in any way?

_____

_____

_____

How do you relate to "when you lose sight of who you are"?

_____

_____

_____

In what way can you celebrate a person close to you as you read about what their Enneagram number says about their healthy self-image?

_____

_____

_____

What are the truths of who God says you are? How are you hearing God speak to you about your self-image?

_____

_____

_____

MEDITATION

Go to page 336 and try the Reflection Meditation exercise.

My prayer this week:

_____

_____

_____

_____

_____

_____

_____

_____

_____

WEEK 52

> MAY THE GOD OF HOPE FILL YOU WITH ALL
> JOY AND PEACE AS YOU TRUST IN HIM,
> SO THAT YOU MAY OVERFLOW WITH HOPE
> BY THE POWER OF THE HOLY SPIRIT.

ROMANS 15:13

JOY
OVERFLOWING

GOD IS YOUR SOURCE FOR TRUE AND LASTING PEACE SINCE HE LONGS FOR A RELATIONSHIP WITH YOU.

You live in a world where an enemy tries to steal your joy and a culture tries to define it. But not today. Today let Romans 15:13 be your call to arms. First, know God is your source for true and lasting peace since He longs for a relationship with you. Second, by the power of His Holy Spirit, know that you can overflow with hope, regardless of your circumstances, past choices, or current concerns. When you root yourself in the Word of God and explore more of your identity through the Enneagram, you can walk confidently into your future with humility and boldness. Each Enneagram type has so much to discover, but the joy is in the journey. Each morning, when you drop to your knees in thanksgiving and when you rise to your feet with expectancy, remember, "The joy of the LORD is my strength" (Nehemiah 8:10). You are beautifully, uniquely, and perfectly complete in your heavenly Father and "are filled with an inexpressible and glorious joy, for you are receiving the end result of your faith, the salvation of your souls" (1 Peter 1:8–9). Now go and live with joy and confidence in who you are!

ONE

ONES live a life full of joy and peace when they embrace their God-given ability of discernment. They understand that everything has different qualities and no longer judge situations and people according to their feelings or beliefs.

Awareness for Ones: Receive the joy of the Lord, knowing you can put your trust confidently in Him. God understands what your heart longs for, and hearing, "You are good and respectable," brings you comfort and peace. Psalm 16:11 encourages you to put your trust in the Lord: "You make known to me the path of life; you will fill me with joy in your presence, with eternal pleasures at your right hand." As you meditate on Romans 15:13, find peace in knowing that you do not have to carry the weight of other people's decisions and opinions. Write down the ways you have found joy in your life when you no longer feel the need to fix every situation or person.

TWO

TWOS find true joy and contentment when they love themselves and others unconditionally. They no longer look for others to validate their worth but instead embrace the value found in them through the love of Christ.

Awareness for Twos: God knows what your heart longs for, and hearing, "You are loved and wanted," brings you comfort. Embrace the access you have to your heavenly Father making your requests known to Him. John 16:24 (ESV) says, "Until now you have asked nothing in my name. Ask, and you will receive, that your joy may be full." This allows you to live your life filled with joy knowing you can trust His loving care for you. As you meditate on Romans 15:13, write down the joy and deep gratitude you feel toward God as he continues to display His love.

THREE

THREES find true joy and satisfaction in their life when they genuinely value themselves and spend time, energy, and resources on developing both their personal and spiritual lives. They no longer chase other people's opinions of them.

Awareness for Threes: Be filled with hope as the power of the Holy Spirit continues to guide and direct your steps. God knows what your heart longs for, and hearing, "You are loved and accepted for simply being who you are," brings you comfort and peace. As you continue to grow on your journey of awareness and spiritual awakening, remember Psalm 118:24 (NLT): "This is the day the LORD has made. We will rejoice and be glad in it." Every day is a new day to live surrendering to the will and the ways of the Lord. As you meditate on Romans 15:13, continue to put your trust in Him. Write down how it feels to live joyfully surrendered to the King of kings.

FOUR

FOURS live full of joy and peace when they learn to accept the past and move forward forgiving themselves and those who have hurt them. They embrace all aspects of life being deeply moved and forever changed by their experiences.

Awareness for Fours: As you put your trust in the Lord releasing your worry and shame, you will find overwhelming joy and an abundance of peace in your life. Psalm 4:7 (NLT) says, "You have given me greater joy than those who have abundant harvests of grain and new wine." God knows what your heart longs for, and hearing, "You are seen and accepted as your unique self," brings you comfort. Embrace God's never-ending and unconditional love for you as you meditate on Romans 15:13. Write down the joy you have experienced in your life when you put your trust in the Lord and let go of past hurts and heartache.

FIVE

FIVES live full of joy and peace as they accept life as it is, fleeting and ever-changing. They no longer feel the need to hoard resources or retreat into the quiet safety of their minds because they realize the value of deep personal connection with whom they care.

Awareness for Fives: Joy and peace are found in Christ when you put your trust in Him. God knows what your heart longs for, and hearing, "Your needs and desires are not too much," brings you comfort. Be filled with hope as Psalm 33:21 proclaims: "In him our hearts rejoice, for we trust in his holy name." Living your life fully present and connected to a life-giving community will allow you to find everlasting joy. As you meditate on Romans 15:13, write down the ways you have let those closest to you know you more intimately and the joy and peace this has given you.

SIX

SIXES live full of joy because their courage and confidence are found in Christ. They no longer look for support or validation from others. They walk out their lives full of faith, trusting in the wisdom and discernment of the Lord.

Awareness for Sixes: When you put your trust confidently in God, you live a life full of joy and freedom. God knows what your heart longs for, and hearing, "You are safe and secure," brings you comfort and peace. As the Holy Spirit continues to guide and direct your steps, be reminded of Psalm 16:8–9 (NLT): "I know the LORD is always with me. I will not be shaken, for he is right beside me. No wonder my heart is glad, and I rejoice. My body rests in safety." As you meditate on Romans 15:13, write down the ways you have experienced joy in your life when you put your trust fully in Him.

SEVEN

SEVENS live joyfully always seeing life full of potential with endless possibilities. As they embrace Christ and put their trust in Him, they experience their full range of emotions, no longer afraid of being trapped in emotional pain.

Awareness for Sevens: God knows what your heart longs for, and hearing, "You will be loved and cared for," brings you comfort. Knowing Christ loves you and desires to care for you makes you want to praise Him. Psalm 71:23 (ESV) says, "My lips will shout for joy, when I sing praises to you; my soul also, which you have redeemed." Trust is what you long for, and Christ ensures you can trust His unconditional love for you. As you meditate on Romans 15:13, allow the Holy Spirit to speak to your heart. Write down the joy you have experienced when you have found rest in God's peace.

EIGHT

EIGHTS live full of joy and peace as they submit to the power and the will of God. They no longer position themselves as the authority on all things. Instead they humbly embrace their God-given strength and leadership skills to make a profound difference in the world around them.

Awareness for Eights: Putting your trust in God and allowing yourself to find rest, knowing He will fight your battles brings you joy and peace. God knows what your heart longs for, and hearing, "You will not be taken advantage of or betrayed," brings you comfort. Embrace Colossians 1:11 (NLT), allowing it to be a constant reminder of where you gain your strength and power: "We also pray that you will be strengthened with all his glorious power so you will have all the endurance and patience you need. May you be filled with joy." As you meditate on Romans 15:13, write down the changes you have experienced in your life as you have sought joy through surrender.

NINE

NINES experience the joy of the Lord as they embrace their own Christ-given identity. They live fully awake and alive to the promises and purpose of Christ. Using their voice and sharing their ideas brings them inner peace.

Awareness for Nines: Receive the joy of the Lord, knowing you can put your trust confidently in Him. God knows what your heart longs for, and hearing, "Your voice and presence matter," brings you comfort and peace. You can live fully present as you cling to the truth found in Psalm 28:7: "The LORD is my strength and my shield; my heart trusts in him, and he helps me. My heart leaps for joy, and with my song I praise him." As you meditate on Romans 15:13, allow yourself to embrace the peace of God. Write down the ways you have experienced God's abundant joy in your life as you have learned to trust Him.

APPLICATION

Now that you've reached the end of this journey, how are you experiencing the joy of self-discovery through the help of the Enneagram and biblical truth?

_____

_____

_____

How can you take what you have learned over this past year and apply all of it to your life moving forward?

_____

_____

_____

As you have read about all the Enneagram personalities throughout this year, in what ways have you learned to grow in empathy and compassion for all the Enneagram types?

_____

_____

_____

Over the past 52 weeks, how have you been filled with hope by the power of God? How are you hearing God speak to you about your joy?

_____

_____

_____

MEDITATION

Go to page 342 and try the Contemplation Meditation exercise.

My prayer this week:

_____

_____

_____

_____

_____

_____

_____

_____

_____

_____

_____

_____

BOX
BREATHING

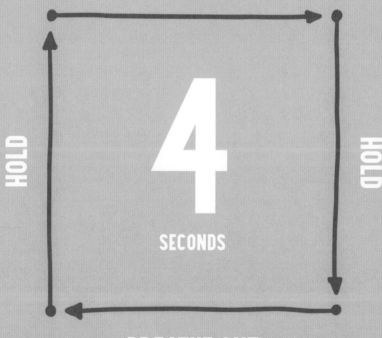

BREATHE IN

HOLD

4

SECONDS

HOLD

BREATHE OUT

BOX BREATHING, also known as resetting your breath or four-square breathing, is a relaxing technique that helps you to clear your mind, relax your body, and improve your focus.

Follow these four steps all in the count of four:

Close your eyes and begin to take a deep breath as you count to four slowly.

1 2 3 4

Hold your breath to the count of four.

1 2 3 4

Begin to slowly exhale to the count of four.

1 2 3 4

Repeat steps 1 to 3 four times.

During your box breathing practice, meditate on the week's scripture while asking yourself what spiritual truths and personal awarenesses you need to breathe in at this moment.

CONCENTRATION
MEDITATION

CONCENTRATION MEDITATION refers to the process of focusing on a single word or passage from the weekly scripture. This helps you to visualize God's Word, breathe it in, and ask yourself, "What is God revealing to me in this moment?"

Follow these six steps:

1 Sit in silence, breathing naturally, while *allowing your mind to focus* on what you have been learning about yourself this week.

2 Next, begin to *visualize a particular word or passage.*

3 As you focus on the word or passage, ask yourself this question: *"What is God revealing to me about this word or passage?"*

4 As you begin to process this word or passage, *recognize where you feel it in your body.*

5 Now, slowly *take a deep breath by inhaling the scripture as your truth,* and then slowly exhale the lies of the Enemy and all negative thoughts trying to hold you back from who God says you are.

6 Lastly, *focus on the part of your body where you feel tension the most* and take several deep breaths, followed by a slow exhale, while focusing on releasing the tension from that part of your body.

REFLECTION
MEDITATION

REFLECTION MEDITATION is a practice that offers a quiet time to reflect on the weekly scripture and to answer one or two of the provided questions below throughout your week:

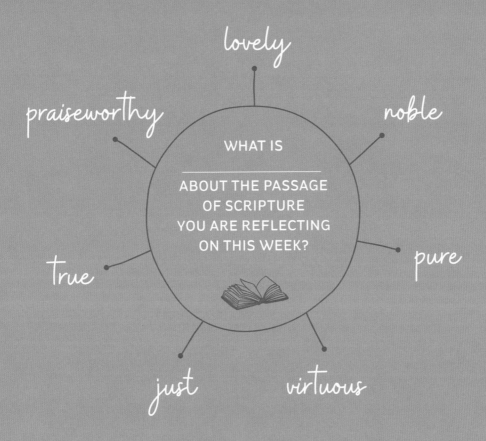

lovely

praiseworthy

noble

WHAT IS
_____
ABOUT THE PASSAGE
OF SCRIPTURE
YOU ARE REFLECTING
ON THIS WEEK?

true

pure

just

virtuous

WEEK 3

What is true, noble, lovely, praiseworthy, pure, just, and virtuous about this week's scripture?

_____

_____

_____

_____

WEEK 7

What is true, noble, lovely, praiseworthy, pure, just,
and virtuous about this week's scripture?

_____

_____

_____

_____

WEEK 11

What is true, noble, lovely, praiseworthy, pure, just,
and virtuous about this week's scripture?

_____

_____

_____

_____

WEEK 15

What is true, noble, lovely, praiseworthy, pure, just,
and virtuous about this week's scripture?

_____

_____

_____

_____

WEEK 19

What is true, noble, lovely, praiseworthy, pure, just,
and virtuous about this week's scripture?

WEEK 23

What is true, noble, lovely, praiseworthy, pure, just,
and virtuous about this week's scripture?

WEEK 27

What is true, noble, lovely, praiseworthy, pure, just,
and virtuous about this week's scripture?

WEEK 31

What is true, noble, lovely, praiseworthy, pure, just, and virtuous about this week's scripture?

_____

_____

_____

_____

WEEK 35

What is true, noble, lovely, praiseworthy, pure, just, and virtuous about this week's scripture?

_____

_____

_____

_____

WEEK 39

What is true, noble, lovely, praiseworthy, pure, just, and virtuous about this week's scripture?

_____

_____

_____

_____

WEEK 43

What is true, noble, lovely, praiseworthy, pure, just,
and virtuous about this week's scripture?

_____

_____

_____

_____

WEEK 47

What is true, noble, lovely, praiseworthy, pure, just,
and virtuous about this week's scripture?

_____

_____

_____

_____

WEEK 51

What is true, noble, lovely, praiseworthy, pure, just,
and virtuous about this week's scripture?

_____

_____

_____

_____

CONTEMPLATION MEDITATION

CONTEMPLATION MEDITATION is an exercise based
on journaling during your quiet time.

Start by writing down your answer to this question:

"What is God revealing to me in this scripture?"

_____

_____

_____

Next, spend a few moments rewriting the scripture in your own words and unpacking what
you are gaining from this weekly Word of God through your specific Enneagram type.

_____

_____

_____

"What is God revealing to me in this scripture?"

_____

_____

_____

Next, spend a few moments rewriting the scripture in your own words and unpacking what
you are gaining from this weekly Word of God through your specific Enneagram type.

_____

_____

_____

"What is God revealing to me in this scripture?"

_____

_____

_____

Next, spend a few moments rewriting the scripture in your own words and unpacking what
you are gaining from this weekly Word of God through your specific Enneagram type.

_____

_____

_____

"What is God revealing to me in this scripture?"

Next, spend a few moments rewriting the scripture in your own words and unpacking what you are gaining from this weekly Word of God through your specific Enneagram type.

"What is God revealing to me in this scripture?"

Next, spend a few moments rewriting the scripture in your own words and unpacking what you are gaining from this weekly Word of God through your specific Enneagram type.

"What is God revealing to me in this scripture?"

Next, spend a few moments rewriting the scripture in your own words and unpacking what you are gaining from this weekly Word of God through your specific Enneagram type.

"What is God revealing to me in this scripture?"

Next, spend a few moments rewriting the scripture in your own words and unpacking what you are gaining from this weekly Word of God through your specific Enneagram type.

"What is God revealing to me in this scripture?"

_____

_____

_____

Next, spend a few moments rewriting the scripture in your own words and unpacking what
you are gaining from this weekly Word of God through your specific Enneagram type.

_____

_____

_____

"What is God revealing to me in this scripture?"

_____

_____

_____

Next, spend a few moments rewriting the scripture in your own words and unpacking what
you are gaining from this weekly Word of God through your specific Enneagram type.

_____

_____

_____

"What is God revealing to me in this scripture?"

_____

_____

_____

Next, spend a few moments rewriting the scripture in your own words and unpacking what
you are gaining from this weekly Word of God through your specific Enneagram type.

_____

_____

_____

"What is God revealing to me in this scripture?"

_____

_____

_____

Next, spend a few moments rewriting the scripture in your own words and unpacking what
you are gaining from this weekly Word of God through your specific Enneagram type.

_____

_____

_____

"What is God revealing to me in this scripture?"

_____

_____

_____

Next, spend a few moments rewriting the scripture in your own words and unpacking what
you are gaining from this weekly Word of God through your specific Enneagram type.

_____

_____

_____

"What is God revealing to me in this scripture?"

_____

_____

_____

Next, spend a few moments rewriting the scripture in your own words and unpacking what
you are gaining from this weekly Word of God through your specific Enneagram type.

_____

_____

_____

ACKNOWLEDGMENTS

We would like to acknowledge that we stand on the shoulders of the Enneagram teachers, experts, and authors who came before us. We want to credit the following Enneagram trailblazers and their published works which have paved an invaluable path that helped guide us in writing this devotional:

- Beatrice Chestnut, *The Complete Enneagram: 27 Paths to Greater Self-Knowledge* (Berkeley, CA: She Writes, 2013).

- Beatrice Chestnut, *The 9 Types of Leadership* (New York: Nashville Post Hill, 2017).

- The Enneagram Institute, www.enneagraminstitute.com.

- Beth McCord, www.yourenneagramcoach.com.

- Don Richard Riso and Russ Hudson, *The Wisdom of the Enneagram* (New York: Bantam, 1999).

- Don Richard Riso and Russ Hudson, *Understanding the Enneagram: The Practical Guide to Personality Types* (New York: Houghton Mifflin, 2000).

- Richard Rohr, *The Enneagram: A Christian Perspective* (New York: Crossroad, 2016).

- Marilyn Vancil, *Self to Lose, Self to Find* (Enumclaw, WA: Redemption Press, 2016).

ADDITIONAL READING

If you would like to continue learning more about the Enneagram, here are some wonderful and helpful resources we highly recommend:

- Beatrice Chestnut, *The Complete Enneagram: 27 Paths to Greater Self-Knowledge* (Berkeley, CA: She Writes, 2013).

- Don Richard Riso and Russ Hudson, *The Wisdom of the Enneagram* (New York: Bantam, 1999).

- Marilyn Vancil, *Self to Lose, Self to Find* (New York: Convergent, 2020).

NOTES

1 This table is adapted from Marilyn Vancil, *Self to Lose, Self to Find* (Enumclaw, WA: Redemption Press, 2016), 147.

2 Marilyn Vancil, *Self to Lose, Self to Find* (Enumclaw, WA: Redemption Press, 2016), 65.

3 James Strong, *Strong's Exhaustive Concordance of the Bible,* (Abingdon Press, 1890), biblehub. com/hebrew/7503.htm.

4 en.wikibooks.org/wiki/Hebrew_Roots/The_original_foundation/Gifts.

5 Zoo Books, "The Bald Eagle's Quest for Flight," my.kwic.com/~pagodavista/schoolhouse/species/ birds/body.htm.

6 Thomas Mabey, *The Evidential Power of Beauty: Science and Theology Meet* (San Francisco: Ignatius Press, 1999).

7 The "hard to believe" characteristics listed in quotation marks for each Enneagram type are from Don Richard Riso and Russ Hudson, *The Wisdom of the Enneagram* (New York: Bantam, 1999), 34, 37-42.

8 J J Stewart Perowne, ed., *Cambridge Bible for Schools and Colleges* (Cambridge University Press, 1884), biblehub.com/commentaries/micah/6-8.htm.

9 Marilyn Vancil, *Self to Lose, Self to Find,* 65.

10 Gary G. Berntson, "Stress Effects on the Body," American Psychological Association, apa.org/help-center/stress/effects-nervous.

11 Marilyn Vancil, *Self to Lose, Self to Find,* 65.

12 T. D. Borkovec, H. Hazlett-Stevens, and M. L. Diaz, "The Role of Positive Beliefs about Worry in Generalized Anxiety Disorder and its Treatment," *Clinical Psychology & Psychotherapy 6,* no. 2 (May 1999): 126–138.

13 Marilyn Vancil, *Self to Lose, Self to Find,* 65.

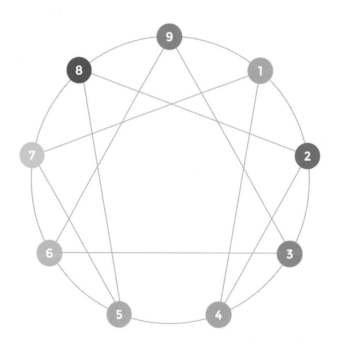